WALKABOUT

Mark Patrick Hederman is Abbot of Glenstal Abbey.
Formerly, headmaster of the school, he has lectured in
philosophy and literature in America and Nigeria, as well
as in Ireland. A founding editor of the cultural journal
The Crane Bag, he is also the author of several books
including *The Haunted Inkwell* and the bestseller,
Kissing the Dark.

The mosaic in San Clemente

WALKABOUT

Life as Holy Spirit

Mark Patrick Hederman

the columba press

First published in 2005 by
τhe columbʌ press
55A Spruce Avenue, Stillorgan Industrial Park, Blackrock,
Co Dublin, Ireland

www.columba.ie

Cover design by Anú Design
Illustrations by Shane Ordovas OSB
Origination by The Columba Press
Printed by ColourBooks Ltd, Dublin

ISBN 1-85607-476-5

For Louise
Walking shoes and all

Veni Creator Spiritus

O Holy Spirit, you have led me for sixty years, even before I was born. I cannot undertake this work, which you have prompted, unless you are with me every word of the way. I am tracing the history of your intervention, not just in my own life but in the lives of many who are, like myself, nonchalant and indifferent workers, pretending to strive for the coming of your kingdom, but, in the end, quite happy if it never arrives.

You can only work through those who willingly co-operate. Your plan cannot be imposed. The mystery of our freedom is the sacred trust that holds you back. How many times have you had to regroup and rearrange strategy because we have been recalcitrant, blind, or in deliberate sabotage of your efforts on our behalf?

And yet in this year of Our Lord 2005 the mosaic scattered around the world in pieces of coloured glass, which we have collected and put together like a complicated jig-saw, begins to take shape.

Writing is not simply recording what happened in the way it might be remembered. Writing is also moving in the Spirit: words are 'written not in ink but in the Spirit of the living God'(2 Cor 3:1).

This book divides into five uneven parts. The first presents an image which symbolises the origin, the paradigm and the purpose of these pages. The second describes a twenty-five year history from 1976 to 2001 during which the Holy Spirit made several unusual incursions into an otherwise unremarkable life. The third is Walkabout: three years at the beginning of the new millennium going wherever and doing whatever the Holy Spirit prompted. The fourth elaborates a more detailed mosaic of time and space as a visible tapestry of the secret workings of this same Spirit, an exegesis of the journey undertaken. The fifth is an unusual alphabet which begins in the middle: HIJKL. Five letters, mostly made up of correspondence written and received. These can be read at any time or not at all. They thicken and expand rather than develop and extend. The end result should spell a clarity of vision or, perhaps more, a direction towards which we should be going, an outline of what we might be doing to promote the work of the Holy Spirit in our world. When I say 'we' I am talking about those who not only believe in, but are in touch with, the subtle yet seismic movement of the Holy Spirit in our midst. And we are indeed many who form this procession. Nor is this an elitist, restricted constituency. It is open to every human being ever born, but by invitation not conscription.

Acknowledgements

Sacha Abercorn, Ciarán Forbes, Fanny Howe, Nóirín Ní Riain and Simon Sleeman are a Cóiced who have helped me to prise this ungainly hold-all out of the depths.

And

TO THE UNKNOWN DONOR

Clematis grows through creepers round these walls
Hundreds of leaves hide endless blocks of grey
Autumn descends in rainbowlike decay
Rescuing evening from the dread footfalls
Littering planetaria with sound.
Edited rows of books envelop us
Shelves full of memories tell of what we found
Fascinating on the transit bus.

Futures are formed by those who read such signs
Ears finely tuned to register beyond
Eyes of a hawk. Magnificence aligns:
Nothing on earth can fail to correspond.
Every minute vibration always links
Yours to the so-called riddle of the sphinx.

I

AN IMAGE

In the Gold Mosaic of a Wall

In December 2001 I was on a book tour in the USA. In Barnes and Noble at Boston University I was given a book called *Churches*, a luxury volume by Judith Dupré, 1 foot by 1.4 feet (30cm x 50 cm) in width and length with gilded double opening doors, reproducing Donatello's Annunciation on the cover. I was travelling light with a knapsack. Could I carry this across America? The inside triptych was a full display of the apsidal mosaic in the church of San Clemente in Rome. About to leave the book behind, something urged me to bring it along. Previous visitations from this wall of images jogged my memory. The book fitted inside the lining of my knapsack. Later looking up missives from the past, I found that the mosaic had been haunting me for over thirty years.

Seven individual cards showing separate details of this apse had been sent to me on different occasions over those years. The mosaic now became an image of the search recorded in this book. It was as if different pieces of a jig-saw turned up at different times without my realising either that they were parts of a whole, or that they might one day create a larger tapestry.

Sometime in the 1960s, a card for my birthday from my aunt, Irene Mullaney: the snake at the base of the cross at the centre of the San Clemente mosaic inside a book on *Mithras, The Secret God* by M. J. Vermaseren, published by Chatto and Windus, London, 1963, same year, same publisher as Iris Murdoch's *The Unicorn*.

A postcard (Rome, 20.8.1977) from Richard Kearney: 'Underground San Clemente to Mithraic tomb. Alleyway between the "Christian" and Mithraic houses.' 'This passage is part of a pagan village which finds itself beside and beneath a Christian chapel of the 8th century which in turn is under the Renaissance Basilica of San Clemente which opens onto chaotic modern Rome. But apart from this brief journey into the earth, it's been all movement and fury along the roads of France and Italy. Give me an open road to an underground passage any day.'

For Christmas 1997, Seamus and Marie Heaney (see Letter H) had a card privately published by Peter Fallon of The Gallery Press: 'The Deer' from the Basilica at San Clemente with a poem: 'Would they had stay'd' inspired by lines from *Macbeth* (Act I, scene iii) which refer in Shakespeare's play to the apparition of three witches from another world:

'What are these/, so wither'd and so wild in their attire/, that look not like the inhabitants o' the earth/, and yet are on't?'

'Stay, you imperfect speakers, tell me more.'

'Say from whence/ you owe this strange intelligence? Or why/ upon this blasted heath you stop our way/ with such prophetic greeting? Speak, I charge you.'

'The earth hath bubbles, as the water has/, and these are of them. Whither are they vanish'd?'

'Into the air; and what seemed corporal melted/ as breath into the wind. Would they had stay'd!

Were such things here as we do speak about?'

1

The colour of meadow hay, with its meadow-sweet
And liver-spotted dock leaves, they were there
Before we spotted them, all eyes and evening
Up to their necks in the meadow.

                        'Where? I still - '

'There.'

             'O yes. Oh God, yes. Lovely.'

                        And they didn't

Move away.

             There, like the air on hold.
The step of light on grass, halted mid-light.
Heartbeat and pupil. A match for us. And watching.

4

What George Mackay Brown saw was a drinking deer
That glittered by the water. The human soul
In mosaic. Wet celandine and ivy.
Allegory hard as Earl Rognvald's shield
Polished until its undersurface surfaced
Like peat smoke mulling through Byzantium.

Senan Furlong had given me the centre-piece of the mosaic in a larger
card: The Crucifixion, including the hand on top and the snake
underneath; Our Lady and St John on either side; the twelve doves
perched on the horizontal and vertical panels of the cross; two magpies
to right and left. On the back he had written a quote from Iris Murdoch,
Henry and Cato, published in 1976: 'Your task is love and love is your
teacher, rest there and wait quietly to be shown truth' (p.178).

Nóirín Ní Riain had given me 'the caged bird', second last image
from the end of the apse on the left hand side. Guidebooks suggest a
symbolism of incarnation. Hardly, in our context. Something about
releasing caged birds and letting them fly. This raised my curiosity about
the corresponding image on the far side of the lower rim. Frank
Lawrence was in Rome and sent it on: *La caccia*, the hunting gear. The
Hebrew Psalm 90 uses similar imagery: 'His faithfulness is buckler and
shield'.

A grouping of lance, broadsword, helmet, axe, towel, horn,
drinking barrel against a thorn-bush recalling the hymn *Vexilla Regis*
(Venantius Fortunatus, 530-609) first sung in the procession (19
November 569) when a relic of the True Cross, sent by the Emperor
Justin II from the East at the request of St Radegunda, was carried from
Tours to her monastery of Saint-Croix in Poitiers.

Only one emblem in the end corner of this section remained to be
identified. Joshua Ordovas went to Rome for the beatification of Mother
Teresa of Calcutta and found a card representing it. A dove swoops
vertically towards a red lizard crawling horizontally. These two figures
and movements became representative of symbolic aspects of our world.

Each emblem held some clue and provided the secret piece of a
wider jig-saw. The seven cards were seven seals, a number representing
completion. Seven days of the week, seven gifts of the Spirit, seven pillars

of wisdom, seven countries visited in 2003 in search of the Johannine. Thus John writes from the island of Patmos, where on the Lord's day he fell into a trance and heard behind him a voice, loud as a trumpet, which said: 'Write down all that you see in a book and send it to the seven churches' (Rev 1:11). And John saw seven stars and seven golden candlesticks representing the angels of the churches which are seven in number. 'Write, therefore, what you have seen, what is now and what will take place later' (Rev 1:19). 'Then he broke open the seventh seal; and for about half an hour, there was silence in heaven' (Rev 8:1).

II

THE BOOK OF ICONS
1976-2001

The Book of the Icons (1976-2001)

Diary entry 1976: 'There are two kinds of diary. One records the life you plan: the concrete you lay in the back garden of your everyday home, the concrete you lay in the front; the other records the eruptions in that concrete: intrusions from another world which seeks to enter yours. This diary is of the second kind. Monastic life is a structure which provides for both; a lattice which gives play to this double history: the causal time sequence of past, present and future, and the breaking through of a time that is 'out of joint'. Time of resurrection. I shall carry on living an ordinary life, doing the things which fill up chronological time. But I shall know that the real service (liturgy), the real work (*Opus Dei*), is to remain (stability), to be prepared, to be ready (obedience) for the advent of this other kind of time. It could come at any moment, it could need me; it might not come, it might never need me. Such things are not important. The important thing is that it is, and that I believe it.'

This story begins in 1976. I had been a Benedictine monk of Glenstal Abbey in Ireland for over ten years. A friend of mine, John Hill, a school contemporary, arrived from Zurich on 11 April, with his wife and her cousin, a professional photographer. They had been sent by the photographer's mother, Joa Bolendas, a visionary living in Zurich, to find icons in Ireland which she had seen in a vision. They were also in search of the spirit of ancient Celtic Christianity which should be exhumed at this time and for which at least three people were already working here, she said. I showed them a collection of Russian icons some of which we housed in the sacristy of the church in Glenstal, but most of which were scattered around various rooms throughout the buildings. We rounded them up and the photographer took pictures of them.

The collection of icons came from Russia after the revolution in 1917 when many so-called 'White' Russians were forced to flee to Europe. An Irish diplomat, Sir Osmund Grattan Esmonde, working in Paris, bought them in the 1920s and gave them to Glenstal Abbey in the 1950s.

When the three visitors returned to Switzerland they were told by the visionary aunt that some of these icons were indeed ones she had seen in her vision. St Nicholas, patron of Russia, had shown them to her and had spoken about them. She later published a book in German and in English using some photographs of our icons. As text beside each icon, she reproduced the words spoken to her by St Nicholas. Some of the icons in her book were not in our collection. Her introduction to the book, published in 1979, states: 'The main purpose of this work is to reveal something of the spiritual and religious value of icons and, by doing so, bring them closer to humankind. In the spirit of ecumenism, this book may also serve as an aid to a better understanding of Christians in the Orthodox Church. The visions themselves present the full testimony of an early Russian saint. "I am Nicholas of Russia, an early saint of the Eastern Church." This was the way he presented himself to me. There are other icons that were proclaimed holy in my visions, but to make them all known would lie outside the scope of this work.

'We searched in Ireland for some of the icons illustrated in this book, following a vision. We found them there in Glenstal Abbey, a Benedictine monastery.'[1]

Joa Bolendas was also in search of the spirit of an ancient Irish Christianity which would be embedded in some of the ruins of monasteries or churches and which would predate many of the later divisions in the church. Reinvigoration of such a spirit would be salvific for our times.

Some time later she communicated to me, through John Hill, that I had, or would have, cancer in the near future. I was to spend some time in Tunisia, put gold foil under the chair where I worked in my room, and keep one of the icons of Jesus Christ giving a blessing close by me. It was a healing icon. I was skeptical about the whole visitation and especially about this last revelation. I thanked her and said that if God wanted me to have cancer that was His affair, I was going to do none of the things she suggested except that I already had in my room the very icon she had mentioned.

About a month later my older brother, John, told me that he had been diagnosed with cancer of the lower abdomen. My sister, Louise, who is a nurse, thought he had little time to live. I felt I had to tell him about the healing icon. He said he was totally agnostic but was prepared to try anything. 'I don't care which firm heals me' he laughed, as he always does, 'I have already been dosed with a hundred healing potions and draped with every kind of sacred linen.' I brought the healing icon to where he was in the Mater hospital in Dublin and left it with him overnight. He is still alive today, thirty years later. No one can say whether the icon was responsible for his cure. One can never be certain about such things. Over the years this icon has healed many people, not just from physical diseases but from mental anxiety and spiritual disquiet. These are private histories which I have no intention of revealing here. But they represent an important fact about these Russian icons, some of which date to the sixteenth century.

Anyway, I began to take more notice of these happenings and to be less skeptical about the spiritual insight of the visionary from Zurich.

Another friend of mine, Ronnie O'Gorman, also at school with me in Glenstal Abbey, came on a visit. I told him the story of the icons and Joa Bolendas. He wanted to get back into his car and bring me immediately a book by Robert Graves which he said I had to read as it was saying something importantly similar. I persuaded him not to be so impulsive, which he always is, and to send me the book when he got home rather than drive back immediately to Galway. *The Crane Bag and other Essays* by Robert Graves[2] arrived within days. The title essay is the review by Graves of a book by Dr Anne Ross: *Pagan Celtic Britain*. Graves believes that this highly qualified academic celtologist is barred from understanding the very material she is writing about because of her scientific education. 'As a girl of seventeen Dr Ross had done what anthropologists call "field-work" by learning Gaelic for six months in a West Highland peasant's hut. Then after graduating at Edinburgh, she took an educational job in the same Goidelic region, but later returned to Edinburgh for a degree in Celtic studies and a Ph.D. in Celtic archaeology'. Thus, according to Graves 'she forgot … how to think in Gaelic Crofter style, which means poetically.' He makes his point by quoting her treatment of an important Celtic Myth about 'The Crane Bag' of the sea-god Manannán Mac Lir. This bag had been made for the sea-god from the skin of a woman magically transformed into a crane. 'This crane-bag held every precious thing that Manannan possessed. The shirt of Manannan himself and his knife, and the shoulder-strap of Goibne, the fierce smith, together with his smith's hook; also the king of Scotland's shears; and the king of Lochlainn's helmet; and the bones of Asil's swine. A strip of the great whale's back was also in that shapely crane-bag. When the sea was full, all the treasures were visible in it; when the fierce sea ebbed, the crane bag was empty.'

Dr Ross is like the rest of us, trained out of our poetic sensibility. She has lost the art of reading the signs of the times. According to Graves she 'can make nothing of such fairy-tale material.' He has to interpret for her: 'What the fabulous crane bag contained was alphabetical secrets known only to oracular priests and poets. The inspiration came, it is said, from observing a flock of cranes, "which make letters as they fly". The letters are formed against the sky by the wings, legs, beaks and heads of these shapely birds. Hermes, messenger to the gods, afterwards reduced these shapes to written characters. Cranes were in fact totem birds of the poetically educated priests ... That the crane bag filled when the sea was in flood, but emptied when it ebbed, means that these Ogham signs made complete sense for the poetic sons of Manannan, but none for uninitiated outsiders. The crane bag was not, in fact, a tangible object, but existed only as a metaphor'.

Dr Ross as an academic archeologist has the job of digging up 'things' from the past, dating and comparing these. But as a trained scientist 'she can accept no poetic or religious magic'. Anything that falls outside the scope of her 'academic conditioning' is 'branded as mythical – mythical being, like pagan, a word that denies truth to any ancient non-christian emblem, metaphor or poetic anecdote'. We too have been overly trained in scientific prejudices. We no longer see the world as symbol. We are incapable of reading the signs of the times, of unearthing the Spirit at work in our world. Our world is like the island of Shakespeare's Tempest: to Caliban a confusion of bewildering lights and sounds; but to Prospero's eyes and ears 'clear signals from a different order of experience'. We have to decide whether 'to turn tail on it all like howling Caliban or to develop new powers of attention and perception capable of orchestrating this mad music.'[3]

Richard Kearney and I were trying to develop such a hunt for the symbolic, such orchestration of mad music, when we began to edit a journal in 1977 which we called, after these recent experiences: *The Crane Bag*. The editorial for the first edition was given to me. It was one of the first times I can remember writing out of another inspiration. The book which supplied the immediate framework for what was trying to edge itself into articulation, and from which much of the material used in this editorial was culled, was also 'given' at this time: *Celtic Heritage* by Alwyn and Brindsley Rees. Here is the original editorial:[4]

The Crane Bag is really a place. It is a place where even the most ordinary things can be seen in a peculiar light, which shows them up for what they really are. There must be a no-man's land, a neutral ground where things can detach themselves from all partisan and prejudiced connection and display themselves as they are in themselves. Does such a place exist? Can such a place exist?

Modern Ireland is made up of four provinces, whose origin lies beyond the beginnings of recorded history. And yet, the Irish word for a province is cóiced, which means a 'fifth'. This five-fold division is as old as Ireland itself, yet there is disagreement about the identity of the fifth fifth. There are two traditions. The first that all five provinces met at the Stone of Divisions on the Hill of Uisneach, which was the mid-point of Ireland. The second that the fifth province was Meath (Mide), the 'middle'. Neither tradition can claim to be conclusive. What is interesting is that both divide Ireland into four quarters and a 'middle', even though they disagree about the location of the middle or 'fifth' province. This province, this place, this centre, is not a political position. In fact, if it is a position at all, it would be marked by the absense of any particular political and geographical delineation, something more like a dis-position. What kind of place could this be?

In Ireland one may still be confronted with the riddle: 'Where is the middle of the world?' The correct answer to the riddle is 'Here' or 'Where you are standing'. Another version of the same idea is the division: North, South, East, West, and Here. 'The figure five is the four of the cross-roads plus the swinging of the door which is the point itself of crossing, the moment of arrival and departure.'

Uisnech, or the secret centre, was the place where all oppositions were resolved, the primeval unity. The discovery of points where unrelated things coincide was always one of the great arts of seers, poets and magicians. Thus, the constitution of such a place would mean that each person must discover it for themselves within themselves. Each person would have to become a seer, a poet, an artist. The purpose of *The Crane Bag* is to promote the excavation of unactualised spaces within the reader, which is the work of constituting the fifth province. From such a place a new understanding and unity might emerge.

The Crane Bag, The Fifth Province and the Cóiced, were three symbols released by the Spirit in our local historical setting in ways for which no one of us was responsible, and no one of us correctly understood, but they eventually worked their own way towards consolidation and clarification. The framework within which a web was eventually woven involved several people and the three identifiable epiphanies which have been outlined above. People played major or minor roles but no one can say which of these was decisive in the eventual emergence of a recognisable pattern. In the chronicle of events which this book records three lily-pads hit the surface of the water consecutively to allow the frog of chance to jump from one to the other.

The three events are important only insofar as they establish the zig-zag of connection which ignites the Spirit's momentum. Ostensibly there is no connection between them. However, the impulse within each person which causes them to do something unusual in obedience to what they perceive to be an inner prompting, creates a platform for the Holy Spirit to take over and forge a link. Such links will be called coincidences by those who refuse any reality to the Spirit, but they are, in fact, the way in which the Spirit moves within our world of perfect freedom without leaving footprints. 'It happened by chance,' we say. But there is no such thing. Every moment of our lives is an opportunity to join forces with the reticent God who works ceaselessly for our completion. The so-called 'visionary' is important as catalyst rather than prognosticator. The breadth of vision disrupting the pedestrian focus of normal day-to-day existence and supplying something akin to 'peripheral vision' acts as counterbalance, but the details of what the visionary sees or prescribes can often be wacky and awry. Such prescriptions should be read poetically, symbolically, not literally. The visionary is used as trickster, as off-beat anomaly, to shake us out of our tiny minds, our short-sighted complacency. As Thomas Mann puts it in a book I was being plunged into at the time: 'The gaze which the departing one sends into the future is impressive and hallowed; much faith may be put in it. Yet not too much, for it has not always been entirely justified ... Jacob solemnly made some solemn misfires – along with some prophecies that amazingly hit the mark.'[5] The cóiced became a configuration which emerged and typified the working of the Holy Spirit in our regard.

In 1978 we met Mícheál Ó Súilleabháin and Nóirín Ní Riain. They were searching for a sound which would incorporate ancient Celtic Christianity in a way not merely archaeological but contemporarily envigorating. The quest was similar to that of the three visitors from Zurich. In 1979 we (twelve monks), directed by Mícheál, recorded *Caoineadh na Maighdine*, ancient Irish religious songs, with Nóirín Ní Riain.

In 1982 we performed a Cóiced rite during the Organ Festival in the chapel at Trinity College, Dublin. Charles Acton writing in *The Irish Times* the next day captured something of the illusiveness and the ambiguity:

Last night's Organ Festival event was in the Chapel of TCD but without any organ, and was a fascinating hour of reading and singing by the Monks of Glenstal and Nóirín Ní Riain. The programme sheet twice spoke of the event as a 'rite', but if it was, it was a very secular rite, or something between all sorts of pairs of worlds. I feel diffident about writing at all, because anything I write must be too literal-minded, too down-to-earth. Who, at the trembling of the veil, should finger the cloth and discuss the merits of the weaver?

Doing just that, however, I must point out that this is part of an 'International Organ Festival', and one must therefore presume that some of the audience that packed the chapel (thank goodness) should have been foreign visitors, to whom the programme sheet must have been remarkably uninformative – but perhaps such visitors will have gone away moved by the otherworldliness of the Celts?

At the risk of damaging a wing started by lifting a stone, I felt that we should have had a much larger and more informative programme ... with something about the various items. As it is, I feel that much of this remarkable performance took place behind the veil and that I experienced it as through a glass, darkly.

In the chapel aisle were a massive wooden candlestick (with candle lit) and sundry other bits of timber as by courtesy of the Forestry and Wild Life Service. At the start 15 men and Nóirín Ní Riain processed in and sang to us around the timber a very long *Caoineadh na Maighdine* from Co Kerry , alternating solo line and choral refrain. This was beautifully sung. Then they moved up towards the communion table and performed before microphones. I am not sure whether these were necessary, but the amplification and speakers were so good (most remarkably) that one had no idea of anything but totally natural sound.

Then we had readings by two or three of the monks individually, all in English, in translations by major names, and singing by the monks or by Miss Ní Riain as soloist, nearly all in Irish. As a very lay Protestant I felt myself uneasy hearing a monk reading about the passion of desire in Frank O'Connor's *The Body's Speech* and occasionally found myself casting Miss Ní Riain as Deanna Durbin to Glenstal's Philadelphia Orchestra in *Fifteen Men and a Girl*, but the sheer loveliness of her voice and the warmth of their artistry and singing were entirely captivating.

It was a fascinating evening and a many-splendoured thing and I am conscious that my clay-shuttered words are inadequate for it.

Au contraire, dear Charles Acton, your words are more accurate than you could have imagined.

Somehow we felt that there was some mystery being worked out through us and that a rite was a more appropriate way of expressing what we ourselves did not understand. Two of the fifteen 'monks' were Mícheál Ó Súilleabháin, as musical director, and Patrick Mason, who directed the rite itself, and who at that time was working with the Abbey Theatre in Dublin. He had been sent our way by Jean-Miguel Garrigues. This enigmatic performance seemed to act as prelude to later elaborations on the theme of the Cóiced as this began to work itself out in our regard.

Five of us, Ciarán, Simon and I with Mícheál and Nóirín began to identify ourselves as some kind of quintuplet – rather like a circus horse for clowns made up of five people inside – with each one providing some portion of the shape. A head + 2 hands + 2 feet would be too simplified a version, but some combination of a larger 'body' than any of the five of us might become on our own, or indeed the sum total of what we all might be if we simply joined forces to achieve a particular goal. Cóiced was more than the sum of its parts and, most importantly, it incorporated into an otherwise totally male monastic community, the feminine principle. I wrote a poem around this time, which is how I cope with what is beyond me:

Cóiced

The word for a 'province' in Irish is 'fifth'.
The fifth one: Meath or 'middle' place,
is secret: drawer, or priest-hole,
Omphallos
a sliding door oiled into space
rock-faced, as in sheer of cliff.

'We'll find them,' callow children laughed
on mid-term breaks
in plastic macs.
'Don't drive. We'll walk.'
They held a compass: North, North-West
and tied a thread to leave a trail.

We found one body in a field
metal-detected teeth through lime
walking-shoes out on a ledge.
One child survived. Now ninety-nine
one plain, one purl, hand-knitted
time of sorrow. For
'Wherever you walk in Ireland
you reach the edge.'

God is also Cóiced. There are five names in the Hebrew Bible: Elohim, Yahve, Jehovah, God and El Shaddai (meaning 'the shadow'); the so-called Pentateuch includes the first five books of the Bible: Genesis, Exodus, Leviticus (Priesthood), Numbers and Deuteronony (the law).

Louis le Brocquy designed the cover for *The Crane Bag* using a simple brush drawing which he originally made for Cú Chulainn's shield in Kinsella's *Táin*. The image is also a province without boundaries: it can be 'an island, a brain, a floating spore, a pregnant cell' in Richard Kearney's elaboration.

By 1982 the first 5 volumes became *The Crane Bag Book*. A preface written by Seamus Heaney describes: 'as much an instrument of divination as a forum for critical thought,' 'The Crane Bag was something conjured in the mythic understanding, a poetic lure to call us beyond our positions towards that dis-position adumbrated in the first editorial.' A discussion conducted 'in the mood of diagnostic reverie'.

In 1983 Iris Murdoch published *The Philosopher's Pupil* and I visited the Skelligs Islands for the first time. The great Skellig is about twelve miles out to sea from Port Magee. We landed in a cove facing east where a monastery was in existence 600 feet above sea level from the sixth century. The island is only about four acres in all but these make up such varieties and extravagances of shape and contrast that they assume archetypal proportion: a mirror of the Celtic psyche measuring the contortions of extremism within a tiny span. A compelling geography of land and sea lends itself as map to heights and depths of a spiritual world. Two peaks, one 600 the other 700 feet, meet at 'Christ's saddle' in the middle of the island: centre of gravity with access to every dimension of surrounding space. The sixth-century beehive cells are rounded stone: outside the dark vastness and murky life of the ocean, inside a smell of confining security in the earth.

The lesser Skellig, hardly possible to reach, but starkly visible from Skellig Michael is mythic also in shape: impregnable fortress guarding secrets surounded by water.

This became one of the places nearest to 'the source' and is mirrored in the passage (in both senses) where Tom 'in the state of restless obsessive nervous energy' goes down to the bottom of the Ennistone baths in Murdoch's novel: 'I must find the source, I must get there' he says and there is a description of his 'going down' (504) which ends with the soliloquy:

Why am I here? There must be a reason. I have got to do something, I have an aim, a task, I must go on down. I've come so far I can't give up now ... I've got to find the place. I've got to see it, the real source ... I must get there and ... and touch it.

This very young, naive male is the one who gets nearest to where Iris Murdoch is trying to reach through her army of flocculent 'philosophers'. And his capacity in this regard is essentially connected with his youth and almost child-like recklessness, abandon and trust:

He came back, stood a minute as if in prayer, and touched the wet concrete floor like a child touching 'base'. He said aloud, 'I did my best,' then hurried back to the stairs.

25 January 1984: John O'Donohue invites me to talk to his group in Galway on 'Masculinity' having had a speaker the previous week talking on 'Femininity.' His invitation came on 13 December, feast of St Lucy, patroness of writers, and the day in 1825 when Pushkin began to write *Count Nulin* finished in two days. I saw Tarkovsky's film *Stalker*. Released in Russia in 1979, it was shown at Cannes in 1980. Half-outlaw, half-saint: his task to guide people to the hidden, secret, forbidden zone.

I am secretary to the twentieth Glenstal Ecumenical Conference taking place in July 1984. This conference originally opened in the year the Decree on Ecumenism of the Second Vatican Council was promulgated. It provided the occasion for Church of Ireland, Presbyterian and Methodist Christians, to meet together with some Roman Catholics for the first time in Ireland on 26 June 1964. The conference has been held every year since then. Before its twentieth anniversary in 1983, I was invited to form an *ad hoc* interdenominational committee to offer suggestions as to the future. Our report was published in October 1983.[6] It seemed to the committee that some radical steps would have to be taken. 'What we propose is that this conference set itself as its immediate task and its longterm goal the study and resolution of the problem of intercommunion between the different denominations which attend. We also propose that the 21st Glenstal Ecumenical Conference should not be held until it is possible for us to celebrate a Eucharist in which all members might participate fully. Such an event would really mark our coming of age and, our opinion is that we should postpone this 21st birthday for whatever time is necessary – even if it be five or ten years – until such a common celebration of our maturity is possible.' A panel of experts was established to formulate an agreed text for a common Eucharist. The Rev. Dr John M. Barkley (Presbyterian); Dean Gilbert Mayes (Church of Ireland); The Rev. Robert Nelson (Methodist); and Dom Placid Murray OSB of Glenstal Abbey (Roman Catholic) drew up and presented to the Standing Committee of the Ecumenical Conference a Proposed Text for a Common Eucharist in May 1985. The text was adopted by the committee and was used for a common celebration of the Eucharist with permission from the then Roman Catholic Archbishop of Cashel and Emly, Thomas Morris, and the authorities from the other four participating denominations. The Abbot of Glenstal, later Abbot President of the Congregation of the Annunciation, Dom Celestine Cullen was chief celebrant, with concelebrating ministers from Church of Ireland, Presbyterian and Methodist clergy, while all members of the conference, apart from two conscientious objectors, one Roman Catholic, one Presbyterian, received communion.

This was certainly a high point of ecumenism in my own lifetime and, in my understanding, a miraculous work of the Holy Spirit.[7]

In 1985 I became headmaster of Glenstal Abbey School. I co-opted Timothy McGrath as co-director. This year marked the end of *The Crane Bag*. Not before I had helped Brendan O'Regan to formulate his ideas about peace both in Ireland and in the world in an article called 'The Third Way' which summarised the work he had been doing since the 1970s in Cooperation North, and outlined a practical possibility for peace in Ireland and elsewhere, between mere protest and impotent politics.

The Good Apprentice by Iris Murdoch accompanied these moves. She reworks the story of the prodigal son with a sensational opening. Edward gives his friend Mark a drug sandwich and kills him, without meaning to. At the end Edward sees his tale as double – as a 'muddle, starting off with an accident … all sorts of things which happened by pure chance' but he also realises that it is also 'a whole complex thing, internally connected, like a dark globe, a dark world, as if we were part of a single drama, living inside a work of art.'

In 1986, ten years after her first intervention Joa Bolendas sent her niece Anne Marie back to Glenstal where she remained for ten days mostly praying in the church. At the end of this retreat she said that we must house the icons in a chapel and open the chapel on 10 April 1988. This would be the feast of the Resurrection in the Orthodox calendar celebrating 1,000 years since Christianity came to Russia in 988.

In 1987 *The Book and the Brotherhood* of Iris Murdoch seemed to be telling our story and the story of this book. Jeremy Williams and I were standing in the crypt of the church at Glenstal Abbey wondering how to turn this space into an icon chapel. He had ideas about creating a Byzantine cathedral like Santa Sophia in bijou style. A man neither of us had ever seen before walked down the steps into the space where we were both standing and told us that he knew what we were doing; that he had been sent to do all the artwork; that no one else was to be allowed to touch anything in this space. We were wondering how to contact the nearest psychiatric hospital until he showed us some of his work. It reminded me of Francis Bacon. But more importantly he reminded me of Tarkovsky's film *Andrei Roublev*, made in Russia in 1969. When the director announced his film about the fourteenth-century iconographer, a man sold his farm in Siberia, arrived in Moscow and told Tarkovsky that he was to play the leading role. Which he did.

I have come to know that James Scanlon, artist from Kerry, is an iconographer. He does what he is told to do by the Spirit and he has all the imagination and technical virtuosity to make happen their combined projects. The icon chapel in Glenstal Abbey is itself an icon. It is visible proof of the existence of God. It is a kind of beauty, as Dostoievsky says, which can save the world. *Divine Beauty* as in the title of John O'Donohue's book published as these words are being typed in 2003.

In 1988 there was the official opening of the Icon Chapel on 10 April, Easter Day in the Orthodox calendar. Joa Bolendas saw three shafts of light entering from above and reaching the floor of the chapel: one for Russia, one for Northern Ireland, and one for Glenstal Abbey as a place where art and religion could meet in a blend of ecumenical and ancient spirituality. Also, three shafts of light for individuals who would visit this place.

Everything about James Scanlon was concentrated on this work while it was in progress. Like Rainer Maria Rilke's solitary confinement in Duino Castle, while he wrote the Elegies: 'I get up day after day and try myself out in the quietest most regular things ... expect nothing of myself ... I have wanted for a long time to be here alone, strictly alone, to go into a chrysalis, to pull myself together; in a word, to live by the heart and nothing else ... That will bring certain regions that have lain there for ages within reach of whatever is beginning to stir in me. I creep around all day in the thickets of my life, shouting like mad and clapping my hands – you would not believe what hair-raising creatures fly up.' Some of these are represented in the cóiced of stained glass portholes above the central dome of the icon chapel.

The floor of the chapel is also a stained glass window into the earth. Glass and sand are similar and this creation is of three different coloured cements. It is wall to wall. Before the cement had set the artist inserted different kinds and shapes of iron: part of the tip of a plough, the corner of an old range, nails, hoops, tools, iron bars. As you enter the chapel these shapes like frozen music, or the letters of some ancient alphabet, lead you from the entrance gate to the holy of holies, where the iconostasis shields the altar in a beehive apse.

At the centre of the floor a large round blue cosmos girded in a band of steel is floating in a sea of green. The edge around the two panelled crucifixes is studded with nails and other instruments of torture and red cement flows from these like blood into a universe.

The icon chapel is also a prison, an undeground cell, from which each person must escape in their own spiritual way. Earl Collins found it so when he visited shortly after the opening. He had first arrived in Glenstal Abbey for Holy Thursday 1980 and later became a monk and priest of the Glenstal community, eventually writing a best-selling *Book of Icons*, in 2002, with each icon produced in colour by The Columba Press. The book provides a theology of the icons but, more importantly a way of praying with the Glenstal Icons.

The icons placed themselves in the positions they now occupy in the chapel. Two are unusually singular on the wall at either side of the nave. The architect said they shouldn't be there. He quoted traditional protocol for his disapproval of such placement. James Scanlon insisted that this was where they had decided to be themselves. There was a row. James removed all his work and departed. But then, again in the words of Rilke: 'When I look into my conscience I see only one law; it stubbornly commands me to lock myself up in myself, and in one stretch to finish this task that was dictated to me at the centre of my heart. I am obeying – for you know it is true, in coming here I wanted only that, and I have no right to alter the course my will has taken, until I have completed this act of sacrifice and obedience.' He returned on time and the icons have remained in the places they chose for themselves.

No one will ever know, except the workers involved, the miracle it was to open this underground chapel on that date and the forces of evil which blatantly tried to prevent it happening. This chapel carries the whole church underground. It is the opening out of a space and, more importantly, the illumination of that space. It is the world of the unconscious and it is the world of feelings, colour, light, which have for so long been closed off and abandoned by many of our churches. In the words of William Blake: 'The rainbow is the symbol of the "opening" of the eternal world into manifestation. Erin opens the centres and is always accompanied by a "rainbow of jewels and gold" which has its doors and windows into Eden. I see a feminine form arise from the four terrible Zoas, beautiful but terrible, struggling to take a form of beauty, rooted in Shechem: this is Dinah, the youthful form of Erin.' When it was completed after working with his team the whole night before, James Scanlon could again say with Rilke: 'At last, the blessed day when I can announce to you the completion … From the last one my hand is still trembling. Just now, Sunday 10th April at 10 o'clock in the morning it is done! That I was permitted to experience this, experience being it. I would not have held out one day longer. All tissue and ligature in me cracked in the storm. I must be well made to have withstood it.' Shortly after completing it James suffered from severe shingles, which in Irish is called 'brush with the devil'.

James Scanlon was the person sent to complete this underground chapel, to repaint an icon within the earth. This meant pitting himself against forces of evil which entered every available person and thing to drive him away or prevent him from carrying out this task. To have this chapel ready for the opening date required a kind of strength and determination which has to be 'religious' in its origin.

Art is truth setting itself to work. The artist is like a passageway that destroys itself in the creative process so that the work can emerge. Something happens through the mediation of a true artist which is then shored up and contained within the work. This something is the emergence of truth; what was meant to be; the future in its appropriate form and shape.

This Glenstal project was James Scanlon grappling with the underground, his descent into hell, his struggle with the darkness. His mother had died of cancer the year before. He believed that she led him to this place.

After this opening I went to Boston and to the USA for the first time. Elizabeth Shannon had invited me. Her husband had been American ambassador to Ireland during the Carter administration in 1977 as this journey began. Their youngest son, David, came to school in Glenstal Abbey while I was director there. I looked up my mother's family in Boston and found her birth certificate and the house where she was born. Bill Shannon was very ill at the time. He died shortly after I came home.

There was a memorial service in Donnybrook Church. Cardinal Ó Fiaich celebrated the Mass. Garret FitzGerald, Gay Byrne and Seamus Heaney gave eulogies. Heaney said in his oration that he was sorry Bill Shannon had died before the publication of the American edition of his book *Government of the Tongue*[8] because he recognised that Bill Shannon was the incarnation of the principles he was outlining in that book. I was able to tell him that Bill had indeed read his book because I had brought it out to him the summer before he died. The day before this memorial service Richard and Anne Kearney hosted a meeting with Seamus and Marie Heaney, Liz Shannon and myself. Seamus Heaney's *Government of the Tongue* contained parallels and correspondences that seemed to describe a blueprint for what we had in mind. The idea was to find some place, structure, method, environment which would allow art to have a voice in the shaping of the world about to emerge in the twenty-first century. Worlds shaped by politics, religion, ethics, economics, have all been too narrow. I began the meeting by outlining the history of, and plans for, such a place in the Limerick/Shannon area. Seamus detected two conflicting imperatives: the first concerns fortuitous energy, a set of accidents discovering purpose; the second involves institution and the actual building or constitution of a movement. These two antinomies might be compared with the kinds of innovation established by Coleridge and Wordsworth on the one hand

and by Yeats and Lady Gregory on the other. We would have to determine whether this 'movement' was based upon a 'religious' or an 'artistic' impulse. Would it be another 'foundation' for Glenstal in the religious sense of these words?

He is afraid of the realisation of the dream. The dream is plasm, what he dreads are bricks and mortar. Let it be nomadic. Tents and teepees rather than towers and tabernacles. We should not foreclose and turn it into an institute. If indeed Paris was the backdrop to such artistic originality at the beginning of the twentieth century this was probably as much owing to the anonymity, vitality and energy generated by a huge sprawling city. What I was describing was the coagulation of two energies: the first was the 'sound' as described by Synge on the Aran Islands and, in this case, by Mícheál and Nóirín, and the second was the institutionalising thrust of an organising genius like Brendan O'Regan: Uisnech versus Ardnacrusha. You do not want this centre to be pedagogical, administrative or promotional. What you need to create is basically an acoustic. The Irish are such that if they hear something exists they are interested, if they are told, they are not. The work of Glenstal should be to establish a transmitter, to allow prophecy to occur, but prophecy without evangelisation, which is a work of art.

My image of what such a centre might do in terms of prophecy was akin to a detective novel where twelve people are invited to a castle, each has a motivation but no one yet knows who will make the kill. It would not be the individual effort of any one artist but something of the phosphorescence created by their mutual presence which might allow one to become spokesperson for the group. Seamus found this of interest and could see a possibility for such a group to disturb the exposed edge of consciousness. It would depend on how the energy was gathered and harnessed. It could even accumulate as an atmosphere around Glenstal.

1989 was the year of Iris Murdoch's *Message to the Planet* and we recorded the third of the musical trilogy with Mícheál and Nóirín: *Vox de Nube*. It contains music from Joa Bolendas and the ancient Russian chant which we used at the opening of the Icon Chapel. The cover represented the icon of Joachim and Anne. These two saints are discussing with the three Persons of the Trinity the birth of the Virgin Mary. Their feastday, 26 July, became a feature in our calendar.

Around this time Brendan O'Regan (BOR), who had founded the Irish Peace Institute (IPI) in the University of Limerick, persuaded me to apply for the job of Professor of Peace Studies at UL. BOR had fundraised the money and set up the chair. The idea was that I would be able to articulate what he is doing and has done to provide a 'hands-on' approach to peace which would help solve the situation in Northern Ireland and then offer brokerage to other areas of the world where ethnic struggle is becoming more and more prevalent and acute. Ireland as test case, with UL as the distillery for such wisdom: I was to translate the practice and the facts into philosophy and pedagogy. It sounded like the setting for what Joa Bolendas had predicted for this Shannon area: the beginnings of a Fifth Province.

In 1991 on 19 February James Scanlon was interviewed on radio about the icon chapel by Gay Byrne. He confirmed what I have written here, saying that he was led there by the Holy Spirit. He quoted me as telling him that if and when the chapel was completed it would do great things for Christianity in Russia.

Three days later the peace professorship in UL was advertised. It seemed clear to me at this time that everything which Joa Bolendas had described about what should happen around Glenstal, this area of Limerick, in terms of the promotion of peace and ecumenism, and with special reference to the situation in Russia, could come into focus through this work. Just as I leave the job of headmaster in the school, this other possibility is created by BOR which would allow me to orchestrate both what has been suggested for here and the work that he has been doing over the years. He asked me to help him with a talk he was giving called 'Harnassing Fire' and this sums up one aspect of the synthesis which we felt was about to take place.

We have had twenty years experience of what is euphemistically called 'the troubles' in the North. Surely, in that time we must have learnt at least two things: that there is no political solution to this problem and that 90% of our people on both sides of the border are prepared to accept that fact and want to live out their lives in peace, harmony and prosperity.

What I am saying to you very simply is that the time is now. 30 years ago on this day the most strife torn land mass on our planet, sown with more blood, hatred and bitterness than fire has ever generated in recorded history, decided to opt for constructiveness rather than destruction. On this day 30 years ago, the European Community was founded. It was not a united political entity, it was a fragile bond of continual dialogue, lasting sometimes into the exhausting hours of the late evening and early morning. But it worked and, more importantly, it healed wounds between Germans, Belgians, French, English etc. etc.

My one suggestion here today is that such transformation is possible for us. The machinery is there, the funds are there, the expertise and the experience are there. And we are the only ones who are not yet there.

I myself have had the privileged experience, on a very much smaller scale, of a similar transformation on this island. 30 years ago, as well, I was appointed Chairperson of Bord Fáilte and I watched the emergence of Shannon Airport, Shannon town, Shannon industrial zone, from a disused area of unlikely desert. Both these transformations, on the small and the large scale, were the result of managed cooperation.

Without wasting time or going into too much detail, I want to sketch for you the possibility for both our communities to achieve a similar kind of cooperative growth which would be mutually beneficial without being individually compromising. I am not offering you pious speculation or political promises, I am proposing hardnosed realism and investment for our children. Invest today in reconciliation and reap tomorrow economic stability, that is my message. And let me remind you: the cost of one day's violence is less than all the monies which have been allocated to date to the business of peace building in the last 10 years.

Funds adequate to the task are certainly available and I am shamelessly proposing that the three organisations which I have been working with over the last 10 years are capable of using such funds in ways that will be acceptable to both communities, both North and South, and which will produce the kind of transformation we all long for.

The combined harvester of the fire which I am here to promote is made up of three essential parts: the reaper, the binder and the winnower of the grain, if I may extend the image. The first is that web of socio-economic relations which make up the organisation we call Cooperation North. We have ten years of tried and trusted experience on both sides of the border. It has dug the ditches and laid down the infrastructure.

The second is the Irish Peace Institute, the binder. It takes the experience of Cooperation North and with the assistance of two universities, one North, one South, distils the formula into a comprehensive and comprehensible package which can be applied in other places where the need is urgent.

The third is the Centre for International Cooperation which uses Ireland's geographical centrality and accessibility to make it into a credible peacebroker in a world where ethnic struggle is daily becoming more prevalent and more violent. Its credibility depends of course upon successful application of the formula to the home country and then its credentials as a successful peace broker rest upon the capacity to adapt and apply this formula to other ethnically unique situations.

We have the funds, we have the formula, do we have the will to harnass the fire?

Brendan used, at my suggestion, Louis le Brocquy's 'Fantail Pigeon No. 3' as emblem for his particular blend of peace brokerage.

In 1991, on 10 June, I accompanied Liz Shannon to the groundbreaking for a new library at the University of Limerick. Ed Walsh, who had no great love for ecclesiastical pomp and wanted his institution to be non-denominational, needed someone to say a grace before the meal. He sprang this on me! 'O Lord, who are known for initiating mad and impossible schemes, such as the creation of this world, bless this work which we now undertake and all those who are making it possible.' I was referring specifically to Chuck Feeney the major donor for this university who was there. I met him afterwards and he said something to the effect that Glenstal would be his next port of call.

16 June 1991was Bloomsday! I had entered a competition at a Texaco filling station. Would you like to have breakfast with James Joyce? If so, complete the following rhyme. I did and got an invitation for two. You had to go in fancy dress: as a character in one of Joyce's novels. I rang Bruce Bradley SJ who was then head of Belvedere and had

written a book on Joyce's schooldays. I asked him what the Jesuits would have worn in Joyce's day at school? 'Just what I'm wearing now,' he said. 'Put it in a plastic bag,' I said, 'and I'll drive round and collect it.' He did (and added a collapsible 'greening' biretta for good measure). I went to the breakfast in the Marine Hotel, Dun Laoghaire with Liz Shannon. She was dressed as Gerty McDowell. We both won first prize there and had to go to the next round in Merrion Square that evening. Again I won first prize for Bruce Bradley's costume: this time it was a return ticket to America!

On 25 June I was interviewed by the board at UL for the position of Professor of Peace Studies. Professor James McConnell was the visiting member from Bradford University, Chair of Peace. I had met him with BOR. He had been an SMA contemporary of our Fr David Conlon. I knew from that interview that this appointment was not to be!

Instead, on 16 August I flew to Boston. I spent the next year teaching English at Boston University, thanks to Liz Shannon who also allowed me to stay in the top storey flat of her house at 25 Lenox Street in Brookline. Seamus Heaney gave me a generous recommendation which influenced the decision of the English Department to employ me as visiting professor. It was the year of Hurricane Bob, of Peristroika, of the collapse of communism and the return of Christianity to Russia. I had one of the most enjoyable years of my life and in 1992 attended a seminar given by Geoffrey Hill on Gerard Manley Hopkins. This became the prototype for such study of poetry in a monastic setting, one of the directions which our new spiritual centre would be taking. Sebastian Moore and Daria Donnelly were also participants. I visited New Mexico with Liz Shannon where Taos, Santa Fe and the area around the Sangre de Christo mountains imposed themselves as another part of an essential horizon.

Back in Ireland for Writers Week in Listowel I gave a talk on Brendan Kennelly at his request, and later at the W. B. Yeats Summer School in Sligo, I led a seminar on *A Vision* where I met Joan McBreen. That November I left for Nigeria to teach at the missionary seminary in Gwagwalada.

During 1993 Frank Wright, the man appointed Professor of Peace Studies at the Irish Peace Institute, died and another search was made for a replacement. I applied but it was not to be. I returned to Nigeria until the summer of 1995.

Mícheál Ó Súilleabháin had been appointed to the Chair of Music in UL and was about to set up a World Music Centre. This tied in with the plans to establish a spiritual and artistic centre in the Shannon area.

MÓS: 'I believe that we could see the rebirth of a distinctive Western chant sound in Ireland. Quite simply, this would come about through an integration of sean-nós singing techniques with the received models of chant as they exist in the manuscript sources. We already know more than enough about the operations of the creative process in oral tradition music to allow us to experiment in that direction with chant. I am talking about linking back to the first thousand years of Western chant tradition before the development of music notation. This process has already begun [mention of 3 records we made]. The kind of rebirth I am talking about will not come about solely through academic endeavour, even though such endeavour may be a necessary stimulus and guiding agent throughout the birthing process. Through her unique positioning between the classical and sean-nós traditions, Noirín has, in my opinion, acted as a spontaneous musical medium, thus allowing the first example of a successful transference of sean-nós technique into chant performance.

The seeds are already sown. It simply remains to be seen whether all concerned will be able to continue the process already begun.'[9]

15 June 1995, I got letters from both Ciarán and Abbot Christopher telling me it was time to come back from Nigeria. Almost a month before this I had written to Abbot President Celestine:

I feel obliged in all 'humility' to let you know a) as custodian of the treasure house of our congregation and b) as my trusted friend, exactly what a precious commodity the Benedictine Order has in my person as we all try to enter the 21st century as gracefully as possible! Because it seems to me, we are neither aware of the challenges ahead nor of the means we have been given to overcome these.

I feel that what I came to do here has been done; that the point I was meant to reach has been reached. Now, I believe, I am ready (having been carefully and painstakingly prepared) to accomplish another task, the shape, form, context of which is not yet clear to me – but the aim of which is abundantly clear: to try to make Christianity an energising, plausible even though 'alternative' life-style for the next century. I believe that few people have been given the opportunities during half of the last century to understand and absorb the meaning of this mystery as have been lavished upon me and if I cannot understand, appreciate, articulate this reality and make it manifest and transparent in a way of life, I don't see how others in this hectic world can be expected to do so.

My own education and religious formation have been essentially connected with Glenstal. However, it may be that Glenstal is too entrenched in obsolete structures and too weighed down by undergrowth, overgrowth, or the impotence of inner complexity, to preside over the emergence of such 'new life' and that my 'task' will have to be accomplished elsewhere; if so, then wherever it will be fathered, fostered, it will still be the direct offspring of Glenstal, as I have found it incarnated in your person and Pope Paul VI-type blend of leadership.

The vague, prophetic contours of this new 'form' which slouches towards Bethlehem to be born has varied and changed from some kind of 'scripture' which might be in poetry or some written form, to an actual community/centre established specifically or symbolically in Glenstal or in Wicklow or wherever is possible. I had thought that a link should be directly to UL. I have been 'in touch' with John Hill, Brendan O'Regan, and others in this regard.

In the meantime, my own preparation has been maturing. I have been allowed to study theology, philosophy and literature in privileged conditions, especially during the last four years, and am aware of certain syntheses which I have almost succeeded in articulating.

Obviously this is valuable to those I am teaching here, as it would be to those whom Christopher intended to commit to my charge if I were to return to Glenstal next year. Frankly, I don't care what I do to earn my living or put down the day, because essentially the real 'work' which occupies my mind and days is at all times going on at the other level which I regard as the *Opus Dei* for me.

I have therefore postponed the decision about next year for myself, which Christopher has graciously handed over to me, BECAUSE I am not yet sure what it should be. IF NOTHING ELSE INTERVENES, then the weight falls on the side of the seminary here. BUT, I am actually expecting some intervention to happen in the very near future which will be decisive and leave me no choice.

So, I am telling you this – I want to share these things with you – because I want you to know what I believe before it actually happens – and because I also know that you are a key person in this adventure: I want you to tell me frankly what your spiritual judgment is about what I have written: is it just presumptuous fantasy or does it ring true and then: have you received any invitations/information/clues which might cause you to say: I know what Mark Patrick should be doing as from this July?

15 July 1995: John Hill writes:

Without knowing anything about you, Joa Bolendas recently turned to me in the church and said: 'Mark's arms are full of light' – meaning 'you are ready to do very important work.' Later she saw that you and several brothers are taking very important steps so as to influence the Church in the right direction. She 'saw' a great light in Ireland.

I have no clue as to what this means. Maybe you do.

In October 1995 Simon heard Enda McDonagh on the radio proposing that a centre be established for the Church in Ireland similar to the one I was suggesting for Glenstal. Timothy also tells me to read Enda McDonagh's article in *The Furrow*, because it's saying the same thing that I am proposing to the community. Later Mícheál sends me an *Irish Times* account of Enda McDonagh's suggestion about an art centre also. And on 15 November Richard Kearney wrote quite independently to say how much he approves of Enda's idea. Another cóiced pointing the way.

So on 18 October, Christopher and I had lunch with Enda McDonagh in the Montrose Hotel where we agreed that Glenstal was the place for his Annamakerrig in the Church and that we should work together. On 8 November Enda gives a talk to the community here on Glenstal as the kind of centre he envisages for the Church and for culture etc. A week later an article in *The Irish Times* summarizes these same ideas. 'Church needs a centre to find itself: A much more critical awareness by the church of its lack of connection with the present artistic renaissance in Ireland and with its equally vigorous intellectual life is much needed.' He suggests 'a kind of Annaghmakerrig in a religious context or with a religious dimension. The Tyrone Guthrie Centre contributed substantially to the present flowering of the arts in Ireland. Without people of talent, of course, no such institution could flourish. But without the support and setting, silence and dialogue, solitude and community which a place like Annaghmakerrig provides for young and older poets, playwrights, painters and musicians for months at a time, the artists themselves would find it more difficult to survive and flourish. The practical and useful is also the symbolic. Ireland's commitment to the arts has this symbolic centre which in no way distracts from the more particular and practical and symbolic centres such as theatres and concert halls and art galleries.

What is proposed here would not be any simple imitation. The inspiration remains while the rationale and form might differ.'[10]

I am reading the book which Joan McBreen sent me sometime recently: *Cezanne in Provence* by Evmarie Schmitt.[11] Apart from being a most beautiful book in itself with stunning reproductions of the work, it also makes connections between Benedict Tutty and myself which I had not understood before. It translates a visual and spatial language which Benedict has always spoken naturally and has been impatient at my not following, into conceptual terms that I can understand. It explains the new epistemology Cezanne was devising by trying to separate perception from abstraction; the connection with music in his use of shape and colour; and the geological description of landscape in terms of *tâches colorées*. This was a breakthrough in understanding between Benedict and myself.

In November 1995 I was in Dublin Castle for a meeting on European routes with Christopher and Mícheál Ó Súilleabháin. Very lavish but not very convincing. How to make Glenstal the centre for a more sophisticated tourism concerning monastic and older celtic religious sites. Prionsias McCana and some other archeologists are interesting. Der Burke said he could get me to Newgrange for the solstice. Michael D. Higgins, dynamic Minister for Arts, Culture and the Gaeltacht, was quite dismissive of the European delegation. He told them that instead of lecturing us about our own culture, which we were perfectly well aware of ourselves, they should be doing something useful like linking or twinning the asylums of Europe. When this was translated, most of the Ronconi team began to suggest that we all wait for a change of government here in Ireland before continuing their idea and this debate!

We visited Tara, New Grange, Monasterboice. Good contact with Peter Harbison who shows interest in our project.

In December Cyprian Love gave a ground-breaking talk on music as intelligence. This lays one of the foundations for the centre which is emerging as a possibility here. This he later developed into a doctoral thesis and a book.[12]

On 21 December Nóirín and I go to Newgrange for the solstice. Claire Tuffy is our guide. The late-Stone Age people who built this monument 5,000 years ago, before the pyramids in Egypt, would have celebrated their new year on this day after the longest night of the year. Professor George Eogan, presently excavating at Knowth, was also present. As were the British ambassador, Mrs Veronica Sutherland, her husband Alex and two visitors from the Chinese Embassy. The sun did not shine, but Nóirín sang *An Caoinead*, the lament for a dead child. It was as if we were switching senses and celebrating the *sol invictus* through sound. Also bringing us back to our first record (*Caoineadh na Maighdine*) and the beginnings of this quest, certainly in terms of sound as far back as 1979.

On Christmas Eve I made out a book of the happenings from 1976-1996 for all those involved, which I gave them for Christmas.

This diary now records events which took place from the beginning of 1996, concerning a new task: to set up in Glenstal, or elsewhere, a centre where art, culture, science and religion can meet.

This, I had felt, was meant to happen in 1992, but either I was not ready for it or the time was not ripe. Missing that take-off time made me fear that the whole thing had been postponed for maybe hundreds of years! It is, for me, the same project that began in 1976, which I recorded in *The Book of The Icons*. I know that it will not be my work, it is something that must happen in its own way, in its own time, taking its own shape and size. However, I am also aware that it cannot happen without the cooperation of those people called to shepherd it into being, myself included. The more difficult task for me is to try to get both myself and the different members of this team to do what should be done at each moment. The intention needs to be taken down to another

depth before it can manifest itself. If this is not achieved we can slow
down or prevent altogether the 'thing' from taking place.

Part of the reason for this log-book is to record those happenings
and the way they occurred so that I can see the extent to which I am
eventually culpable, but also to divine the next step from the sequence
of their unfolding. The privilege is being present to 'that decisive
moment when what has been given to you to live, as corporeal destiny,
personal adventure, as well as historical event, cristallizes into "the
motive" (whether that means a "style" in writing or a plan to be put in
place) and becomes the bread which your work consecrates.' (Rilke)

John Hill had asked me (and also Nóirín) to write a blurb for his
forthcoming English translation of the visions of Joa Bolendas:

Visionaries are never guaranteed that what they say or what they see
are divinely inspired or adequate to the impulse of the Spirit. All
images and words are taken from the tiny cupboard of our own
limited and blighted experience. Many misfires can accompany some
cannily accurate shots at the moving target of our future. Theirs is
an unenviable task of concentrated love, ever-renewed humility,
scrupulous daring and quaking self-confidence.

Although temperamentally affronted, agnostic and aghast at
such phenomena, I am forced to admit, after 20 years experience,
that the source, the energy and the direction of the recorded visions
of Joa Bolendas seem to me to be ungainsayably trinitarian, even if
the details and the directives in some instances leave me
disappointed and nonplussed.

What she says has had so many coincidental connections with
my own life that I am forced to acknowledge my Lord and my God.

In February 1996 I had just finished *The Green Knight* by Iris Murdoch
when Ronnie O'Gorman sent the first reply to my book of the icons:
'Am reading your diary(?) "quest", "voyage" with fascination. There
really is a wonderful interweaving of different threads and one strong
gold one leading inexorably to a rational celebration. You make life
exciting. I am happy our threads still cross on occasions. I am not
surprised you are getting support from the community – it will give the
monastery stunning relevance in a world which has become "mentally
ill" (well put by Soedjatmoko).

'This project will proceed to success; I feel its spirit. It's already at work. It has its origins in pre-Christian times, something from Newgrange, Lugnasa, St Brigid and firelight. Watch out for shadows! But it's emerging into wood and stone.'

My immediate job was to articulate a vision for the future. This was done after consultation with many people both inside and outside the Glenstal community.

Ausculta, the Latin for 'listen,' is the first word in the Rule of St Benedict. Since the sixth century, communities have followed this Rule, as do the Benedictine monks of Glenstal Abbey in Ireland. Ireland is situated in a pivotal position off the mainland of Europe. Glenstal, in southern Ireland, and within easy reach of Shannon Airport, is ideally placed as a centre for spiritual revitalisation.

Monasteries, like the ancient hill-forts of Celtic Ireland, provide access to a spiritual realm. A monastery is a listening ear for the world around it. As such, the monastery is an essential part of society, providing a place to be in touch with our deepest selves, with nature, and with God.

Hospitality, an essential feature of the Rule of Benedict, is also a hallmark of Celtic culture. After careful consideration, the monks of Glenstal Abbey feel that they are being asked by God to listen more intently to the needs of society and have decided to make themselves, their grounds, the ethos and atmosphere of their monastery, more available to people assailed by a world of unprecedented stress.

The monks themselves have no great gifts to give away; they offer instead a place and an atmosphere conducive to the discovery of personal value and inner peace.

Monks are those who take a step away from the world around them. They strive to preserve what is best in the heritage received, while remaining open to what other cultures and traditions offer. They welcome with enthusiasm and discernment the advances of technology and science, and try to weave these into a wider and more ancient understanding of the universe.

Seventy years ago five founding monks took over an abandoned castle and four hundred acres of unproductive land. Today, a vibrant community of forty-six has built up a self-supporting monastery.

A daily round of prayer and liturgical celebration combines with work in education, ecumenism, care for the homeless, pastoral ministry, counselling, farming, bee-keeping, gardening, woodturning, forestry and silviculture, research, scholarship, writing and the arts.

Over the years, rare books, private libraries, archives, and icons, have come into the care of Glenstal Abbey: a heritage to treasure and to share.

Farm and woodland, castle and gardens, inspirational surroundings for monastic life, must be preserved, even when offered to a contemporary world eager for genuine spirituality and inner peace.

An architectural strategy has been devised to ensure that monastic life, as it has been lived for centuries, continues undisturbed no matter how many guests or visitors come our way at any given time.

A new guest house will be for those who wish to spend some days within the monastery, participating in the liturgies and dining with the monks. Such involvement requires restriction of numbers to a dozen at a time.

Professional and business groups, families and associations, will reside separately in appropriate locations on our grounds. Interaction with the monks and the life of the monastery would be elective.

Comfortable, self-contained hermitages, modelled on the ancient beehive cells of Irish monasticism, will be constructed for those who wish to spend time on their own.

The abbey church will be redesigned for better participation in liturgical celebration.

The monastery itself will be renovated and expanded for a growing community, complete with health and fitness centre.

Existing accommodation for homeless 'men of the road' who keep returning, will be upgraded.

A new library will house precious collections, rare books, manuscripts and archives. Modern technology, equipment and design will enhance research and scholarship.

A new entrance courtyard and reception area will ensure individual care and assistance for each guest as well as undisrupted tranquillity for all.

A flexible multi-purpose convocation centre, modelled on an ancient Celtic meeting place, will host conversation and dialogue and present works of art, theatre and films, which explore existence and sound its depths.

Experts in the arts, business, science and the professions, will be enlisted to gather at Glenstal and confer among themselves, with the monks and with invited guests.

The vision is of the monastery as a beehive of the invisible, distilling wisdom from many sources, searching out a new cultural perspective: a new way of hearing, seeing, and being in touch with life. The search is for a fresh articulation of traditional beliefs and values, towards a better quality of life in a new century.

Gregory Collins tells me his dream in February 1996. A voice tells him to go to Sutton Hoo. Paul looks it up in the encyclopaedia on his computer. It is some burial ship for Vikings. I tell Gregory he should read Iris Murdoch and John Moriarty (even though I haven't yet read *Dreamtime* myself). Gregory reads *Dreamtime* and finds both Sutton Hoo and many other threads of this story: 'Imagine another Patrick. A Patrick in our time for our time. A Patrick who not only seeks to bring a richer Christianity to Ireland, he seeks also to bring what is best in its Celtic and pre-Celtic inheritance to Ireland ... Imagine it: an Ireland whose centre is at Uisnech ... Imagine it: the numinous new chapter which might one day be added to our Lebor Gabala Erenn.'[13] I find a card I had given to Simon in 1976. It described 'this' and John Moriarty, who, in 1982, had planted a map at Uisnech, the centre of Ireland, after having prayed at Clonmacnoise :

There the wrinkled, sagging strong man,
the old one, only drumming now;
shrivelled up inside his great skin as though
it once contained *two* men, but one now
lay in the churchyard, and he had outlasted him,
deaf and often, in his widowed skin,
a little bit confused.

But the young one, the man, as though he were
the offspring of a neck and of a nun: taut and vigorously
filled with muscle and simplicity. (Rilke's 5th Duino Elegy)

Important confirmation comes from Nóirín, who never writes and who
had been saying that she would have no further part in all of this:
Dromore, February 29th, 1996, Feast of St Romanus, ad 460:

At age 35, Romanus headed to the Jura mountains between
Switzerland and France to live as a hermit. For a time he was
blissfully alone, then his brother arrived, followed by a couple of
other men. Then his sister and a group of women joined them.
Soon there were enough men and women to build two monasteries
and a nunnery. St Romanus, who wanted nothing more than to be
left alone, spent the rest of his life surrounded by people!

Our doubts are traitors and make us lose the good we oft might
win, by fearing its attempt. (Shakespeare)

Patrick a chroí,

Some personal afterthoughts in the shadow of our words today
... Any hesitation or negativity springs from a deep, earth-bound,
self-centred fear of being a weakling, a complacent one, a dreamer,
a WOMAN all at the one time and fulfilling no particular driving
force at any particular moment. Although this may seem narcissistic
and inward based, I feel the obligation is now to confront an
intense, mysterious instinct which Heaney terms, as he refers to the
poetry of Emily Dickinson, 'crystalline inwardness'. In being truly
crystalline, I have to be totally and vulnerably honest, from the heart
and the psyche and I'm sure that the feminine and male
manifestation of this transparency will be totally separate yet ONE
at the same time. Being convinced, from the most direct pain of my
heart, that things have 'moved on', the ultimate stepping-stone to
the destination of moving towards oneness of vision and reality,
both now and beyond, lies at YOUR feet. As Mick said today when
we spoke after your 'call', you remain firmly in the role of 'God's
earthly investigator'.

I hope I won't be found totally guilty!

We shall not cease from exploration, and the end shall be to
arrive where we started and know the place for the first time. (T. S.
Eliot)
Rath Dé ort go deo!

In March I decided against holding a meeting of the Cóiced in Louise's
house to meet with Richard Kearney. Too many things militating against
it at the moment. Instead I met Richard and Anne for dinner. Richard
asked me to find a letter he had written to me in 1976. I found the letter
on Dostoievsky, *Jane Eyre* and *The Portrait of a Lady* that he had written
twenty years ago. Still very exciting. I send it back: 'What a tall order –
so typical of you – "Can you find me that letter I wrote to you twenty
years ago on prolepsis/epilepsis?" Well here it is! Today ... was the
perfect day to go through all that correspondence which dates from the
same period as 'The Book of the Icons' which I sent you. You were only
21 at the time and I exactly 10 years older. The correspondence
(especially two letters of it) is interesting proleptic discourse on your
novel *Sam's Fall*. There is something happening at this time which is the
fruit of all that and you are important to it in a crucial way. So, don't
neglect it. You are right that some incisive move has to be made and
maybe you are the one to make it'.

Meeting this weekend of 2 March in Chancery Street with potential
protagonists in a new TV programme called *The Blackbird and the Bell*.
I have a flaming row with John Moriarty. He is too seriously 'spiritual'
and over-sensitive. His condemnation of Brendan Kennelly infuriated
me. He seems to be talking from the higher moral or spiritual ground. I
wrote to him: 'I continue to believe that our meeting – however
traumatic and boneshaking – is providential. I have read the introduction
to your book. The real questions about it are the ones which Æ asked
about Yeats' *A Vision* when it appeared in a limited edition of 500 copies
in 1925: "How is this knowledge possible? Is there a centre within us
through which all the threads of the universe are drawn?" and "Out of
how deep a life does he speak?" The secondary questions are about style,
presentation etc. I say you need to be edited. If I hear once more that
anyone is "Grand Canyon deep in the world's karma" I shall vomit
Grand Canyon deep myself. What you say about Turtle was gone a long
time: "The book makes no claim to aesthetic dignity. Its urgencies and

anxieties are to say something, not to say it beautifully" is precisely what I was trying to say to you about Brendan Kennelly's *Book of Judas*. BUT I recognise that your work is also from Him and that, as Monet says, "the light is the real person in the picture".'

8 March: Jennifer Johnston came to Glenstal Abbey for the weekend. This had been brewing for a long time. She came ostensibly on the Department of Education programme to give a talk to the school. But it was so much more than that. It was a homecoming. There were privileged encounters between her and Ciarán and Benedict. Ciarán had introduced us all to *The Invisible Worm*. It was a fullness of time. She went down into the icon chapel also.

17 March: Marie Hughes had given me a book called *The Second Coming* by Leon Moscona. I glanced through it. It talks of the opening of the seventh centre and the 'third eye' (agna chakra) and more or less uses the eye metaphor where I was using the ear in my description of the Glenstal centre. At the personal level he describes a cosmic openness by using the spine and achieving a number of resurrections. Blessings are like keys for opening the centres which are situated in the legs, the stomach, the chest and the head, which eventually becomes an outlet for the column of air, created by the breathing.

Benedict showed me his latest work which is a head that has a flap at the top which he told me was the release of the spirit in Yoga. He was sending it with two other pieces to an exhibition in the RHA.

I wrote a blurb for John Moriarty's book, *Turtle was gone a long time*: 'This is the log-book of an Irish Orpheus. Notes from the underground. Descent into hell. It describes a mysticism that journeys back through evolutionary layers and delves into prehistoric silt, which has congealed into the average Irish psyche. At its most dangerous and exciting it probes "adultery with the abyss". It is neither entertainment nor literature. It is a concatenation of words where meaning has ceased to inhabit sentences: "soundings off the coast of consciousness". As such, it can be incantatory and repetitive. But those who have the patience and the thirst will recognise the authenticity of the struggle and be rewarded with an insight as rare as it is restorative. A solitary fragile reaper, John Moriarty has harrowed our collective hell. Those who read this tale of the turtle will be grateful for the knowledge it brings and the propitiatory rite it enacts; obviating for some, perhaps, the necessity of making quite so hazardous a journey ourselves. It is sufficient, hopefully, for one turtle to dive to the bottom for the rest to avail of the cable he has laid. John Moriarty, on halloween night of our century, has made himself into the "scooped out turnip of our tribe". His book is addressed to the deepest anxieties of our seeking. Brother to dragons and companion to owls, he has opened his skull to "a new vision of what we are, a new experience of what we are, a new approach to what we are." For which can we be anything but grateful?'

19 March: Letter from Jennifer Johnston: 'I have so much to thank you for and mere words are not flexible enough to express what I want to say – only in novels can I manipulate language; when I start to write a letter my mind and my hand become stiff!

'I found Glenstal such a joyful experience. My short stay has given me an energy and a bright spark in my head. I would wish to thank you all for your kindness and for knowledge that was impressed upon me that good, if not God, exists. We all need to re-discover this quite frequently.

'Please would you give these two books [copies of her last novel *The Illusionist*] to Benedict – I have put his plaque on the wall above my work table – and Ciarán. My last view of him covered from head to toe in wood shavings and sawdust is in my mind.

'I hope all your plans come to great and glorious fruition.'

21 March: Benedict's feastday. Timothy's fiftieth birthday.

22 March: This morning Benedict died. We were walking down the corridor towards my room. He said he felt a bit weak and he sat down at the window just opposite my door and began to breathe heavily as if snoring. He tried to open the window and his nose flattened up against the pane. He began to gasp and went blue. Seconds later he was unconscious. I held him in my arms and called out to Ciarán who was in the courtyard.

He got Hannah. We laid him down in the corridor outside my room. He was already dead. Dr Paddy Moroney arrived later. He wanted to try artificial resuscitation. I said not to bother. Benedict wouldn't thank him if he did bring him back. This was the most perfect way for him to go. He had always been so fearful of it. Now he was at the other side without a struggle. And he had done everything he had to do. Ciarán had delivered his pieces to the RHA exhibition the day before. I had typed up his interview with Richard Hurley and he had approved.

Just before he died he had been at breakfast. He said to Brian: 'I had a wonderful dream last night about the future of this place. I'll tell you about it later.' There was a self-portrait in his room with a garish light bulb over his head. It reminded me that Goethe had died on this very day and his last words were: 'More light.' *The Illusionist* was on his desk. Terence and Gregory were in the room also.

23 March: I was haunted by Brian's account of Benedict's dream. Perhaps it was better that he never told it. I had this feeling he would try to contact me. I remembered in 1984 when I was doing 'Thought for the Day' on RTÉ radio and was visiting him in London, he suggested that I tell them the story of Dun Bó. He had given me a sculpture of 'the singing head' which I still have in my room. Dun Bó was the greatest poet of Ulster and the night before a great battle the king asked him to sing them a song. The poet said his heart was too heavy but that he would sing for them the next day at the same time, wherever he was and wherever they were. The battle was lost and the poet was killed with all the others. His head was brought back on a spear as a trophy and placed in the celebration tent where the winners were feasting. At the appointed time the head began to sing.

I had done that story on Friday 16 November 1984, and Nóirín and I had arranged that she would sing *An Caoineadh* the next morning on *Smaoineamh* (the Irish version of *Just a Thought*) at exactly the same time, so that the severed head might sing. I'm sure no one in the country noticed. You would have to be bilingual and listen to Radio Éireann at 7 o'clock in the morning – a pretty unlikely combination. However, the deed was done and it was Benedict's idea. I was convinced that he would try to contact me this morning at the time he died. It was the same day my father had died in that same year 1984. I was wondering how he would do it, when Henry O'Shea rang me at exactly the time to tell me to turn on Radio Éireann. On the radio there was the only recording of Joyce reading 'Anna Livia Plurabelle' from *Finnegans Wake*.

24 March: Again picked up *The Second Coming* by Leon Moscona, which Marie Huges and Jim Lillis had given me. The page I opened said that 22 was the important number and from 22 March until 22 September was the time of the Circle Dance (Paneurythmy) or sundance which the Hopi performed to dance their dream awake.

August 1987 was the end of a 22,880 year cycle of time and the beginning of a new 2000 year cycle. This is the dawn of the epoch of aquarius which is that of the Holy Spirit. Dance introduces the cosmic spiritual rhythm that allows the kingdom of God to emerge. This is threefold. The microcosm of each human being reaching its perfection. This is described in terms of the opening of our chakras and the shaping of a 'body-mantra', the cosmos of a culture, and the macrocosm of the whole world and the universe.

When nature thus renews itself, there will be a new song for the coming epoch. At the beginning of every divine culture human beings sing. The dance involves a pentagram: 5 couples and in each one the 5 of 2 hands + 2 feet + head. This accomplishes the opening of the seventh centre. All this was an interesting commentary for me on the Cóiced. It did not have to be any particular five people, it was a pattern of five which could be any grouping or different combinations of five. It would lead towards the number of seven.

25 March: Ciarán and I keep vigil together in the church with Benedict in his coffin. We discussed my sermon and also the change which Ciarán detects in me. He is trying to achieve some change in himself through psychotherapy. Neither he nor Benedict accept that such change can be 'religious' although they both know that something has happened in my case which involves a certain integration.

Benedict's funeral today complete with his self-portrait and chakras head. My words after the Gospel seem accurate and appropriate although long. So many things in the ceremony were made by him: red ciborium, copes, ambo cloth, virgin and child in the sanctuary, sanctuary lamp, stations of the cross, stained glass window, crucifix etc. Large crowds.

26 March: Letter from Margaret Nugent: 'I was so sorry for you when I heard of Br Benedict's death. I'm sure he was intended to be a cornerstone of your artistic enterprise and it must have been shocking to have him literally die on you. Maybe he will blaze a trail in the other dimension and test your powers of perception to pick up his messages.'

In April Joan and Joe McBreen took me to London for the day to see the Cézanne exhibition. Flew from Shannon and back the same day. Lunch with Ted and Clare Barrington, Irish ambassadors. Discussed *Jackson's Dilemma* by Iris Murdoch, which Joan had read in America. She gave me Rilke's letters to Clara on the first Cézanne exhibition.[14]

Cézanne teaches us how to see. Rather, as Lacan says, he makes us see what prevents us from seeing. His paintings are metaphors for feelings. Benedict everywhere. Later Joan sent Helen Vendler on Heaney and Hopkins. I wrote to Heaney (Letter H) trying to organise a seminar on his work which would inaugurate the centre here for distillation of wisdom from every available source: East, West, religious, scientific, cultural, artistic. A place where science, art, religion (of every denomination) can meet is more likely to give birth to a more imaginative century next time round.

28 April: Letter from John Hill in Zurich: 'Thank you for your comment on Joa Bolendas' book. It was appropriate, fair and heartfelt. It is now with the publisher ... There is an introduction by Robert Sardello ... In fact, several of your ideas about the future of Glenstal Abbey find expression in the works of Sardello.

'Your article on the future centre at Glenstal is inspiring and links many strands of our Christian and pagan heritages, forming them into a message which is desperately needed today. I hope you can engineer it into a reality. If I can be of any help, let me know. 'Desperately needed' – in the past few months many individuals here are becoming aware of an inhuman attitude that is pervading all aspects of life in Europe. This new spirit of the times uses such words as 'rationalization', 'economic', 'efficiency', and 'success'. This attitude is not new but the intensity with which it is applied, sweeping aside all other human values, is frightening. Not only are the achievements of the welfare state being undermined, but anyone who cannot produce immediate proof that verifies the success of whatever undertaking, is dismissed sooner or later. Smaller organisations are in trouble. Art and culture have to submit to commercialisation, if they are to survive. This affects my profession as well. Psychoanalysts are not efficient enough and therefore are not eligible for support from insurance companies. The behaviourists can prove their success by changing people in 40 hours. In midlife, however, these same people come to us for deeper work. I just hope that you won't be overtaken by this spirit in Ireland. It is quite ruthless. Your centre with an inner ear, as a place of welcome and peace, really needs to happen.

'It was nice to hear from Gregory, and I look forward to meeting him. Sad to hear about Benedict's death.'

20 May: Mike Shiel, a photographer sent by Bill Gates to photograph the modern equivalent of The Skelligs here at Glenstal, is staying. I show him round. Joan McBreen also in Glenstal. We three visit the Bible Garden with Brian. This becomes the scene for Joan's poem:

The Bible Garden

In a year, a decade or a century,
the photographer's presence will be clear.

Here is the picture.

Four people are in the Bible Garden.
Two of them move from plot to plot;
One is naming herbs, plants, vegetables and trees,
sharing each one's symbol and metaphor with the other.

The one with the photographer is near
the farthest edge of the wall.

What is said between them is being
listened to intently.

The camera is only used once.

For you this is not enough. You demand more
than the sky darkening or the rain falling,
cooling the hands, faces and necks of those
in the picture.

You want them running from the Bible garden,
desiring more than they have.

What follows is not easy to say:

Here time has stopped. For some this joy,
for better, for worse, for love of God,

is never enough and this, the world
knows, is the sorrow of the story.

5 August: Roland Moser sends the brochure of 'The Tent' made for 1000th anniversary of Berne by Mario Botta, one of their most famous architects.[15] Although it looks like a state of the art conference centre, it is built so that the Swiss Army can move it to any other site whenever that is appropriate. Corresponds to Heaney's idea of 'tents and teepees'.

6 August: Transfiguration. Went to Ballyneale with Christopher, Nóirín and Mick, to have dinner with Loretta Glucksman. Magical evening – horses – Knockfierna – walk by the kitchen garden. Loretta a sensitive and mystical presence.

We had an unexpected and seminal conversation about Glenstal and the University of Limerick. Loretta believes that the realisation of our plans in Glenstal will be the leaven which will raise the batch around the Shannon area including UL.

9 August: Michael D. Higgins came to spend ten days with us. It was a creative time for us all. He fitted into the community easily and sensitively and responded appropriately to each one individually. It was again like a home coming. He wrote some fine poetry[16] and had interesting interaction with many of the community. We visited the site of the film *The Serpent's Kiss* and met John Boorman's son and Donal McCann, who is 'saving up' his visit to Glenstal! For this film they had created a two-acre dutch garden on stilts. It was like visiting the under side of the world in creation. We were invited to the destruction of the garden by thunderstorm the following Tuesday.

Michael D.'s visit is something of a proleptic prototype. He is the spy going into the promised land and being hidden in the house in the wall of the town by Rahab who puts a scarlet thread on the window through which he escapes by being let down the wall in a basket! The centre will take on the shape of such precursors. On arrival, I gave him a page from a book about Rilke (*The Beginning of Terror, A Psychological Study of Rainer Maria Rilke's Life and Work* by David Kleinbard) which Ciarán had given to me: 'He needed to be alone in order to molt, to fall apart in order to come together again as a writing poet ... [He] believed that he had to go through a kind of mental disintegration as a preparatory stage for the emergence of his unique gifts of seeing and saying … At such a time he had to be alone, because, in the radically undifferentiated and unintegrated state which he needed to rediscover his genius, he felt extremely vulnerable to the impingements of other people upon his internal freedom, his unique sense of himself, and his emerging work. At such times the capacity to be alone, as Winnicott defines it, was essential to him, because it meant that he could feel sheltered and protected as he came apart, lost himself, and dissolved into the undifferentiated state which he celebrates and praises as "das Offne" ("the open") in the eighth Duino Elegy, in "An Experience", and in a number of the Sonnets to Orpheus.

'A child feels that he can be alone in himself because someone else is there who asks "nothing but to be there functioning and protecting at the border of the invisible". (Rilke's fantasy of the perfect companion.) Only the individual who has developed the capacity to be alone in this way, by internalizing or creating such a "protective environment," "is constantly able to rediscover the personal impulse …"'

Such would be the kind of artistic safety net which monasteries might provide for artists. Our Rule (chapter one) warns those who wish to become hermits that they must first go through a certain amount of training in community, so that 'having learnt to fight in the consoling confines of community life, they may develop those inner resources necessary for single combat in the desert.'

I went to America promoting these ideas in October 1996. I met with Patrick F. O'Leary, originally from Skibbereen and now a leading spinal surgeon in New York. We met in his rooms. His secretary is from Limerick and had visited Glenstal. He is interested in our capacity to be a proactive force in the renewal of value systems. The church, in his view has failed us miserably to the point of being in breach of contract. A philosophy of economic expedience prevails and the church continues a ritualistic deception. He admires Cardinal O'Connor and the Pope. His hero is Don Hinfey SJ whom he treated on one occasion – DH happens to be the person whom I replaced in Nigeria when teaching in the seminary there. O'L reads voraciously and spoke of tapes called *Intellequest* which teach history, philosophy, literature etc. which he uses in his car. He was interested in Glenstal but also said that if anyone from Ireland asked to meet with him he would make time to do so. We had a considerable argument about religious attitudes and I suggested that his standards were perhaps too high and his 'God' somewhat daunting. He says he has always had an inferiority complex and perhaps this is what has driven him to succeed as much as possible. At 52 he is entering the last quarter or third of his life maximum and must therefore begin preparing for whatever the next stage must be.

Malachy Glynn and I went to the new play by Wole Soyinka called *The Beatification of Area Boy* at the Brooklyn Academy of Music. Brilliant satire by the Nobel prizewinner of 1986 on the present state of affairs in Nigeria. The scene was the square outside a nightclub with automatic doors. The subcommunity of vendors, beggars, visitors which formed itself in this space, is engineered into a 'gang' by the porter of the club who becomes a self-appointed mafia boss. This was the first and the only time I had seen a play of his performed. I had read the others and written about his work but had never seen a production in Nigeria.

Flew to O'Hare, Chicago. Lunch with Fr Andrew Greeley in the Ritz Carleton Club. He was about to do an interview with Cardinal Bernardin, who is dying of cancer. AG coming to Dublin in November, giving a talk on the difference between Catholics in the North and in the South from a sociological point of view. If Glenstal can do anything to make Ireland what it should be, 'the imaginative capital of the Catholic world' he will give us any help he can.

Saturday 19 October 1996: I flew to Denver. It is a new airport and strikingly designed like a series of teepees in the stunning setting of the Rocky Mountains. I was invited to the Gala Dinner Dance for The American Ireland Fund by Susan Morrice, head of the Denver chapter of the fund and president of her own company. There were 400 guests. Very interesting meeting with C. W. Fentress and his wife Barbara who, as a team, designed the new airport and many other major buildings in Denver. She is especially interested in culture and ethnic aspects of architecture. They are working in Korea at the present time and have also worked in Africa. She wants to be kept in touch with developments in Glenstal. The major event of the evening was the presentation of the 1996 Humanitarian Award to Kevin McNicholas and of the Leadership Award to Senator George J. Mitchell. Both were impressive people to meet. Mitchell is of Irish and Lebanese origin. He began life in an orphanage. He is quiet and deep. Every child, he believes, wherever they are born in this world, should have the possibilty and the space to realise their full potential. He found this in America. He wants to make it available to all children in Northern Ireland.

I rang Fanny Howe, another poet and writer who has been connected to the project and who is working at Mills College in San Francisco. Her friend Gertrud Muller had visited Glenstal and Dromore just before this trip. I left a message on her recorder. Then I rang Carroll and Nancy O'Connor. He is one of the most successful Hollywood and American TV actors and directors. He has a degree from UCD. His wife Nancy is from the Sioux Native American Tribe. She has a degree from Trinity College. I got her on the phone. She was interested and said she would ring back. I had a real contact with her on the phone, I thought. She says she is a convert to Catholicism. We would try to meet the next day. Carroll is very busy filming a show called *Party of Five*. Fionnuala Flanagan (the actress) and her husband Garrett O'Connor from Ireland were with them.

Malachy and I crossed the Golden Gate Bridge and spent an evening overlooking the bay at San Francisco. Visited Chinatown. Dinner in Hunan Home Chinese restaurant in Jackson Street. My fortune cookie at the end of the meal told me in Chinese and in English: 'Your present plans are going to succeed!' In the Fairmont Hotel there is an external glass elevator which goes sixteen stories up. It eventually bursts into a panoramic view of San Francisco at night. It is like a child's dream. Also frightening. This could be the one day that the glass cube falls! Met John Ryan, formerly from Tipperary, whose firm Macrovision is going public. Great friend of Malachy who organised fishing trips in Ireland, while the best party he and his wife were ever at was put on by Trish Taylor. Three years later I meet him again at Creekside, Cupertino. Since the last visit, his company has increased and multiplied exponentially. Malachy had backed him as a winner and bought some shares in his company which have since become very valuable. John had given UL some shares while Malachy was their fundraiser. Last year John had rung Malachy, not realising that he had since left UL, to say that these shares were now worth almost $1 million and why wasn't anything being done about them. Limerick University were quite unaware of their existence or their value. They have since been sold and are going into another building there.

I found the visit strange in terms of some *déja vu*. We were retracing footprints exactly as they had occurred three years before. Even to the extent that we couldn't get into the restaurant that had been booked for lunch and so doubled back to the one we had visited last time: Faz at 1108 North Mathilda Avenue, Sunnyvale.

I told him my intimations. He said rubbish. That was all pure chance. There was no such thing as either providence or synchronicity as some kind of secret significance waiting to be read. The facts of this meeting were simply that he and Malachy had made contact. He had heard that Malachy had been ill also and Malachy had said that he was going to be in the area, that I would be with him so could he bring me along. I found myself saying to him, as if it came from somewhere else, embarrassing even myself, 'Poor fool you if you think it's all as easy as that.' I said he was ripe for this meeting for some reaon, that there was a divinity that shaped our ends and that he would know in some years from now why this meeting had taken place. He said I was right about one thing. He was bored from making money and now was wondering what to do with the rest of his life. I noticed as we came that he had the most jazzy sportscar which he actually didn't like driving. In fact he hated driving cars as his mind was always engaged elsewhere. He said that he was enjoying this conversation because, despite his apparent skepticism, these were the subjects that really fascinated him and he was a voracious reader. I promised to send him some books.

Fanny Howe got my message and phoned back. Told me that the O'Connors had had a great tragedy recently. I was upset, especially as I had known nothing of this when I first contacted them. Nancy rang again and would ring back between 2 and 3. The hotel failed to put her through. Eventually her husband Carroll told me they had been trying to get me all afternoon even though I had been waiting for the call in my room. It was too late then to meet. There is a spiritual desert all around me here – nowhere more apparent than from the top storey of an office block skyscraper, surveying the concrete jungle of lighted cubicles in a million oblong boxes stretching to the sea. I left with the feeling of something undone. I wanted to give Nancy O'Connor a copy of Iris Murdoch's *The Good Apprentice*.

Mary Ann Smith, looking radiant after her one-woman-play performed in nearby Austin collects me at the Stonleigh and we drive to the most fashionable home in Dallas for 'tea'! This is the only place in town where they mow the driveway. The house is owned and has been 'done up' by Gene and Jerry Jones and is a palace of marble and genuine antiques. Gene Jones owns the Dallas Cowboys. As we drive there Mary Ann's mobile sounds. It is her old friend Zandra Rhodes, one of England's most famous fashion designers. Where is she? Two blocks away at Lily Dodson's. Good, we'll collect her. Mary Ann parks illegally and tells me to go and get her. 'How will I recognise her?' 'You'll know her immediately.' I march into Lily Dodson's demanding audience with Zandra Rhodes. A chorus of her admirers points my way through acres of the Escada clothes line. Eventually I hack my way into a back room where several Southern Ladies are taking notes. I do know her immediately. She has purple and orange hair twisted in fantastic note-pad clips around her head, tri-coloured lipstick and eye shadow with casual but elegant woolens and trousers tapering into untied Dick Whittington London boots. She allows herself to be kidnapped and we arrive at 'tea' to which every other person in Dallas has been refused entry by Billie-Lee Rippey, unless they have paid up in full for the opera ball. We are shown the house, including the air-conditioned wine cellar and the children's theatre, and 'tea' is everything you can imagine on silver plates (and I don't mean silver plate!) and 'Aren't you just the most precious thing' and 'Where did you get that precious dress?' Zandra Rhodes, the most qualified opinion in either hemisphere, declares all the furniture and art decor to be the real McCoy. I later discover that Zandra had been in the Royal College of Art when Iris Murdoch was on the staff in 1963. She and Ossie Clark were fashion designing, while Bridget Riley, Kitaj, and David Hockney were painting.

Bobby Sue introduces me to the guest of honour, Maria Cooper, daughter of Gary Cooper. She met her through Mary Ann Smith. Maria tells me that her best friend is a Benedictine nun in the Regina Laudis Community, Connecticutt. Her name is Dolores Hart. Bobby Sue has been telling me for a long time now that our meeting has got to take place (that it is the ultimate purpose of this visit) and I realise that there is a heap of synchronicity and the rest of it about to explode. I tell her I haven't time to give her all the low-down on Regina Laudis and Glenstal but that she has to come and visit, which she will. She later sends me *The Holographic Universe* by Michael Talbot which I use in my book on the Tarot.

Mary Ann Smith and I race off to be on time for the meeting with Angela Lansbury, being presented with the 1999 Algur H. Meadows award for excellence in the arts at Southern Methodist University. She was on a panel with B. Arthur and William Eckart discussing her Broadway career 'From Mame to Sweeney Todd'. Two years previously the same award was made to Stephen Sondheim. All this for Paul Nash.

5 November: Lunch at Nieman Marcus for book signing with Maria Cooper Janis. Her book contains a letter to her father, an introduction by Tom Hanks, a series of wonderful black and white photos of their life together as a family of three. Visited by all the great contemporary stars of Hollywood and such famous artists as Hemmingway and Picasso, with identifications and commentaries from Maria herself, it is an intimate album without being coy, which generously shares the magic of a glamourous and privileged childhood. Mary Ann Perryman bought me a copy which Maria signed. The cover has a picture of a little girl on the set of *High Noon* being fed ice cream by the famous marshall, her father.

Tuesday 29 October: Met Geoffrey Hill at Boston University. Also Cleo Webster in her home. Both have connection with our plans.

Wednesday 30 October: Meeting with Kingsley Aikens in his office. He advised against setting up our own foundation in America. You have to go through legal procedures for every state. It costs. Why not use the already existing American Fund for Ireland. There was no danger about not getting donor advised grants, even though this was not possible to specify in writing; the donor has to make an unconditional donation to the fund for tax recuperation purposes. However, in practice the fund never deviates from the suggestions of the donor.

1 January 1997: Gregory came back from Zurich for Senan's ordination as deacon. He had met Joa Bolendas and their meeting was significant for him. She had had a vision previous to their meeting in which Nicholas of Flue had spoken of Gregory. This saint, one of the patrons of Switzerland had his feastday on the day Gregory arrived in Zurich.

He told me he had a dream while he was there in the place of dreams. My head was half eaten away with cancer. It was as if I was going to have to die in order to let the message spread. This was what Joa Bolendas had originally sent John Hill to tell me in 1976. After initial feelings of fear and especially about such suffering and ugliness, I find this a disappointing contribution on my part to the project. However, I am ready for whatever role is mine and I am grateful for this preview because, if such were to happen without it, I, and certainly others, might take it as proof that the whole venture was fantasy on my part.

9 March: President Mary Robinson presents one of Ciarán's bowls made of Irish yew to the Pope. A lot of publicity. Brilliant photograph in the *Irish Independent*.

In Dublin at 6.30p.m. Richard Hurley gave me definitive plans for the Development Control Footprint plan for our new building programme for Glenstal Abbey in its first stage.

10 March: Excellent meeting and Chapter vote in community on the Development Control Plan. All in favour except three. Very encouraging. Fr Vincent Ryan makes a significant intervention supported by four people publicly and many others later:

I like the overall concept, it is imaginative and well worked out. There is a creative use of space and levels. The architect manages to pull together disparate buildings and gives them cohesion. He cleverly solves the problem of circulation. Features that I like:

1) the imposing but welcoming entrance court and hall.
2) the apse, Blessed Sacrament Chapel and other features of the church.
3) the pivotal position of the library – no longer on the periphery.
4) the little gardens and patios and other features which give a lightness and grace to the architecture. Avoidance of all that is heavy and institutional.

On the broader issue of whether we should build or can we afford to, I have the following observations:

1) The signs of the times are not auspicious, but I sense a mood of hope and confidence in the community which augurs well for the future.
2) We are not building just for ourselves: the motivation seems to be a sense of mission in the Irish church; to provide a certain kind of hospitality of which Fr Enda McDonagh spoke in his address to the community.
3) I am a little scared by the magnitude of the operation to be undertaken, but am heartened by the energy and sense of purpose shown by the planning and development team. We seem finally to have got our act together, and the time is now

ripe to move forward.

4) As monks and religious we need a vision and a sense of purpose if we are to survive into the next millenium. Br Patrick's document seems to provide us with such a vision. Let us go for it. *Prospere procede*!

31 March: I show Gregory the twelfth century Byzantine cross in the icon chapel which is not on display and which he had not known. This was, somehow, an important discovery – as if, as yet undisclosed treasures were hidden in these vaults.

Simon and Christopher went to Switerland. Meetings with the Russian Church and with a parent, Atanase Tonchev, who is both interested and able to further our plans, especially on the ecumenical front. The priests of the Russian church although initially hostile were eventually enthusiastic. They recognised, embraced and 'loved' Simon, according to Christopher's startled account.

10 April: Letter from John Coyle: 'I have read your diary and thank you for your confidence in me. I have been trying to assimilate it and gain an overall impression of what is happening.

'First of all, my committment to the "visionary" plan for Glenstal – yours, Christopher's, and now much of the community's – is very strong. I say this, not out of an interest in what to do next with Glenstal, but out of the Church's need now and the obvious spiritual vitality that is in the Benedictines in Glenstal. Glenstal is not unique, thank God, but there aren't many groups like it in evidence at the moment. The lack of direction, the disarray of the Church is alarming. While my response to critics is to reassure and refer to historical cycles, one has only to look at church attendances, the actions of one's friends and children's friends and of a demoralised clergy to read a very different story.

'Religions can disappear. In Cyprus once I visited a shrine of Aphrodite which had been a main religious centre of the Greek and Graeco-Roman world. The outlines of the Temple are left. The central object of worship was a large ovoid stone – some primitive representation of the Goddess – that had cohorts of priests and priestesses attending it and hordes of worshippers. It was discovered during excavations and now stands on a plinth in a corner of the local museum, ignored.

'There are always people with reservations. But there comes a time when adequate consensus has been achieved and then it is time to proceed. In the secular world that would be called the "political will", usually based on the vision of one person or a small group who are sufficiently convinced that they are doing what is right. As for myself, I do my best to shed the business rules and general skepticism or cynicism in order to see the religious or spiritual needs. If Glenstal has a reason beyond being a generally well-bred, well-behaved curious club for gentlemen it is to stand clearly for our fundamental beliefs and open the doors to so many people – individuals and groups – who need to discuss and express their spirituality and religion. If that means more buildings, then that's fine.'

13 June: I collect Fanny Howe at Shannon, we had lunch in the Hunt museum and visited the icon chapel. She says she wants everyone she knows to visit it. She had forgotten to bring me Pavel Florensky's *Iconostasis* which she knows I must read. Then she found it 'miraculously' in a bookshop in London.

15 June: Drove Fanny to the airport. She left some 'notes':

'The Ikon room is like the parable of the mustard seed – read tonight – buried treasure that is filled with intense spiritual power – something about it being underground like minerals really adds to its force. The hiddenness of that, too. I think its being from elsewhere is important to this power – transplanted like those trees – and I feel it gives power to a body to introduce foreign and even destabilizing elements. So the Russian influence is very deep and good for this place.

'In the same way another similar dark room that exists for light – a screening room – could be exciting. Showing films from elsewhere (peace as communication) on a smallish screen, projected from a VCR – would be great – a little archive of films from around the world that feed the spirit of this place.

'Perhaps try a preliminary low-key event – like a screening of *Andrei Roublev* with a short talk about Tarkovsky – or a slightly more ambitious Bresson retrospective, maybe he himself would come from Paris! – would draw film buffs from all over. A small controlled event might help you move your project forward to a new stage of development ... Would Limerick University have equipment for a low-key screening? Projectors can work wonders now ... Just some thoughts! from Fanny.'

She also had this pressing intuition that Glenstal should connect with a place in San Francisco, California, which she describes:

'Sky Farm sits on 50 acres of rolling mountain meadows 1 hour north of San Francisco in wine country. Created by Fr Dunstan Morrissey, a Benedictine monk, over the past 25 years, it is now complete.

It contains:

2 guest houses (made from wine vats)

1 cottage

a refectory

a chapel

a main house with 2 additional guest rooms

and a large library of theology, philosophy and mystical literature from all traditions,

a large vegetable garden.

Fr Dunstan, 75-years-old, wants to have guests come indefinitely who are able to live in silence a good deal of the time – who might want to do scholarly or creative work there – He wants to withdraw himself from the day-to-day running of the place· and find someone to help with that (general maintenance + the garden) and he is still developing a purpose for Sky Farm that will continue its devotion to silence, but include some other practices. Could it be a liason place in America for Glenstal?'

14 July: Collected Sacha, Duchess of Abercorn, at Shannon Airport. She is related to both the Romanov· dynasty in Russia and the poet Pushkin. Brought her to the icon chapel and gave her a key.

21 July: 'Dear Patrick, It is early a.m. I am awake with too many thoughts in my head to let me rest – (so, as Pushkin so often did when inspiration struck) – I am putting pen to paper from the warmth of my nest!

'"Thank you" simply does not express what I feel – in fact you know when a tap has not been turned on for some time – how spluttery and even rusty the water is when it first comes out – that is how my thoughts and words will emerge, I fear – but I trust that if I leave the tap on, the airlocks will eventually disappear and the flow will find its own pace.

'That you should have invited me "out of the blue" to Glenstal at this precise moment is one of those synchronous or meaningful coincidences, which it seems we both understand. The extraordinary connection with the icon chapel, which I need to try to explain to myself more coherently – its beauty was quite overwhelming, as was the power of the tension of opposites which it holds – the two icons of St Nicholas guarding the gateway of the inner sanctum brought many things into focus for me. This is the first piece of a jig-saw puzzle that has presented itself to me. Where it is to go in practical terms I await to see. I feel I need to hear more from your side as to what the next step should be – but I am prepared and willing to offer what I can.'

22 July: Have been collecting first editions of Iris Murdoch novels which seem to turn up in each of the places I travel, signalling that I am in the right place at the right time. I now stumble on Eamonn de Burca's antiquarian bookshop in Priory Avenue, Blackrock. Many interesting possibilities for our new library, including himself!

Fax from Susan Tew to say that the man we had prayed for in the icon chapel and to whom I had sent a copy of the icon book had been 'miraculously' cured of his malignant tumour.

John Hill arrives with his translation of the book by Joa Bolendas, *So that you may be one* (from the visions of Joa Bolendas with Essays by Robert Sardello, John Hill and Therese Schroeder-Sheker). He has copies for Celestine, Christopher, Gregory, Terence, myself and Gregory insists that a copy go to Placid.

John visits Nóirín who tells him that a really exciting and original version of Christianity is being hatched in Glenstal. John had been sent to Ireland with Joa's book 'to bring these words to the UR KIRCHE, the original Irish Church. From here the light of creation, through Christ, will go out over the whole earth. He is a messenger. He wipes the first book with his tears (in the Spirit). Joa had a vision of one risen from the dead, Frederick of Oxford, telling her this and that her message was to invite everyone (theologians) to the eucharistic table to break bread and to drink. The "new" church involves a full and comprehensive understanding of what it means to be human, which must therefore include religion, psychology and Menschsein. Give thanks'.

Main strategy meeting with J. Hill. He wants to leave here tomorrow and bring a copy of Joa's book to Sacha Abercorn. I arrange that very easily. He tells me that when Christopher arrived in Switzerland it was 11 o'clock at night and he rang John from the airport – even though he hardly knew him – to say that he was lost and couldn't get a room anywhere. John had to drive to the airport and bring him to his rooms. He was in the middle of changing house and could offer him nothing except his psychoanalyst's couch where Christopher stayed the night. When he brought him to their home in Einsiedeln, Christopher left his pectoral cross behind and it was there for a week until John eventually got it back to him via Gregory. John Hill found all that symbolic!

30 July: Fanny Howe writes: 'I talked to the film curator at Harvard and he said you'd need to order 16mm films from an archive over here, probably, like Harvard's, and show it on a smallish screen there. Bresson retrospective in Toronto. I wish we could go! It has been a bit tumultuous since I left you, but I am hoping that August first will bring a month of cheer out on the Vineyard. I wonder how things have been going for you.'

Book on Synchronicity as a new form of leadership by Joseph Jaworski comes by post from Sacha's son Jamie.[17]

2 August: I flew to Geneva. I had one moment of panic as I got off the plane. I had not even brought Atanase Tontchev's address or phone number, I was so convinced that this meeting was meant to happen. He was there. We drove to meet the Panins, Alexander and Elena. She is a personal friend of the Patriarch of Moscow. We had dinner speaking in French.

3 August: Mass in the little church which Atanase had built in his ski resort development. Then a day in the thermal baths which Caligula had given to his sister! Very sunny. Dinner in a restaurant where they catch for you the mountain trout you are about to eat. Most of the discussion Atanase and I had centred on the art centre here and the possibility of a visit to Russia from Glenstal with special reference to the church there and the Patriarch of Moscow. I had written down the following which AT asked me to read out to him. I then gave him a copy: 'Atanase and I have been talking to one another in different ways and at different levels; we have been talking directly, communicating indirectly, picking up bits of conversation with other people, hints, premonitions, signs.

'We have been alert, attentive, anxious to decode messages and understand the real meaning and the full import of our meeting. If I have understood correctly then these last four days have been some of the most providential and fruitful of the whole adventure so far.'

I am to DHL from Glenstal to Atanase an official letter to the Patriarch of Moscow, outlining who we are as a delegation from Ireland, asking him for an audience and explaining why we believe this should happen.

6 August: Feast of the Transfiguration. Senan's ordination.

7 August: I had to get the official letter to the Patriarch of Moscow written and signed by Celestine and Christopher before noon today because DHL could not guarantee delivery to Switzerland before Saturday after that time. Much pressure right up to the last minute but it got there. Malachy had organised DHL. Letter read as follows:

His Holiness Aleksij II
Patriarch of Moscow and all Russia
Cistyj Pereulok 5,
RUSSIA – 119034 Moskva.

6/8/1997

Your Holiness,

We are monks of a monastery in Ireland, following the Rule of St Benedict, who feel prompted by the Holy Spirit to ask you for an audience when we come on pilgrimage to Russia either at the end of this year or the beginning of next year (1998). Our journey would depend upon whether or when you might consider our request. If it were convenient for you this year, then at some time during the month of September, or during the second half of November would suit us best.

We believe that there is some mysterious bond between the Celtic Christian Church and the Russian. We also believe that because of its suffering the Holy Church of Russia has been able to guard the Spirit of Christianity like gold that has been refined by fire (Rev 3.18), in a way that is most holy and, at the same time, most necessary for the troubled peoples of our day.

Our monastery has a substantial collection of Russian icons, which were given into our care in the 1950s. We were again prompted by the Holy Spirit to place these in an especially built crypt which was blessed and opened on the 10th April, 1988, Easter Day in the Orthodox Calendar, in the year which marked the millennium of Russia's allegiance to Christ.

Now, ten years later, we feel called to make a pilgrimage to Russia itself and to pay our respects to yourself, as leader of the Church in Russia, if it is possible for you to respond favourably to our request.

There will be three monks of this monastery on this pilgrimage, the present abbot, the previous abbot and one of the monks. None of us speak Russian, but we would hope to be able to communicate with you somehow, in English or French, and through the Holy Spirit.

We remain your brothers in Christ,
Christopher Dillon,
Abbot of Glenstal Abbey.

Celestine Cullen,
Abbot President
Benedictine Congregation of the Annunciation.

Mark Patrick Hederman
Monk of Glenstal Abbey, Ireland.

I rang John Hill who was just leaving Ireland for Switzerland. He had been staying with Louise and Risteárd and was now staying with Peter and Elizabeth Gill. He had had a very warm meeting with Sacha Abercorn and was bowled over by Barons Court where he had stayed the night. He felt he had distributed the book throughout Ireland and that the journey from Glenstal to Tyrone in the one day had been symbolic of that complete spanning of the country.

I told him of my visit to Geneva and asked him to ask Joa Bolendas some questions:

1) Should we accept the money offered from this source?
2) Was it appropriate for us to visit the Patriarch in Moscow?
3) Who should be on the delegation – I mentioned the possibilities: Celestine, Christopher, Gregory, myself and Sacha Abercorn.

13 August: John Hill's letter arrives (dated 10 August).

Dear Mark,

This last trip to Ireland was not easy but done out of inner necessity. As soon as the book was published, I knew that I would bring it first to Ireland. When I returned, I felt something had been accomplished. There were some moments of delight: the visit to Sacha, and a deeper contact with Louise and Risteárd than before.

Your trip to Geneva seems to have been successful! I will now enclose Joa's response to your questions. When we went to the church, it was Mary who spoke, so I enclose all the visions of that visit. I also enclose five icon books as you requested.

I hope your vision of a peace center is now somewhat closer to realization. Remember from earlier visions, Joa has always supported this work and seen it as your great task in life.

God be with you and joy be in your heart.

(Friday, 8th August 1997

Mary, the mother of Jesus, looked at me, then spoke with joy and peace: John Hill set foot on the Irish island with God's message. He touched the earth of Ireland with his feet and brought light and blessing to the peoples of the world. He brought the book to the churches of the Protestants, the Catholics, the Anglicans – also to the Russian Orthodox Church, which will accept this work later.

The offering has happened! Angels rejoice and give praise for the presentation of the book. Tell John that I and my son greet him and thank him. Amen!

(to Joa)

Have courage and continue on your path! John should take time so that body and soul may recover.

(My comment: It did strike me how, in a symbolic way, I did bring the book to all the churches – to Glenstal, to Sacha (Russian connection), and later to the grave of my grandfather (Presbyterian), and to the Anglican church (St Anne's bookshop in Dublin, the person in charge received it with great cordiality). After these words were spoken, something in me expressed the desire to serve God, Christ and Mary, despite all my shortcomings.)

Later Mary continued:

'And now to the questions:

'Mark should say to the one who has given him money: We thank you for the generosity of your offer. With pleasure, we accept your offer, as long as it is without conditions, and just for the new spiritual centre. (Here Joa added that it is important to remain spiritually free, without bondage to some other principle.) The millionaire with his money may want to influence the Russian Church, may want power over the Russian Orhodox Church. His hands are dark, his feet are dark, the surface above his head is dark. This has something to do with power. The period of power in the church is definitively over. Living with Christ *is* the new Church.

'On the other hand, the Russian Duchess in Ireland is one who truly seeks God. Her hands, her feet and her forehead are full of a bright light. Behind her head is a light. Trust her.

'However, with regard to the proposed visit to Russia, do not include the Duchess from Northern Ireland in this matter. Otherwise she will lose confidence on a political level, and will have less strength. It is very important that she stands there where she is with her spiritual strength!

'(My comment: I don't know what 'political' means here and I would have to ask further. This part of the vision does not refer to Sacha's connection to Russia but, I guess, just to the proposed visit to the Moscow Patriarch.)

'Later an Irish saint spoke about Mark's questions; who should go to Moscow:

'Abbot Celestine – No

'Abbot Christopher – No.

'Mark – Yes.

'Gregory – with Mark – Yes.

'Those who go must work with great care on a theological level.

'(Here Joa saw in vision how the Patriarch would reflect about all that was discussed in the innermost levels of his soul. For example: he would say yes to seventy per cent of the revelations of Joa Bolendas' work and it would take days or weeks to discuss the remaining thirty per cent. Much time is needed to think through everything that would be said.)

'Whoever goes to Moscow must be strong and confident.

'Whoever goes must, in spirit, be able to stand authentically and truthfully before God. It is not so important to seek what is "the true church" but "the truth in religion".'

(Here Joa commented: it is important not to get bogged down discussing the truth of the Catholic and Orthodox churches, but the truth of the Spirit of the Christian way.)

(My comment: the 'no' to Celestine and Christopher I do not understand. I know it has no bearing on their mission and holiness before God. Several times Joa has had very positive visions about them – too many to keep sending. Has this something to do with a unique opportunity of a breakthrough in the relationship between East and West?)

Later the Irish saint continued:

'The meeting can take place now but not necessarily. Whoever goes needs three months to prepare himself.'

I gave this text to Gregory and Abbot Christopher and sent a copy to Atanase Tontchev with the following letter:

'I know I am supposed to send you these. I am on retreat, praying for you also, and giving thanks for the gift of our meeting. I think that the two abbots make it too official (i.e. the institutional Catholic church) and that it should be just "monks" (Gregory and I).'

14 August: Michael Paul Gallagher SJ, who is giving our retreat, and I go to the icon chapel. Especially relevant is the Descent into Hell. His talks on Thérèse of Lisieux and mysticism are important. James Scanlon rings to say that he is going to Lisieux.

18 August: In Dublin. Ciarán rang. Could I order a book on St Thérèse de Lisieux's last days by a French author Six, and collect his diary which he left in Waterstones. I ask in Waterstones if someone left a small pocket-diary, blue? They give it to me immediately. I take it back to Louise's. Decide to check if it is Ciaran's. Find it belongs to someone else! I return it to Waterstones, and as I do, realise that the real diary I should be giving to Ciarán (for his birthday tomorrow) is this one: what has been happening to the Cóiced!

21 August: Letter from Ed Walsh thanking me for good wishes on his retirement from UL. He has been a giant in this county, developing the university from nothing to its resplendence today. Nora and John Lambert are staying. They show me and Fr Peter how to make rosaries out of fishing cord to start a new industry in our shop. Something about them, these rosaries and the fact that we met in Mejugorje, pulling me

in an untoward direction! As Fr Andrew Nugent has said: 'Your appearance in Medjugorje must have been almost as miraculous as her own!' The Lamberts are seriously linked to the Holy Spirit.

11 September: I get news that Mícheál O'Regan, Dominican priest and psycho-synthesis pastor at Eckhart House died suddenly. (He used to stay in Puckane beside Glenstal after Christmas and attend liturgies here. He was counsellor to Barré Fitzpatrick, Richard and Anne Kearney, and Nóirín among others.) I had never actually met him, except to say hello once or twice.

13 September: Very good talk with Gregory. He tells me that Mícheál O'Regan, shortly before he died, had told the guest who is presently staying in our guesthouse to come to Glenstal to meet me. This man, Dermot Rooney, had told this to Gregory as they both went by car with John Hannon to the funeral.

14 September: I meet Dermot Rooney. Walk down back avenue. I tell him that I have no idea why Mícheál O'Regan would have told him to come and see me. In such unusual circumstances I believe that the purpose must lead to the icon chapel. He has an experience in the chapel in front of the icon of Christ the Healer which is either a real vision or else the ravings of a very disturbed person. I feel afraid for him but am aware that I have done nothing to promote this meeting. I have been forced into it. I bring him to lunch. He is in tears.

17 September: Dermot Rooney tells me what happened in the icon chapel. It was an initiation rite for him. A similar experience to one he had at Newgrange. He touched the stone and another world, an older one, invaded his vision space. He thought of Ivor Browne. My prayer that he had asked me to say became a mantra that helped him to survive without drowning. I was godfather at the initiation ceremony striking a balance, he felt. I was unaware of any of this.

22 September: Nóirín launches her book and CD on plain chant in Taylor's Hall, Dublin. Brian Keenan is present. Simon and I are there.

25 September: Bobby Sue Williams is staying in Glenstal for the week. It is very good for us and for her. We walk to the garden and up the Clare Glens. Peaceful times.

26 September: Bobby Sue leaves. I have another mind-blowing session with Dermot Rooney. It's as if I am being used to tell him things and I just find myself saying them and they surprise me as much as him.

I give him *Dreamtime* by John Moriarty, Yeats on the Vortex and *Jackson's Dilemma*.

29 September: Henry O'Shea back from Zurich, where he stayed with Gregory, brings me greetings from Christoph Schonbörn (Dominican friend of mine from Le Saulchoir in Paris in 1968) who is now Cardinal Archbishop of Vienna. I had been quoting him these days in talks and articles on icons.

6 October: Drove with Dermot to Enniscorthy to give a talk on Heaney. He wanted me to bring him somewhere sacred. We went to Knockfierna and walked to the fort. The lecture I gave on Heaney was uncannily descriptive of all we had been saying and of what had been happening since he arrived. In his diary Dermot (who wants to call himself Diarmuid if he joins the monastery) wrote (in between inverted commas made of musical notation): ' 6th October: Knockfierna – the hill of truth. The passage way – light. The ship is coming in for landing. Prepare the altar.'

17 October: Letter from John Bayley telling me to come and see Iris Murdoch.

19 October: Dermot told me another dream. He had met Louise. Louise had told him 'I've met you before in Waterloo Lane.' We then discover that his (Dermot's) family live in Waterloo Lane very near my Aunt Irene's old house and that they knew her and her dog! Wierd connections.

Anyway I go to America and he goes to France to do a retreat under Thich Nhat Hanh.

October 24: Flew to Denver. Biggest snowfall since 1982 for this time of year. Thousands of cattle die. Met by Alex Cranberg. Four hours to get eventually to his home (10 miles away!) at 2a.m. Roads littered with cars and lorries unable to continue. Alex's generosity and four-wheel drive get us there.

Susan Morrice, his wife, had organised several meetings for me which had to be cancelled. We were more or less cabin-bound for the weekend. So, nothing happened as planned in Denver. Susan lost her voice and was in bed for one day.

Showing Alex our Ausculta brochure, he was struck by the Shema Israel palimpsest. His father was originally Jewish and worked as a physicist in Los Alamos, New Mexico, where Alex spent his childhood. Fascinating carved wooden doors brought from Pakistan to Santa Fe,

New Mexico, by the German firm Serat & Sons, hang in his living room. The message of the brochure was similar to that put forward in a book called *The Turbulent Triangle* by Isaac Rottenberg. I thought of Sacha Abercorn's sensing a triangle of energy between Glenstal, Baronscourt and Russia. This Denver triangle concerned Christianity, Judaism and the state of Israel. Alex had the book in his library. I read it. Crash course for me in ecumenism in this direction. Judeochristianity as one. There has never been a revocation of the covenant with the chosen people. Their way and ours is an exodus towards the same God. Theirs is the apophatic path. They are the original monks. Their God is the God of our mystics also. Christianity is the introduction to Judaism and not the other way round. But a Judaism purified of local, ethnic, geographic, political narrowness. A Judaism in and of the Spirit. The Jews have always known the way to the Father; only the Gentiles needed Jesus Christ to be that way, to open that way! Rottenberg quotes a prayer of Pope John XXIII a few days before his death (4/6/1963): 'We realise now that for many many centuries our eyes were so blind that we were no longer able to see the glory of your chosen people, nor to distinguish on their faces the signs of the special status of our brothers. We have come to see that the sign of Cain is on our foreheads. Century after century our brother Abel lived in blood and tears on account of our trespasses because we had forgotten your love. Forgive us the curse which we have so unjustly inflicted upon their flesh. We have crucified you for a second time, because we did not know what we were doing. Lord, help us turn from the evil way we have gone in history and in Church history. Let our conversion consist of a concrete renewal. May the peace of God, which guards our lives and thoughts, fill our hearts in Christ Jesus our Lord.'[18]

Alex said that the author of this book was in Denver. He arranged for us to have dinner with him and his wife Malvina. Both their fathers converted to Christianity in Poland. Her mother and herself were expelled from their home on this account. Neither of them had been taught anything of their Jewish culture and now deeply regretted this omission. Conversion to Christianity had made no difference to their identification by the Nazis. Their families were killed in concentration camps and Malvina had been in a concentration camp in Poland from the age of 16 to 18. It was as if we had reached a level beneath each of our separate lives reserved for very few and privileged encounters. It was part of the 'meaning' of my visit to Denver. The other part was building up the connection between Susan, Alex and what we are trying to become in Glenstal. As if this network makes up a larger more widespread community of like minds and hearts. The airport in Denver continues to inspire architecturally. The Tents and Teepees that Seamus Heaney prescribed.

28 October: Landed in Dallas. Stayed with Phil and Bobby Sue Williams. Another home of deep contact with Glenstal. Beside my bed I find a book called *Small Miracles* by Yitta Halberstam and Judith Leventhal. This records coincidences as in the book which Sacha Abercorn had sent me on synchronicity by Joseph Jaworski. Both books saying: 'Maintain a certain rhythm and harmony with the universe. Don't try to rush things. Go with the flow. Allow things to happen. If you stay rooted in the intellect only, and disregard the spiritual aspect of life, you won't have them. If you get onto the wavelength of the universe then coincidences happen.' Bobby Sue is on this wavelength. The first thing I notice in their garden is wisteria.

We met the group who had been to Ireland this summer. All believers in our project. Mary Ann Smith is foremost in this regard. I find an immediate and down to earth connection with her in so many wavelengths and levels of sensibility. I stayed for a night with Gene and Mary Ann on their ranch where the first episode of *Dallas* was filmed.

Mary Ann Perryman is an impressive and witty person who has understood with some secret intuition what we are trying to do.

I was brought to the Mick Jagger and Rolling Stones concert in the Texas Motor Speedway. 'Bridges to Babylon' was celebrating thirty years of their music in a technological extravaganza. 250,000 were expected in the newly-built gigantic motor racing stadium. 40,000 arrived. My hosts bewailed the fact that, under these circumstances, had we known, we could have traded our $75 tickets for seats right up in the front row. I thanked the many stars in the firmament that beautiful evening that we didn't have to take advantage of that offer. My eardrums were already under severe pressure even at the huge distance we were away from the stage, where the group looked like intoxicated ants shrieking and gesticulating. Above, on massive screens we were treated to close-ups of their facial expressions and physical gyrations. They looked ancient and unhinged. The music was totally unfamiliar to me and not one decibel of it approximated to what my ear would identify as either beautiful or meaningful sound. Mick Jagger who has often been to the Smith Ranch where he was famously addressed by Gene as Mack Jigger is the same age as myself! He certainly needs to get something done about it, if he is to continue at this pace and with such total exposure. The wrinkles are grand-canyon deep, as John Moriarty would say. The drummer in the group is apparently a great-grandfather.

4 November 1997: Flew to San Francisco to attend a conference 'Toward a New Civilization' hosted by the State of the World Forum. It was a week-long session held in the Fairmont Hotel. Susan Morrice was also attending. She introduced me to Tom Jordan, a great friend of Connie Ryan and one of the original team to set up the American Ireland Fund with William Bourne Vincent. We were soon big into the world of coincidences, which is the way Tom Jordan sees his life also.

Redressing the balance of our divided world began with an opening night gala Mediterranean dinner, consisting of pasta ravioli filled with three cheeses garnished with toasted pinenuts in a light pesto sauce, followed by Chilean sea bass with a kalamata olive tapenade, roasted ratatouille sauce, grilled artichoke with garlic, olive oil and fresh thyme, marinated baby fennel and a parmesan reggiano polenta triangle, followed by cappuccino ice cream truffle served with a mocha and chocolate sauce, all with Wente Bros Reserve Semillon 1993 and Ivan Tomas Zinfandel 1993 or Domain Carneros by Taittinger, Brut 1992 or Greengulch Hills Fume Blanc 1995 as choice of wines. Then we were treated to no less than five speeches, ending with Marian Wright Edelman and Walter Cronkite (celebrating his 80th birthday). Far too long. Most people were dead and buried before it ended.

'A Walk Through Time' was a mile-long labyrinth with posters marking one foot for every million years of history, illustrating major events of evolution on planet earth. From Star Dust to Us, the title read. It took two hours. It was interesting, instructive, undifferentiated, and ultimately unconvincing: potted science and anthropomorphic agendas hitched to evolutionary events, through what is intended to be catchy commentary underpinning photographs, illustrations or diagrams on each poster, resulting in a scripture of the world which reads as combination of the Biological Book of Exodus and Beatrix Potter. Thus:

'Beings with hard parts have favoured histories'; 'Life is a story of permanence and change. Exuberant and innovative, it is also deeply conservative'; 'Organisms and species do not just evolve or become extinct they anastomose (fuse together)!'; 'All life forms are consortia. We are all chimera, composites of many life forms and many mergers'; 'Life originates in greasy, bubble-like, pre-life droplets which provided hospitable enclosures. Their surfaces permitted communication and exchange between inside and outside.' This last coagulation of metaphors (certainly the least 'scientific' account of the origins of species that I have read) might be the new theological jargon or an explanation of what our brochure is trying to express about the connection between monasticism and the world outside! However, the language becomes even more personificatory and pregnant with pathetic fallacy as the story nears its anthropomorphic goal: 'Bacteria aren't just fast; they're also loose. Gene traders and swappers, they do not just create the next generation – they can become the next generation. "Horizontal" evolution yields brand-new kinds of beings.' But when the vocabulary gets into the groove of fairytale, horror movie or war story, it becomes politicised and tendentious as Battler Briton or Star Wars: The earth is Goldilocks surrounded by three kinds of porridge: Venus being too hot and Mars being too cold! We hear of 'Horde havoc' and 'vampire-beings' that 'suck life from victims' and 'clones munching from inside out'. But the prize for latterday propaganda must go to this 'scientific' description of millions of years of geological evolution: 'In one of nature's luscious ironies, the outcome of invasion, followed by truce, will produce a grand blossoming in the history of life.' So, ride on symbiogenesis into Pearl Harbour etc. etc.

As I did the Walk through Time myself, some garbage collectors were arguing angrily with their boss about the impossibility of carrying out their functions with this trail of cardboard littering the sidewalk accompanied by a constant stream of pedestrian driftwood. He assured them that the interruption would only last a day and then the whole pavement could be cleared, posters and all, by the trash compactor.

This walk through time was packaged by 'employees of Hewlett-Packard Laboratories in Palo Alto, California, to provide a context for decisions about their future direction as a corporate entity.' Well it certainly gave them permission to increase and multiply and expand over the face of the earth. Manifest destiny. It was presented by Lewis Platt, chairman, president and ceo of the company and then discussed in hushed tones of awe and admiration by selected participants. Lunch was devoted to further eulogisation of the 'walk' while devotees munched 'Crab meat with a split half leg of fresh cracked crab' sponsored by the Hewlett Packard Company.

This opening phenomenon symbolised, for me, the State of the World Forum as a total entity: Too big, too much, too many, too often. 'It is our task, the president, Jim Garrison, told the membership, over the next several days to consider in a collegial fashion those principles, values and actions which should guide humanity as it moves into the next phase of development.'

Very worthy and very ambitious. However, few of the movers and shakers who were listed as patrons and who might conceivably produce the influence which such a benevolent hi-jack of the planet would require, were present. In the vacuum created by their absence, the helm seemed available to the highest bidder. And, thusfar, Hewlett Packard were pretty much alone in the field. Significantly, though plausibly under the circumstances (his wife, Raissa was seriously ill at the time), Mikhail Gorbachev, whose foundation underpins these proceedings and who was billed to appear on the last day of the conference, sent his apologies.

There was an idiom of bland bombastic self-congratulation at some of the public sessions: an aura of the enlightened ones, 'we' against 'them'. As if even constructive criticisism, questioning or deconstruction would be apostasy.

Nor was there any attempt to foreshorten or curtail. People who were programmed to speak for limited periods extended their mandate unconscionably and no attempt was made to spare the sometimes large and always unfathomably patient audience, many of whom were not completely fluent in English, although this was the only language used in the forum. (Another question-mark over its presumption to speak for the planet.)

But there were so many extraordinary presentations and such a galaxy of well-known world figures from every walk of life: it was a sumptuous daily feast of knowledge and insight. Marian Wright Edelman, president of the Children's Defense Fund, and Walter Cronkite, famous American broadcaster and jounalist, were my pick for the opening session.Wednesday gave us Stephen R. Covey of *The Seven Habits of Highly Effective People*, moderating a discussion on climate change, and Ben Zander, conductor of the Boston Philharmonic Orchestra, leading the 700 participants in a performance of Beethoven's *Ode to Joy*. Thursday found the 700 participants on an interactive multimedia experience which meant that we, as a group, drove a plane over a number of mountaintops and through certain target areas. Each participant received a baton with red plastic at one end and green plastic at the other. One side of the room could make the plane go up if they raised the red end of their batons in the air, and make it go down if they raised the green end; the other side of the room could make it go left or right by raising the green or red end of their batons in the air. The plane was on a very large screen and we, as viewers and active participators, had the impression that we were inside it, in charge of the controls.

The point of this exercise was to show how a group of 700 people who had never met before could cooperate in a relatively short time to achieve certain identifiable goals. It worked impressively as an exercise and the idea was that if this 'plane' was the planet, we could, by taking certain simple steps and making some clear and identifiable moves, change the direction we were presently moving in.

Among the star-studded cast for today was Muhammad Yunus, founder and director of the famous Grameen Bank in Bangladesh, Andrew Young, US Ambassador to the United Nations, Fritjof Capra of *The Tao of Physics*, and discussion ranged from 'Medical Leadership and the Drug Crisis' to 'The Growth of Microenterprise and Corporate Social Responsibility.' Friday was dominated by a discussion on crimes against humanity in which Arn Corn Pond who had escaped the killing-fields of Cambodia, another who survived the ethnic cleansing in Bosnia, a girl whose family were wiped out under a South American dictatorship, Alexander Yakovlev, who had spent all his life in Russian concentration camps and José Ramos-Horta, last year's Nobel Prize winner for Peace from East Timor, participated.

Ms Leslie Danzinger was billed to speak about 'Science and Society: How Technology is Shaping our Future'. Her company produced a kind of glass which was able to bend light. This is apparently a difficult accomplishment but important in areas such as optics etc. In the middle of her rather technical explanation she stopped and said: 'Here's where

RONNIE SMITH PAINTING SERVICES

Wallpaper Stripping Service Available

Only Quality Materials Used
No Payment Required Until Work is Complete - References Available

Tel: 086-196 3547   01- 459 6490

Interior
Exterior
Offices
Houses
Warehouses
Shops

I let my hair down, literally' and she let a mass of chestnut hair fall over her shoulders by removing one pin on top. The gesture caused a massive silence. Then she said: 'The real reason why I know how to make glass bend light is that it was revealed to me in a vision. No one can tamper with light unless God shows them how, because light is essentially from God.' Her mother was Jewish and kept on asking this question: 'Why did we all get into the trains that were taking us to Auschwitz? Why did we not refuse to move. There weren't that many soldiers herding us into the carriages.'

My own contribution was to a seminar on Monks without Monasteries chaired by Alan Jones, dean of Grace Cathedral, and Spirituality in Social Action. There were representatives of many world religions. In the second one, Arn Corn Pond, who had escaped the killing fields in Cambodia, broke down in tears while he was speaking and most of the participants found themselves joining him, not out of sympathy or sorrow, but some deeper gift of tears for humanity. When I spoke after him he came over and put his arms around me and everyone went back to their kleenex again. Anyone at this session came out a slightly different person. Susan Morrice was also there and the meeting deepened an already accelerating connection between us. John O'Donohue's book *Anam Cara* was mentioned as one of those works which made Christianity attractive to many.

But the real surprises were meetings that took place by chance in between the official sessions. Joseph Jaworski of the book *Synchronicity: A New Kind of Leadership*, which Sacha Abercorn had sent me, was at this conference and met Susan Morrice. Mark Luycks of the European Commision (from Belgium) who had tried to get all the Benedictine Abbots of Europe to meet Jacques Delors, when he was president of the EC, to examine how spiritual values could best be promoted in the structures of Europe. He was also a fan of Nóirín Ní Riain's music. The presiding poet of the State of the World Forum was David Whyte. It was my first time seeing him in action. His book *The Heart Aroused, poetry and the preservation of the soul in corporate America*, is a convincing attempt to allow the poetic imagination to influence the world of business and work.

There was a large contingent from Northern Ireland including the lord mayor. This conference is being hosted in Belfast in 1999, Jane

Morrice, Susan's sister is the co-ordinator, and they hope for help from Glenstal.

8 November: Flew from San Francisco to Santa Fe. Stayed with Sandy and Jim Fitzpatrick. Liz Shannon was with them. Snow on the way here. Very high up and cold. Beautiful drives through the Sangre de Cristo Mountains. Met with Bernard Pomerantz, author of *The Elephant Man*, among other books, and Jan Loco (native American silversmith, whose grandfather was one of the chiefs advising Geronimo. He was so in favour of negotiation with the white people that he was christened Chief Loco, thus her name.) She does all her work on granite rock and regards it as religious activity: combinations of sun, stone, silver, light. Made me think of Leslie Denzinger's light-bending glass.

13 November: Fanny Howe drove me to Los Angeles. I went to a poetry reading she did and visited her publisher. She has written about thirty books of poetry, literature and mysticism. She is still trying to make a link with Fr Dunstan Morrisey's sixty acre monastery in San Francisco, Sky Farm, where visitors stay in hermitages constructed from wine vats!

She brought me to an art exhibition in the LACMA: Video art by Bill Viola. A series of square rooms in darkness with video projections on various walls. This is what she had in mind for a room corresponding and adjacent to the icon chapel in Glenstal, where introductions to the icons and art movies with spiritual purpose might be shown.

Fanny told me that after the first time she met me in Cork in 1995, she had returned to America and Gertrud had told her that she must visit an Irish psychic who had set up in San Diego. It cost $100 and seemed an awful waste of money. She never usually does such things. The woman was gaudily 'celtic' and dripping with earrings and ghastly jewelry. Anyway she startled Fanny by a number of revelations. She saw her surrounded by vines: Fanny had just spent that summer trying to set up a house for herself in Martha's Vineyard. At the end of the session the psychic told her that there was a man in a cassock in Ireland called Patrick and that she was to ask him to pray for her because he walks in his dreams!

I stayed with David Nash (Glenstal old-boy, 1968-1973) and his wife Fiona and their baby girl Hannah.

16 November: Flew Los Angeles to Boston. Stayed with Liz

Shannon. Met Cleo Webster. I knew there was something to find out there. She showed me two beautiful icons she has. Her father was a Greek Orthodox priest. The icon represents the Trinity but on equal terms in a straight line of three. It became one of the major icons of this journey. Cleo is going to leave it to me in her will.

20 November 1997: Flew to Chicago to meet Fr Andrew Greeley again. On the flight read the book he had written for Christmas: *Star Bright*. It was about a man studying in Boston who falls in love with a Russian duchess! The man goes on the same walk I went yesterday along the Charles River and flies from Boston to Chicago. I land and forget that I am an hour out of sync, and so am late for our meeting. His staff are all in a flap. We have lunch. He takes me to St Patrick's Cathedral recently restored, Henry Moore's sculpture of Nuclear Energy and Crystara. All symbolic. I find Rilke on *Love and other Problems* in the university bookshop. Getting into a taxi I hear John O'Donohue's voice in the back seat. It is a radio ad for his book! He has been following me.

25 November 1997: Met Sacha Abercorn in Buswells and planned a trip to London to inaugurate a seminar in Glenstal on sacred space with Peter Hunter, environmental architect.

Attended the Pushkin Prize fundraising dinner in Trinity as Sacha's guest. Abbot Christopher also. Seamus Heaney read and spoke. He was in plaster with a broken leg.

10 December 1997: Van to Dun Laoghaire to cross to Hollyhead on Stena line. Too rough to cross. Stayed with Louise and Risteárd. Wrote cards from the van in Dun Laoghaire to Seamus Heaney and Chuck Feeney. There is a conection between these two. Somehow they will converge.

11 December: Crossed England in the blue van. Stayed in Coventry.

15 December: Met Sacha and her son Nicholas at her appartment mews in Little Chester Street, off Buckingham Palace. Taxi to Peter Hunter's office, 30 Regent Street. Very good discussion about sacred space and the Glenstal project. They would come and do a seminar on this subject next April or May. Sacha and I talk afterwards and she describes herself as someone walking through the desert and every now and then coming across a Bedouin tribe encamped around a fire. She joins the group around the fire and feels very much welcome and at home. This is how she feels about Glenstal at this time. There is some

reason for this mutual presence, something to be done. What she describes reminds me of the atmosphere of the Rembrandt in the National Gallery of Ireland, The Rest on the Flight into Egypt.

16 December: Ealing to Oxford by blue van. Met Iris Murdoch and her husband John Bayley in their home. House looks unkempt and deserted, like something described in her novels. She is beautiful. She has Alzheimers and like my own mother she cannot find the words she wants, so she fumbles for them and tries to hold up the fumblings to express to you what is deep in her heart and soul and mind. If you understand and reply in words that make her know that you have heard and understood she looks at you with such depth of communication it is sacred, an icon. 'You have such beautiful eyes' I tell her. She agrees by not withdrawing them. 'Yes, Iris, you always had beautiful eyes' John Bayley says, as if talking to a child. He fusses and interferes and looks very scattered himself. She kisses me so gently and with such communicative tactility. We kiss three times. I hold her hand. I give her the book of the icons (Joa Bolendas'), the tape and CD of *Vox de Nube* and some Butlers' Irish chocolates. I could be bringing gold, frankincense and myrrh. She says, you must must come back again. 'You are doing something important in your beautiful monastery in the centre of Ireland.' They have to leave for a dental appointment. He leads her to the car. She stands with me as he backs the car out of the tiny drive and almost runs over a crocodile of school children passing by in pairs. She rushes to save the children. He tells me that he first met Sacha Abercorn (he is an expert on Pushkin) at Sutton Hoo! (He has actually made a mistake it is called Luton Hoo and is Sacha's old home, she told me later) but the slip is meaningful also. I felt such immediate love for Iris Murdoch and that she was there, so present, and so cut off, but living in a monastery of her own where her communion with God was transparent. She was radiant with that presence. I later found three first editions of her books in Oxford: *The Philosopher's Pupil*, *The Black Prince* and *Bruno's Dream*. I bought these. I had to leave *The Italian Girl* behind as I could not afford it.

19 December: Card from John Hill: 'It was good to see you in the summer – a symbolic and meaningful encounter. I hope you found the words of Joa Bolendas helpful. Many times in the last months she sees a rainbow of light from the church of Ireland to the Russian church. It is

getting stronger. This is your work and she sees you searching for a way to do it.'

21 December: Meant to meet Nóirín outside 2 Temple Villas at 6a.m. Went to 2 Temple Gardens instead! We were round the corner from each other for a half an hour. Then I discovered my mistake and collected her. We both believe that such things are providential, so we didn't much care. Today was the solstice and the advent antiphon 'O Oriens'. We both knew we were meant to celebrate the rising sun. I turned up towards the Silvermines and the sun rose as we arrived on top of the ridge. We left the car and walked together arm in arm towards the rising sun. It was dancing and pulsating in front of us in a way I had never seen before. It was a divine showing and we were left silent and awed by it. The sundance was a phallic throbbing movement and the words of the Benedictus came into my mouth: *Erexit cornu salutis.* It was saying to us both: You can't not believe now. We were like children of some new forest who had stumbled on a divine ritual and it hadn't been by accident. On the way down the hill three horses stopped us. Another Cóiced. They too were messengers.

22 December: San Clemente card of the deer from Seamus and Marie Heaney: 'Dear Mark Patrick, I owe you a letter. But in the pelt and blizzard of card time, I signal the season's blessings.'

23 December: Nóirín and I drove to Belfast to John Barkley's funeral in Belmont church. We left at 7a.m and arrived at the church at 1.30p.m. just in time for the service to begin. Three angels led us there. It could not have happened otherwise. He was one of the great priests in both our lives. Carrie was delighted that we came and told Nóirín it would have made John's day that she was there. We drove back immediately, going via Athlone and reaching Dromore where we had supper with Simon and Micheál at 8.30. I don't think I have ever been so long in a car.

1998:

22 January: To Galway to meet John Coyle. Two more Iris Murdoch first editions in Kenny's. John is ready to be our flagbearer. He believes in us and believes the time is ripe. Who does he want to help him? What member of the community would he choose? I had always imagined that this was going to be Timothy. No, he wants to work with Simon. 'Has

he stopped building his own little empire down there? Is he with you? If so, we'll work together.'

24 January: Gregory came back. This was important for me as stabilising presence. He has been in Beuron and confirms the connection between our roots there and a whole spirituality left unexplored in the recent post-war ambiguity. He had a dream about the Church that Benedict had shown him a tile in the sanctuary which he had lifted to find an undergound church beneath. He looked up and saw golden telescopes in the sanctuary. It was about access to the icon chapel and then its power moving outwards towards the universe. Also his connection with Edith Stein through a very old nun contemporary of hers; Fanny Howe had just sent me her reflections on the same Edith Stein.

20 February: I wrote to Iris Murdoch and John Bayley, saying how moved I had been to meet her, how beautiful she was, how I knew that behind the walls of Alzheimers she was in a monastery with God and that wonderful wisdom was being secreted there. If any manifestations of this wisdom should emerge, in however garbled a form, I would like to be privvy to them. I also gave him a dig about the *New Yorker* article saying that he did not believe in God and had persuaded Iris to adopt this view!

12 March: Malachy and I meet Bobby Sue Williams and Dolores McCall at Shannon airport. They had come from Israel. We had lunch in Dromoland Castle.

14 March: I showed Dolores and Bobby Sue the icon chapel having told them the story and shown them Joa Bolendas' book. I then drove them to meet Rita McConn Stern and Ted in Kinvara. Rita took them over and showed them her house. We were meant to have tea at 4 and then go to supper at Paddy Burke's at 6.30. By 6.00 they were still swopping stories about houses and furnishing and decorating. Ted and I are left to preside over the abandoned tea table. We have huge strawberries and chocolate cakes before leaving for dinner. Dolores told us her story. She had been working with a big firm in New York. Apparently, they lost everything at that time. All the big customers were trying to meet her boss and she was holding the fort for him in the office. Mr McCall, their biggest client comes in. It is around lunchtime. He says he wants her to go to lunch with him. She says she can't leave the office, he knows that. She has a choice, he says, either she takes him to lunch or he withdraws his account from their firm! She decides to go.

He keeps her at lunch for two hours. He insists on having coffee, desert etc. When eventually she insists that they must return together to the office, she is in a panic. What on earth can she say to her boss. When she gets back, there is pandemonium in the office. Her boss cannot believe that she walked out like that. She turns to present Mr McCall to him, their biggest customer. There is nobody there. He has deserted her. She turns and runs. She goes to the lift, down into the lobby, out into the carpark. No sign of him anywhere. Nothing for her to do but go back upstairs and face the music. When she gets back into the office she finds him hiding behind the door, laughing. Some time later they are married. Five years later her husband dies and she is left with a considerable fortune. From her earliest consciousness she has wanted to become a missionary. All that has happened in the meantime must have some purpose and she has been waiting to find out what form her life, already given to God, should take.

16 March: Richard Hurley presented plans for the guest house to the community very competently and successfully. This will go through in a fortnight's time and if Marcia O'Brien comes up trumps we're on our way. Richard also brought sketch plans for the library.

10 April: Tenth anniversary of the opening of the icon chapel. Louise sees Ballyneale up for sale in the property section of the *Irish Independent*. I give two talks to those on retreat here. Timothy has asked me to do this as Margaret MacCurtain who had been booked can't make it. I say I haven't time to do something new so I'll give them what has been on my mind. Gerard (later Br James) McMahon produces a very beautiful programme: *Heaney, Silence and the Empty Tomb*. After the second talk, Brian Carroll asks me very directly if there is not some reason for these talks, 'As Marie Heaney says, have you not done some journey similar to that of Seamus Heaney, and what is the secret of that discovery?' I agree to answer him tomorrow. Almost miraculous agreement reached in the multi-party negotiations in Belfast that day.

11 April: After morning prayer I know that I have to tell them the story of the icon chapel in response to Brian Carroll. I listen to the radio again at the time of Benedict's death to get some message. They are telling us what the papers say and quoting Seamus Heaney in today's *Irish Times* in response to the possibility of peace at last in Northern Ireland. I know that this is a direct answer to me. The talk advertised for

me in the programme is : Obedience: listening to the music of what happens. I do just that. I answer five questions put to me yesterday and then I say why I am going to tell them the story – because Brian Carroll's question was exactly the one I had put to Heaney and he asked it on the tenth anniversary of the opening of the icon chapel. So, I tell them that I feel Glenstal has had a similar vocation to Seamus Heaney and is being asked to be the place where the altar can be anchored. The altar in the icon chapel like the altar in his poem is to be hauled up into the main body of the church and out to embrace the larger context, to connect with UL and Shannon and to help this mid-western region to become the fifth province which will eventually bring peace. I tell of the first arrival of John Hill and his news of the visionary aunt in 1976, *The Crane Bag* in 1977, the three records with Nóirín and Micheál, the building of the icon chapel and James Scanlon's arrival. The opening on the feast of Russian Orthodoxy in 1988 and Joa Bolendas' vision that three shafts of light: one to Russia, one for peace in Northern Ireland and one to particular individuals visiting the chapel, fell on the floor that day. I showed them John O'Donohue's *Anam Cara*, Nóirín's *Gregorian Chant Experience* and Joa Bolendas' *That You May Be One*, as signs that things were speeding up and what was foretold was about to unfold.

There was an article on Glenstal Abbey as it is emerging in the music world especially, and the statement by Seamus Heaney in the same *Irish Times* this morning. Heaney's piece was directly apposite: 'If revolution is the kicking down of a rotten door, evolution is more like pushing the stone from the mouth of the tomb. There is an Easter energy about it, a sense of arrival rather than wreckage, and what is *nonpareil* about the new conditions is the promise they offer of a new covenant between people living in this country. For once, and at long last, the language of the Bible can be appropriated by those with a vision of the future rather than those who sing the battle hymns of the past.'

Some of those present at the retreat are disgruntled. They have not been able to understand or appreciate what I am talking about. In fact, because of Timothy's invitation to me they have been overhearing a conversation of the Cóiced. Some find this a privilege, others find it a pain and are ready to say so. I am sorry for them, but it hardly costs me a thought.

James Scanlon and Maura come for the vigil and he brings me a biography of John Cage and two beautiful framed pictures of the future 'ecopods' (Simon's word for our convocation centre) in Glenstal. We visit the icon chapel. Great and beautiful energy.

Mícheál O Súilleabháin has now got the chant course organised and is advertising for a lecturer. Christopher is approached about this. Cyprian is back for this weekend. His new record/CD of organ music with the icon of St Nicholas on the cover has been released.

16 May: I had arranged to meet Fanny Howe and Dermot Rooney in the Fairmont Hotel, the only place I knew in San Francisco. Fanny drove us to Sky Farm, one hour from San Francisco, crossing over the Golden Gate Bridge and heading for the Napa country which is the wine making area. Sonoma, a famous cluster of vineyards is the neighbouring town. Here on a sixty-acre mountainy site, Fr Dunstan Morrisey, a Benedictine hermit, has built what he calls a hesychasterium, on land which was donated to him by a parishioner who believed in his vocation to silent meditation. The hillside now has a refectory with kitchen, built in Tibetan-style architecture, a chapel and two hermitages made of wine vats, a guest quarter and library, where Dunstan also lives, and a cabin where two caretakers are living presently. He was on retreat so we had the place to ourselves, apart from his Russian wolfhound, Sophie. Susan Moon, a Buddhist friend of Fanny, came to join us overnight. There had been so much rain in the previous days that rattlesnakes were more plentiful than usual.

Fanny has been sure since she visited Glenstal last year, that there is some connection to be made between Glenstal and Sky Farm. Dunstan is over 70 and has been here for twenty-five years, living on his own. By a series of unusual occurrences, Dermot Rooney decides that this is the place he wants to be for the next few weeks, so he can decipher some possible connection which might be revealed. We all happened to be here at this time to inaugurate together this experiment. Fanny had met Dunstan at a Simone Weil conference where she had presented a video. Sue Moon, who edits a Buddhist journal, has written a monograph on Dunstan: *To Hear Thoroughly*.[19]

At the entrance to Sky Farm, Sam Kean, author of *Fire in the Belly*, a work on masculinity, has his centre. He had been invited to Ireland to speak by Dermot, some years ago. Not that relations between him and Dunstan are very cordial. Dunstan sold him the land but since then there have been difficulties. Difficulties also with the local bishop who wanted the property handed over to the diocese. When Dunstan refused he cut off contact. So, there is no recognition of the place or its tenant at official church level, apart from the contact with Dunstan's original monastery.

17 May: We went to Green Gulch, a Buddhist Center in Muir Woods, to hear Norman Fischer, Jewish-born abbot of this community, giving a talk before we had lunch with him. His talk was on the connection between art, poetry and spirituality. After it we had an interesting session: The equivalent of The Holy Spirit in Buddhism, he thought, might be described as 'suchness'. This reminds me of Hopkins' *haecceitas*.

Susan left and Fanny drove us to Berkeley. It is rakish and like the 1960s – as if Fanny's historic home town. It is my past too – France in the times of student revolt, and Dermot's, a throwback adolescence from the same era! It cements us together and Fanny is exhausted. We go to Mass to rest. Hateful folksy mish-mash music. Joa Bolendas' book is in one of the shops. We buy nothing.

21 August: Letter from John Hill answering my questions to Joa Bolendas:

'Your letter was timely. I was just about to leave for New York: a conference on Revisioning Death. I was apprehensive about my talk and meeting a new group of people. What a surprise! The conference was a great success and my talk went well. We had fun, there were many artistic intervals and the whole set-up proved transformative for many who were present, which rarely happens in such large gatherings. This group, formed around such people as Robert Sardello, Chris Bamford, Therese Schroeder-Sheker are dedicated to a spiritual renewal in psychology, philosophy, theology, art, etc. Most of them are scholars in their own right with a lot of experience in their own fields, and are really good people. They avoid an ideological, dogmatic, or pseudo-scientific approach that one tends to find in groups dedicated to spirituality. They have a deep respect for the work of Joa Bolendas. I felt that something I have been groping for these past years has now become manifest. I am sure I will continue to work with this group.

'Before the conference I stayed some days with Chris Bamford – a really wonderful man. He is a Celtic scholar and was involved in the

Yeats school in Sligo some time ago. You might already have met him. Recently he has gone through a spiritual crisis, owing to the death of his young wife and this has changed his whole outlook on life.

'With the advent of your letter and my overall impressions, I believe that you too, sooner or later, will find a connection to this work. I kept thinking of your goal of a peace center. Of course it would be wonderful at Glenstal, but it might manifest where and when the spirit so wishes. In fact there was a strong suggestion that the next conference of this group could be held in Ireland and, quite independent of me, perhaps at Glenstal! Treasa O'Driscoll, who knows Fr Simon, will be in contact with him, if plans go in that direction. If they do, I recommended to Sardello that you be invited as one of the speakers.

'Joa Bolendas prayed for your three questions. I will just print out my translation of the answer of a risen one, that she heard in vision:

Hilarion is a man of truth.

John will also have contact with him later.

Give him some of your work. (The Icon Book?)

Hilarion will become a new person, a spiritual awakening is possible.

Tell him the man and woman of today are seeking the mystical.

For the psychologist 'Dermot',

Yes – God has called him,

but he should work for Christ and for humanity!

This work for God, Christ and humanity has to be learned and worked through.

He has to change and be active!

For the three people:

Three to seven people must be called by God independently for the great work that is to be done in the church – for the renewal and unity of Christians. Ask the Holy Spirit of Pentecost for this renewal!

It is important to work further on:

Who is Christ?

How is the Holy Spirit active in our lives?

What separates us? What unites us?

John will be in Ireland (perhaps next year).'

In October 1998 Harry Bohan organised a conference in Ennis asking

'Are We Forgetting Something? Our Society in the New Millennium'. I gave a talk 'Climbing into our Proper Dark'. After the talk Maura Hyland of Veritas asked me to write a book expanding on this topic. The book *Kissing The Dark* came out during this pre-millenniel year. It was listed as a bestseller for non-fiction paperbacks and I had no problem publishing books I wrote since then. Before this I had spent twenty years trying to get some of my writing accepted by publishers.

In March 1999 I attended 'Thanksgiving: Spirit of 1,000 years' a conference of religious leaders held at Thanksgiving Square in Dallas. The Archbishop of Canterbury, Rabbi Adin Steinsalz, Cardinal Arinze, Dr Seshagiri Rao, president of the World Hindu Federation, Dr Siddqqi, president of the Islamic Society of North America, Venerable Achok Rinpoche, representative of the Dali Lama, Jagad Guru Ramananda Charya attended, among others. A delegation was led by Ronnie Appleton, QC, from Northern Ireland. They had been persuaded to build a similar Thanksgiving Square in Belfast.

Met Cardinal Arinze in the lift on the way to breakfast, he remembered being at Ewu, our monastery in Nigeria. With Sir John Templeton at breakfast. His foundation awards prizes to religious endeavours. Keynote address by Dr Louise Cowan: 'Our Need for Thanksgiving in the New Century.' She compares our situation at the brink of a new millennium to the sixteenth century Renaissance when the whole of human life was revisioned in new and different terms. Ships and printing revolutionised the world of that time; spaceships and computer technology revolutionise ours.

The closing ceremony was a multimedia pageant at the Meyerson Symphony centre. It was impressive with representative musical instruments accompanying most world religions. The Archbishop of Canterbury addressed the gathering. Disappointing attendance. A long time was spent working out the order in which the dignitaries of the world churches would walk in the procession through the beautifully designed Ian M. Pey auditorium. More were on parade than in the auditorium watching.

A number of worthwhile events in this conference. Most impressive was their having persuaded the United Nations to declare the year 2000 an International Year of Thanksgiving, during which there will be a stamp made of the stained glass 'Glory Window' spiraling upwards into the chapel ceiling at Thanksgiving Square. But, in the end, I ask myself what is it all really about and what are these people doing here?

The delegation from Northern Ireland made it quite clear during the interviews they gave for television during the St Patrick's parade day: they were here for dollars. They had brought with them a brochure showing the proposed scheme on Sand Quay, near the Waterfront Hall, half an acre bounded by the River Lagan. The design was the result of an architectural competition won by Brian Paul of Hurd Rolland of Edinburgh. On the back of it they show pictures of the Eifel Tower, the Pey Glass Triangle in front of the Louvre, the dome of St Peter's in Rome, the Atomium Ball and the standing stones at Stonehenge, so they have ambitions for its grandiosity and durability. It is not going to be cheap. Having set up the Square in Northern Ireland they, of course, hope to attract more dollars to the province by business and tourism. serious reasons for thanksgiving.

Some of the Indian participants were there to propose a similar square in India. Everyone thought this was a marvellous idea. Some pointed out that it need not be a very complicated or expensive structure, just a square marked off. Nonsense, whatever they had in Dallas was going to be bigger and better in India. And they too needed American dollars to build it.

Representatives of the Dali Lama are everywhere and they are looking for the release of Tibet from Chinese domination, so any publicity in America is pertinent.

Cardinal Arinze is there because he is president of the Pontifical Council for Interreligious Dialogue and this is a perfect platform for promoting this without getting into problems of intercommunion etc. He has also been browbeaten by Fr Luis Dolan, an Argentinian of Irish parentage who has embraced this cause and is promoting it very successfully. He works with Elizabeth Esperson, who runs the centre of thanksgiving in Dallas, and has brought both the Vatican and the UN on board.

Interesting connection between John Templeton and Peter Stewart. They came together when they were young men and founded the YPO (Young Presidents' Organisation) for the whizz-kids of business management, and when they were too old to be members of their own club they founded another for more ageing magnates. Now they seem to have come together to market a new product which is 'Thanksgiving'. Templeton gave the same speech at least three times during the weekend. When you hear it first it sounds plausible but the third time it begins to fade. 'When I wake up every morning I say, wow! Another day to be of service.' He started the Templeton Foundation because the Nobel foundation had left out what he considered to be the most important area of human endeavour: religion. And he wanted it to be a bigger prize than any they distributed to give it prestige and publicity. That makes it worth over $1,000,000 at this time.

Peter Stewart, who is behind Thanksgiving Square in Dallas, and he, are trying to be religiously 'original' and unite the world under one banner. The trick is that 'thanksgiving' is something everyone must subscribe to and you don't even have to belong to a religion to do so. Using a broad-grain shotgun they can shoot the planet. It is almost the Cocoa-Cola ad: 'I want to teach the world so sing in perfect harmony.' Get them all to say thank you and that will bring them together. During the weekend we thanked everyone all the time: the sponsors, the speakers, the coordinators, the organisers, the facilitators, and ourselves for being there. Everything was dealt in superlatives and 'If they get me to say thank you one more time' I overheard a woman from Northern Ireland hissing, 'I'm going to hit somebody. Anyway, what have we got to be thankful for in Northern Ireland.'

At the closing ceremony everyone had to put a beautiful piece of paper on the altar with their reason for giving thanks written on it. We read out our sentiment publicly and then reverently placed it on the altar. Delegates represented Zoroastrianism, Hinduism, Jainism, Buddhism, Judaism, Christianity, Islam, Sikhism, the Baha'i Faith, with the Indigenous Peoples of the Americas. Sentiments ranged from: 'I invite everyone, including the environment, into my heart', to 'I see gratitude when I give a bone to my dog. He cannot speak but he shows his gratitude with his body language by the way he looks at me and the way he wags his tail.'

1999:

19 March: Hopkins seminar in Denver. So, why Hopkins? He, almost unbeknownst to himself, is the Holy Spirit, like a Trojan Horse, entering the contemporary artistic tradition of the Catholic Church, and bringing

with him the riches and the mystical strain of English literature, or rather, literature in English.

My own initiation to this dimension of his work came through a seminar in Boston with Geoffrey Hill in 1991-92, which I stumbled upon through Eddie Holt, the Shannon fellow from Ireland (currently *Irish Times* columnist) whom I met chez Liz Shannon when I was at Boston University.

I applied to the Monasterevin Summer School to publicise these ideas but got no reply. When I met Dennis Gallagher in Ireland the last time he was here he gave me his new card. It had an advertisement for the Hopkins seminar in Denver. So I wrote to Victoria McCabe and she put me on the programme. My talk explains this role of Hopkins but in a technical way.[20]

As this was the occasion to offer an honorary doctorate to William H. G. Fitzgerald, former ambassador to Ireland, for largesse bestowed, I offered a prayer of the faithful for all those Americans who had helped Ireland, especially Senator George Mitchell and Ambassador Fitzgerald. He came over to meet me afterwards and will come to visit Glenstal in the summer. Both he and his wife belong to a group of Republicans who believe in the Reaganite economy which allows for accumulation of vast wealth in few hands, but who then feel obliged to be philanthropic with this abundance especially in the area of education.

Hugh Kenner gave the after dinner speech with amusing anecdotes about his meetings with T. S. Eliot, Samuel Beckett, Ezra Pound and William Carlos Williams. His philosophy: meet the creative people alive in the world in which you live. You can't meet the great people of the past but why pass up on the ones who are your contemporaries?

1-5 August: The Fifth Annual Sophia Conference, honouring Joa Bolendas, was held at Glenstal Abbey. 'The intention of these conferences is to deepen understanding of Divine Feminine Wisdom, Sophia, as an actual spiritual presence ... to foster the forming of a Sophianic culture. Such culture comes about primarily through those perpetual researchers, often writers, artists, musicians thinkers.'

John Hill, Ronnie O'Gorman, Miriam Mason and Simon Mason, grand-niece and grand-nephew of Joa Bolendas, John O'Donohue, and Sacha Abercorn were present from our corner of the mosaic. Robert Sardello, Cheryl Sanders, Therese Schroeder-Scheker, Christopher

Bamford, Anne Stockton, Treasa O'Driscoll made up another corner introduced to us via John Hill. This meeting was an important piece in the jig-saw. As recipient of the 1999 Sophia Award from the School of Spiritual Psychology, Joa Bolendas was described as follows: 'In 1957, as a mature woman of forty years of age, the Swiss mystic Joa Bolendas first began to see in vision, dimensions of God's light. It was streaming from above and surrounding the dedicated individuals and activities of those within the Swiss Reformed Church and other Christian communities of her village. As the spouse of a pastor, and a mother of three sons (one of whom she buried and grieved) this life of revelation was not something Joa sought.

'Sensitive and deeply intuitive as a child, she nevertheless was of vigorous constitution and in every way healthy. She participated in and loved the beauty of nature, art and music, and had never sought visions. God gave them to her, although not out of the blue. The living word of the Gospels and the rhythmic life of the liturgical year had formed the very fibre of her life and meaning. Gradually, over time, these first "beautiful experiences" of light and specific signs of God's presence in the village setting began to deepen and expand.

'These epiphanies were not unrelated to the mysteries of the liturgical year, and came into being no doubt because of the capacity Joa (in particular) and her family and community circle had to follow the life, passion, death and resurrection of Jesus Christ in their daily lives. Eventually the revelations (visual and auditory) included Christ, Mary, angels, the saints, the evangelists, numbers, hymns, living images and symbols.

'For forty years, she has sustained this deep inner work, maintaining diaries and journals of visions, struggling with, praying over, receiving, trusting and loving the life and work God gave her. It has always been Joa's wish to write under a pseudonym. The first book of some of these collected writings came out in English in 1997 under the title *So That You May Be One*, published in the USA by Lindisfarne Press. A second volume of her writings will be forthcoming.

'Anonymity is characteristic of her charisma. She is in her eighties, has a vital family circle, and spends the remainder of her days reading, writing, painting and praying.'

John O'Donohue was the only outside speaker from Ireland to address the group.

My talk to the Sophia Conference was called 'The Limerick Tumblers: Choreography of the flight-pattern of a local breed of pigeon.' It tried to give an overview of our part of the jig-saw which by now seemed to have taken some shape: 'This meeting does not take place by chance. It was meant to be, but has only come to be, because a number of circumstances have cleared its way, and because a number of people have followed the clues which led to its emergence.

'It is as if four groups of people were burrowing their way through a mountain and at last they meet. There is a stream from anthroposophy, there is a visionary stream from Zurich, there is the School of Spiritual Psychology from America, and there is the local stream from this source in Ireland. The object of my talk is to give an account, which is a personal one, of the local breed of pigeon. Those of us who have been working on the ground here and are, therefore, not surprised that this conference is taking place here at this time, have been aware of a certain consistency of presence, a detectable pattern of movement, an identifiable posture, which allow for progress. All of which resemble a dance or flight-pattern.'

In September 1996, Professsor Mícheál O Súilleabháin invited us to the Irish World Music Centre in Limerick to a celebration of new Irish expressions in music and dance. Two new dance sets were premiered at that performance. The choreography for these pieces was inspired by the unusual flight-pattern of a local breed of pigeon called the Limerick Tumbler. This local breed is a variety of the Short Faced, English, Tumbling Pigeon, so-called because of its peculiar tumbling flight-pattern. After thirty years of selective breeding, during which time the pigeon loft was vandalised at least once in 1986, reducing the whole movement to a minimum number of two birds left on the planet, they are now a recognised and established colony.[21] They have managed to change the original species into a much more 'showy' type of bird. So much so that this was the first time a breed of pigeons had been honoured by having music and dance commissioned in its name. By the end of this talk you may understand the many and varied reasons which suggested this title: 'The Limerick Tumblers: Choreography of Flight-Patterns in a Local Breed of Pigeon.'

My story begins forty years ago when at least five of the people in this room were at school here together.[22] I went on a school trip to

Engelberg in Switzerland with John Hill. I remember wondering what kind of a wierdo he was when he began to describe the strange call he said he heard from that place, and began answering it with a cow-horn that he had bought as a souvenir.

We left school. I decided to join the monastery here, a comfortable and cowardly way to do what we both said we wanted to do: follow the direction of the Holy Spirit. He was much more adventurous and unusual. He went down to the sea on Killiney beach and promised to go wherever the sea wished to take him. His mother had an army of right-wing stalwarts to shake him out of this foolishness and make a man out of him. Elizabeth and Peter Gill were seen as corrupting influences as they tried to help him find out where the sea wanted him to go. Feichin O'Doherty, Professor of Psychology in UCD, believed there was great danger of heresy here; Fr Matthew Dillon, his former headmaster, thought he should go to Dalgan Park as a Columban missionary, and General Moore, a friend of John's mother and a member of the Greystones Golf Club thought that if he got toughened up a bit he could join the British Army.

Meanwhile the sea beckoned and told John to go to America. When he arrived, there were people waiting for him. He did an MA in philosophy at the Catholic University of America in Washington DC. I remember that he was required to read Heidegger's *Being and Time* in three weeks and do a paper on it. I was in Paris studying philosophy and theology during the student revolution of May 1968. So, it was over thirty years ago that John and I met in Paris. His mother in desperation had gone to America to bring him home. I think the bank was the preferred option at this time. Just before she arrived, however, the sea communicated its wishes to John who was told that he should go to Paris to a place called La Maison de Toute Detresse where he would meet someone who had been sent to provide him with the next clue for his journey. Walking along the Boulevard Saint Michel, or some off-shoot, we passed a patisserie and were overwhelmed by the delicious scent and irresistible sight of strawberry and apricot gateaux. We had only enough money to have one between the two of us.

The Maison de Toute Detresse was a hostel for down and outs run by Jesuits. John met Anne-Marie his future wife in this hostel where they were meant to be voluntary workers. The Jesuits soon got rid of them as the last thing they wanted was a pair of star-crossed lovers dealing with the overflow of drop-outs in the Paris of the late 1960s. Anne-Marie brought John back to Zurich where he was introduced to Joa Bolendas. She told him to apply to the Jung Institute. He presented himself at the formidable portals of this Mecca of psychoanalysis and was told to readjust his flight-pattern and come back when he had received a doctorate from some recognised university. The pigeon went home with his tail between his legs if that is possible. Joa Bolendas told him to go back again the next day and reapply as if nothing had happened. I'm not sure how many times he reluctantly agreed to undertake this humiliating exercise, but one Saturday morning, I think it was, he was waiting in the ante-room when a Jungian analyst from China met him there and told him he had been expecting him. After a certain amount of examination it was discovered that John Hill was exceptionally gifted at dream analysis. He was accepted by the Institute and is now one of their revered pantheon.

I was invited to his wedding. Joa Bolendas said I should be there. I was a monk of Glenstal Abbey by now and could not have afforded a ticket. The day after the invitation came I met a man in Dublin, a friend of both our families – John Hill's mother and my mother were close friends – who said he had bought a ticket to go to the wedding but now could not go, and would like me to represent him. I was John's best man and I met Joa Bolendas very superficially and briefly.

Now the first point I have learnt, and which I make here in anecdotal form, is that John Hill is not just the translator of Joa Bolendas; he is, in fact, a collaborator. In his translator's foreword to her visions he tells a significant story:[23]

> When I started my training as a Jungian analyst, I was afraid that the analyst I chose would expose my faith as a fraud or a massive defence system. I feared that I would be unable to articulate or defend my own religious belief. To my surprise, these fears were alleviated by the unconscious itself, which came to my rescue by means of a dream. In this dream I saw a large stone altar surrounded by four pillars supporting a roof, a simple version of the baldachin of St Peter's, Rome, which was in need of repair. A voice said, "The altar is religion, the four pillars are psychology." When I awoke, the holy atmosphere surrounding the altar impressed upon me the necessity

of maintaining my religious perspective, and I understood the altar to be a symbol of my own immediate relationship with God. I recognized the mandala structure of the baldachin as a symbol of the wholeness of the personality. This would be the subject matter of analysis. It could be renewed and strengthened so as to act as a support, protection, and means of communication of the altar mysteries, which at times were too powerful to be contained and expressed through faulty structures of my personality. This dream has remained with me throughout my life, pointing to a distinction between religion and psychology and the need to recognise their complementarity.

The first fact of the particular local flight pattern I am trying to describe here, is that Joa Bolendas is essentially connected to John Hill, and that symbiosis, from my point of view, is symbolic of two dimensions: those who see visions and those who dream dreams on the one hand; and the complementarity between religion and psychoanalysis on the other.

About ten years later in 1976 John arrived in Glenstal with Anne-Marie and her cousin Sami, Joa's son, a professional photographer. They had been sent by Joa because she had had visions about Ireland. There was a spirit of Celtic Christianity which was hidden in certain places: monastic sites, ancient high crosses, early medieval churches. This spirit of Celtic Christianity must be released and become a source of renaissance for the whole Judaeo-Christian culture. Specifically she had seen in a vision some icons that were in Ireland and these were going to be powerful vehicles for the release of this hidden spiritual energy.

Joa Bolendas identified from photographs our icons as some of the ones she had seen in her visions. She and Sami brought out a booklet on *The Icon and its Significance*[24] which included photographs of all the icons she had seen, (9 of the 16 in this book were from our collection) with, as text, what had been said to her in her visions. The book was published in 1979.

Since that time many people have found healing of one kind or other from one icon in particular, and from reading the book with the picture of that icon and the following prayer of St Nicholas:

It is the icon of the church
for every kind of sick person!

Everyone - who contemplates the icon -
begins spiritually to adjust to Christ -
Thus you receive light and spiritual strength.
What happens then is most holy.
By this experience, not every sick person will be healed;
but they will begin to become holy.
This icon must not be lost!
It is most sacred!

John Hill had communicated to me around that time that Joa was sure that the spirit of Celtic Christianity which needed to be tapped and channelled would be greatly helped by three people in this Shannon area who were already working in that direction. I believed, at that time, that one of these must be Brendan O'Regan, the father of Shannon Airport and all the development in that surrounding region, with whom I had been working very closely as he set up the Irish Peace Institute within the newly burgeoning University of Limerick. I was also involved with Brendan in his work for Northern Ireland, Co-Operation North, and his plans in Shannon for an international centre for co-operation which was focused primarily on Russia and on trying to end the Cold War. There was a very pronounced ecumenical dimension to Joa's visions and she kept on stressing that Russia would be affected by the release of Celtic Christianity, which predated all divisions between Orthodox and Catholics.

In 1982 the flight pattern shifted. The Joa number became 5 instead of 3: The Cóiced. This was the old Irish word for a province. It means a fifth, even though there were only four geographical provinces in Ireland. The Fifth Province, the middle, Meath, was the spiritual centre which was hidden. This fifth province of the imagination where unity could take place, became a theme in the 80s both through *The Crane Bag* and *Field Day*. In the strange way that these events unfold and corroborate each other, the sermon in our church on the Sunday morning that this conference began, by Fr Vincent Ryan of our community, was about a very early mosaic in the floor of the church in the Holy Land at Tabgha where the multiplication of the loaves and fishes took place. Vincent described how there were only four loaves depicted on the basket in the floor because the fifth loaf was on the altar everpresent and everywhere.

But for us, at that time, in the 1980s, it meant a group of five people. A dance of five. This was more precisely and biographically made up of the interchange at many levels between three members of the Glenstal community, Simon, Ciarán and myself, with Nóirín Ní Riain and Mícheál Ó Súilleabháin. But it also overflowed into the wider community. I have learnt that all these images and hieroglyphs, these dance-patterns, derived from Joa's visions and sayings, are symbolic. They are not meant to be taken literally. The dance involves a pentagram: 5 couples or 5 people and in each one there is a bodily reality of 5, as in 2 hands + 2 feet + head, representing different gifts, different personalities, different roles. This dance of five then accomplishes the opening of the seventh centre. It did not have to be any particular five people, it was a pattern of five which could be any grouping or different combinations of five.

For instance in the community here in Glenstal there were five ordinations in the 1990s which were seals on that altar of five wounds which make up the reality of the mystery which is here involved. Five loaves on the altar to feed the five thousand. A mystery which combines all that makes up the particular genius of human being: the five ordinations were Simon and Basil, and then a new trio which formed an important group of stained glass windows in the emerging cathedral of the Transfiguration: Gregory, Paul, Senan. They seem to have been sent at this time with very different but exceptional gifts which could help the Johannine church to manifest itself. And this community has recently been expanded symbolically by Joa Bolendas, to the sacred number of seven, as in seven planets, seven days in the week, seven sacraments, seven deadly sins, seven gifts of the Holy Spirit, the Heptateuch (first seven books of the Hebrew testament). Seven people are meant to perform a kind of symbolic dance. This represents, in some way, the seven Chakras. There is a new 'spirituality' maybe it is a very old one, but it leads to communion with God and wholeness of the individual person. This wholeness involves a clearance and connection of the seven chakras of our 'subtle' bodies. However this is being achieved in us by a special kind of community of persons (seven in all – although not to be taken literally) each one corresponding to one of these chakras. Joa Bolendas specified that seven people would 'turn up' – not to be press-ganged or head-hunted. They could be groups of people as in a family or community, or an individual; the identification should not be too literal or numerically confined; and just as the chakras themselves cannot be identified with biological parts but yet are situated in certain areas, so this whole movement is meant to take place fully in each one of us, but each of us is more identifiable with one of the seven chakras.

One of Grimm's fairytales describes the kind of community which was emerging. And even finding this story was an exercise in what it is about. I put a notice on the community board asking if anyone had a copy of Grimms' Fairytales. The brother librarian, Colmán, found a copy of *Jacob und Wilhelm Grimm Volksmaerchen* in a bilingual series Verlag, Hamburg, 1947, which Fr Philip Tierney had bought in 1951. This contained one version of the story in German with an English translation. Br Anselm Hurt also gave me a copy of his Grimm's *Household Stories* printed in London and New York in 1896 by George Routledge & Sons, which he bought in a second hand bookshop for £2. It contained an entirely different version of the same story. The one I give here is a combined version of both.

What it describes is a community which is not a company of chosen friends; not not a cabal of gifted initiates, not a clique of high-minded reformers. It represents a community of searchers for the truth. They are sent, not elected. Not everyone has the same gifts. This folk tale of the Grimm brothers called 'How Seven travelled through the World' tells you something of what I have found about such a 'virtual' community:

There was once a man who understood a variety of arts; he had served in the army, where he had behaved very bravely, but when the war came to an end he received his discharge, and three dollars only for his services. 'Wait a bit! this does not please me,' said he, 'if I find the right people, I will make the King give me the treasures of the whole kingdom.' Thereupon, inflamed with anger, he went into a forest, where he found a man who had just uprooted six trees, as if they were straw, and he asked him whether he would travel with him. 'Yes', replied the man, 'we two shall travel well through the world.' They had not gone far before they came up with a hunter who was kneeling upon one knee, and preparing to take aim with his gun. The master asked what he was going to shoot, and he replied, 'Two miles from hence sits a fly upon the branch of an oak-tree, whose left eye I wish to shoot out.'

'Oh, go with me', said the man, 'for, if we three are together, we must pass easily through the world.'

The huntsman consented and went with him and soon they arrived at seven windmills, whose sails were going round at a rattling pace, although right or left there was no wind and not a leaf stirring. At this sight the man said, 'I wonder what drives these mills, for there is no breeze?' and they went on: but they had not proceeded more than two miles when they saw a man sitting upon a tree, who held one nostril while he blew out of the other. 'My good fellow,' said our hero, 'what are you driving up there?'

'Did you not see,' replied the man, 'two miles from hence, seven windmills? it is those which I am blowing, that the sails may go round.'

'Oh, then come with me,' said our hero; 'for, if four people like us travel together, we shall soon get through the world.'

So the blower got up and accompanied him, and in a short while they met with another man standing upon one leg, with the other leg unbuckled and lying by his side. The leader of the others said, 'You have done this, no doubt, to rest yourself?' 'Yes,' replied the man, 'I am a runner, and in order that I may not spring along too quickly I have unbuckled one of my legs, for when I wear both I go as fast as a bird can fly.'

'Well, then, come with me,' said our hero; 'five such fellows as we are will soon get through the world.'

A while later they came upon another man who was lying with his ear to the ground. They asked him: 'What are you doing there?'

'I am listening,' answered the man.

'What are you listening to so attentively?'

'I am listening to what is going on in the world. My ears hear everything; I can even hear the grass grow.'

'Come with us,' the others said, 'six fellows like us will travel usefully through the world.'

Soon they met a man who had a hat on which he wore quite over one ear. The captain said to him: 'Manners! Manners! don't hang your hat on one side like that; you look like a simpleton!'

'I dare not do so,' replied the other; 'for if I set my hat straight, there will come so sharp a frost that the birds in the sky will freeze and fall dead upon the ground.'

'Then come with us,' the others said, 'for seven people like us should travel smoothly through the world.'

These seven new companions went into a city where the King had proclaimed that whoever should run a race with his daughter and bear away the prize, should become her husband; but if he lost the race he would lose his head.

The seven companions bade their runner buckle on his other leg. The wager was that whoever first brought back water from a distant spring should be victor. Accordingly the runner and the princess both received a cup and both began to run at the same moment. But the princess had not proceeded many steps before the runner was quite out of sight, and it seemed as if but a puff of wind had passed. In a short time he came to the spring and filling his cup he turned back again but had not gone very far before, feeling tired he set his cup down and laid down, making a pillow out of a horse's skull, to take a nap. Before long he was snoring loudly. Meanwhile the princess, who was a better runner than many of the men at court, had arrived at the spring, and was returning with her cup of water, when she perceived her opponent lying asleep. Emptying his cup she ran on faster still. All would have been lost if the man with his ear to the ground had not heard the snoring. He summoned the huntsman who was able to see with his sharp eyes. He loaded his gun and shot the horse's skull from under the runner's head. this awoke him and jumping up he found his cup empty and the princess far in advance. He ran back to the spring, filled his cup and returned home ten minutes before his opponent.

The king was disgusted and his daughter not less and they consulted together how they should get rid of the suitor and his companions. At last the King said, 'Do not distress yourself, my dear: I have found a way to prevent their return.' Then he called to the seven travellers: 'You must now eat and drink and be merry.' He led them to a room with a floor of iron, doors of iron, and the windows guarded with iron bars. In the room was a table set with choice delicacies, and the King invited them to enter and refresh themselves, and as soon as they were inside, he locked and bolted all the doors. That done, he summoned the cook and commanded him to keep a fire lighted beneath till the iron was red-hot. The cook obeyed and the seven champions sitting at table began to feel warm. They rose to leave the room and found the doors and windows bolted fast. Then they perceived that the King had some wicked design. 'But he shall not succeed,' cried the man with the hat; 'I will summon such a frost as shall put to shame and crush this fire.' He put his hat on straight and a frost fell and all the heat disappeared and even the meats on the dishes began to freeze. Two hours later the King, thinking they would be suffocated, caused the doors to be opened and he went inside. As soon as the door was opened there stood all seven fresh and lively. In a great passion the king turned on the cook and scolded him. The cook pointed to the fire saying: 'There is heat enough there I should think.' And the King was obliged to own that there was and he saw clearly that he would not be able to get rid of his visitors in that way.

The King now began to think afresh how he could free himself. 'Will you not take money and give up your right to my daughter?'

'Well, my lord King,' they replied, 'Give us as much as one of us can carry and you are welcome to keep your daughter.'

This answer pleased the king very much and the companions said they would come and fetch the sum in fourteen days. During that time they hired all the tailors of the kingdom to sew them a sack. The strong man who had uprooted all the trees took the sack on his shoulder and carried it to the King. The King put a ton of gold into the sack which required sixteen men to lift. But the strong man lifted it up with one hand. By degrees the King caused all his treasures to be brought but they did not half fill the sack. 'Bring more,' said the strong man, 'these are only crumbs'. Then they were obliged to bring seven thousand wagons laden with gold and all these the man pushed into his sack, gold, wagons, oxen and all. Still it was not full. When everything they could find was put in, the strong man said, 'I must make an end to this; and, besides if one's sack is not quite full it can be tied up so much easier!' and, so saying, he hoisted it upon his back and went away with his companions.

When the King saw this one man bearing away all the riches of his kingdom, he got into a tremendous passion and ordered his cavalry to pursue the seven men. Two regiments accordingly pursued them and shouted out to them: 'You are our prisoners! Lay down the sack of gold or you will be hewn to pieces!'

'What are you saying?' asked the Blower; 'you will make us prisoners! First you will dance on air!' So saying, he held one nostril and blew with the other the two regiments right away into the blue sky. So the seven companions took home all the wealth of that kingdom, and, sharing it with one another, lived contentedly all the rest of their days.

The community which I am trying to describe which infiltrates and overlaps the actual physical community of monks at Glenstal Abbey, is a component part of Glenstal and has always been supported and ratified at various levels by the different Abbots. Abbot Augustine sponsored and actively participated in the recordings we made with Mícheál and Nóirín; Abbot Celestine presided over and preached at the opening of the icon chapel. Abbot Christopher was here with us at the opening of this conference.

During the 1980s there was a very definite presence from Northern Ireland, first of all through Fr Terence Hartley who was ordained the same year we opened the icon chapel and had been in Einsiedeln for his theology and worked with John Hill and Joa Bolendas. Later Fr Gregory, who came from the Falls Road, the same street as Terence, found the icon chapel like a sluice gate in his own journey towards God. He joined the community with a doctorate in Byzantine Theology and is one of the foremost experts on icons, the liturgy and theology. He also spent a year in Zurich. He later wrote a best seller called *The Glenstal Book of Icons*.

In 1997, Sr Jo O'Donovan, a constant presence in theological investigation in our region, who had been introducing the community to Buddhism, brought William Johnston, the writer and expert on Eastern mysticism, to Glenstal. We discovered that he too was born on the same Falls Road as Terence and Gregory.

It somehow became apparent that the opening date for the Icon chapel in the crypt under our church must be 10 April 1988, Easter Day in the Orthodox Church, in the year they were celebrating 1000 years since Christianity first came to Russia. One of the iron crosses on the eastern door of the Icon Chapel is the same age. It comes from Crete.

The third recording we performed with Nóirín and Mícheál, called *Vox de Nube* (The Voice from the Cloud),[25] contains much of the music we sang on that day. So, the two points of reference for me are the icon chapel as the visual symbol of this incarnation of the Spirit in this locality, and the music of *Vox De Nube* completing the trilogy of records which we made with Mícheál and Nóirín in the years preceding the opening of the chapel, aural icons of the new music, audible sounds of the inaudible. And this, again is something local, something idiosyncratic to particular cultures. John Hill again mediates an important anecdote in his introduction to the visions of Joa Bolendas:[26]

> I remember the day when Nóirín Ní Riain, Joa Bolendas, and I went to church and prayed. Quite spontaneously Nóirín began to sing the hymns of Joa. I was struck by the beauty and deep Celtic resonance of Nóirín's interpretation. Joa was impressed by the quality of Nóirín's singing but upset because her songs were not sung in the way she had received them. As we continued to listen, Joa passed me a note containing the following words of a saint: 'It is the Irish soul that sings your hymns in this way. In Africa you will experience them in still more different ways – with drums and movements of the body. Give thanks!'

The message is clear: Give thanks for pluralism, for cultural difference, for each breed of pigeon finding its own flight-pattern. There is no definitive way, no univocal interpretation, no dogmatic directives. And yet there is a Celtic Christianity which is going to give life not just to us but to many others when its beauty and freedom of spirit are released. This will be in the form of a culture which is a way of seeing, hearing, touching, tasting.

So the third truth which emerges in my consciousness from this contact with Joa Bolendas is that there is a community here which has already been formed and is expanding, but the focus, the hearth, the temenos, is the icon chapel.

In 1991 and 1992 I was drawn to the Yeats Summer School in Sligo and lectured and learned about his work *A Vision* and his involvement with hermetic religion through The Order of the Golden Dawn. I met Joan McBreen, poet and psychic, who began to write a series of poems[27] which traced the unusual flight-pattern of the local breed of pigeon. Five of these poems: 'The Bible Garden', 'The Wisteria in the Courtyard of Dromore House', 'The Half-Heard Lament', 'The Other Side of the River', and 'Remembered Time' were emblematic.

Wisteria became a code word, both as flower and emblem. Mary Ann Smith: 'My mother had a wisteria to stop the traffic. It bloomed all summer long. She put a teacup of fertilizer on the roots.' Outside Pamela and Pat Mulcair's house, Elisabet Bernie's first garden after she got married, 25 Lenox St, the E-Bar-S Ranch, Isabella Lane, Rita's Roost, The Glenstal 17th century walled Garden, 16 The Palms, San Antonio, I found it in every significant place I went.

The Wisteria In The Courtyard
Of Dromore House

The wisteria in the courtyard of Dromore House
is yearning towards its own shadow.
Evening. Two women are also yearning
towards one another. One is hiding her face.

It is growing darker. The women leave the courtyard
and enter the house. A moth is shivering over
a candle-flame; small rolls of bread are offered
to the man who appears in the tableau.

His eyes are blue, do you remember?
The women are careful not to look at them,
looking instead at the single branch
of white blossom they carried into the room.

The man is lifting his head; he reaches
for the flowers: "Tell me how long
they last, my dears, how long?"
The moon has lit the courtyard. Music

Is playing in the house, the beat insistent.
Candle-light, lamp-light, moonlight . . .
on the table wine in a stone jug, purple grapes.

Suddenly everyone is older. There is a wind
starting to blow, the door is swept open
and the rest of the story is repeating itself …

The actual deed which was the conference itself, held in Glenstal Abbey
and honouring Joa Bolendas, was a footprint of the Spirit on the journey
being recorded here. Miriam, Joa's grand-niece, worked miracles to get
here. Her brother Simon and his wife Sibylle made a point of being here
also. Miriam's voice left imprints in the walls of the church with her
singing of the music which Joa had retrieved from visions. At one point
during the conference Miriam was singing in the main body of the
church and Sacha happened to be in the icon chapel underneath.
Hearing the sound Sacha was aware that this music needed to be
grounded or earthed from down below. It was heavenly music, music of
Ariel. Another voice from down below needed to be sounded.

19 September 1999: Asked to speak at the opening of our new guest
house, which was so generously paid for by Dolores McCall, these words
were given to me: 'Strange date, almost like science fiction and yet we
are here. The future has caught up with us. The ancient Celts would
have seen it as a symbol of perfection – nine being the nearest
approximation of unity. On this day, 19 September, in 1803, Robert
Emmet made his speech from the dock: 'When my country has taken its
rightful place among the nations, then let my epitaph be written.' Many
have tried to write that epitaph and might have expected to finish it
before we stepped into the new millennium. Soldiers, statesmen, civil
servants, politicians, churchmen, have all tried their hand. The stamp we
used to invite most of you here today bore the features of Seán Lemass,
grandfather of the Celtic Tiger. We rejoice in all of that: it has made
possible the prosperity we see around us today, including our own.

Limerick has sprung up like a phoenix out of *Angela's Ashes* to
become the mouth-piece of the Shannon. For the last fifty years, at least,
people of the Shannon region have been trying to build here an estuary,
where the river meets the ocean. Estuary comes from the word for the
tide, *aestus*. Estuary is where the local meets the global where tide meets
current. The Shannon estuary has also been turned into a runway where
dreams take off and fly. This region has become the place of our future,
the place where we welcome the tidal wave that comes.

Some are afraid of the future. They fear it as a destructive force, as a hurricane off our coast. People call it the abyss. They see nothing but chaos for the future. Some are too confident about it. The century we are leaving was a century haunted by the Titanic. It began with the tragedy of over confident and arrogant hubris swallowed in the waves. It ended with the largest audience ever assembled on this planet watching the rerun of the movie.

Others believe in the future and are ready and waiting when it comes. Such people have no time for the abyss. Whenever they are confronted by what others call the abyss, their only thought is where can they build the bridge. We have been blessed with many such people in this region. They have taught us that managed co-operation can conquer any situation. They have created around us here a whole region where the future will be made welcome, will be made prosperous, will become our future together. 'There is a tide in the affairs of men which taken at the flood leads on to fortune'. How do you take the tide at the flood? How do you lead it on to fortune? By being prepared. By building watch towers, bulwarks, filters and spigots to distribute the water as it hits the shore.

But when it comes to writing, whether an epitaph or a dream, we have learnt at last to turn to the poets. It is not for us to write the future. It is for the future to find its finger in us. 'Between my finger and my thumb, the squat pen rests.' The finger is the Spirit, *Digitus Dei*, the artist is the thumb; when writing the future, they are writing an icon. The future is a vision or a dream. Artists must be prepared for such a task.

Irish poets learn your trade
sing whatever is well-made ...

The holiness of monks and after
porter drinkers' randy laughter

Monks have their place in such a work. We are preparing that place here at this time.

Tuesday 26 October 1999: Flew to New York and then to San Francisco. Met with Tom Jordan. He spoke of his disappointment with the Catholic Church and disillusionment after the promise of Vatican II.

He felt that ecumenism was really important and specifically the root connection with Judaism. I told him about Christoph Schonbörn, the Cardinal Archbishop of Vienna who had been in Le Saulchoir with me in Paris in 1968. When I got back to the Maxwell Hotel I found some mail that I had brought with me and hadn't yet opened. One was a letter from Frank Lawrence in Rome with the following on a separate sheet:

Intervention at Second Special Assembly for Europe of the Synod of Bishops, 7 October 1999 – Afternoon session – Synod Hall, Vatican. H. Em. Card. Cristoph Schonbörn, O.P., Archbishop of Vienna

Vienna is midway between Moscow and Madrid. Is it in the middle of Europe? Where does Europe begin? And where does it end? Till ten years ago, Vienna was at the Eastern extremity of free (Western) Europe. After the fall of the 'iron curtain', a new boundary was born: the Schengen boundary. Should we be content with this de facto division? The 'Europeanisation' of the European Union can be achieved only if integration is supported by spiritual renewal, and Jesus Christ is the key to this. I would like to mention explicitly three wounds, and I invite the Synod to pray and work for their healing:

1) While the crimes of Nationalsocialism have been discussed and overcome, those of Communism are often still veiled in a 'cloud of unknowing' and in silence. Should we, the Christians and Bishops of the West, perhaps also particiapate in this silence? Should we not ask for forgiveness for this in the present Synod, so that the memories of the martyrs can be celebrated with a pure heart?

2) The Holy Father always speaks about the two lungs of Europe and of the Church: the Eastern and the Western Church. The tradition of the Eastern Church has been, I must personally acknowledge this, of great help in the serious crisis of the Western Church. The Western Christian needs a vital contribution of the theology of the Fathers of the Church, of the monasticism of the Eastern Church, of the solemnity and the beauty of the Divine Liturgy and the icons. How much of the ecclesial renewal is due to the Churches of the East! But also the Eastern Church needs the Western lung to be more

incarnate in the visible structures of society and overcome the serious danger represented by the national Church, for whom the referral to Peter, the center of unity, is undeniable.

3) Prophetically, Wladimir Soloview felt that the Schism of Christianity between East and West can be overcome only by a new referral to the mystery of Israel: the root must sustain us, we do not sustain the root. Our belonging to the only People of God is not due to language, culture or nationality, but by the choice and the calling of God, who from our differences invites us to His 'holy meeting' in the 'Israel of God'. [Original text: German]

It was almost exactly what Tom Jordan had been saying to me in the car. I sent him a copy.

29 October: Met Fanny Howe at the Fairmont Hotel, which is being renovated for the millennium. She was, as usual, correcting hundreds of scripts for her students. We had met at the same time in the same place with Dermot Rooney in May of last year when he began his retreat at Sky Farm. The rain had stopped and it was the most beautiful day. Autumn colours and candescent light. We drove over the Golden Gate Bridge and along the coastline through Sausalito and San Rafael to Petaluma where Fanny had booked us into a motel. There were no rooms available in Sonoma as some kind of festival was in progress. We stopped at nearly every point along way to look out at the ocean and back over San Francisco. It was a magic drive, as if we were being shown it at its most spectacular. Motel 6 on the highway, past the Alzheimers Centre, was too awful an end to such a gifted day. (My archetypal motel is the one in Hitchcock's *Psycho*.) We drove on to Sonoma in the middle of the wine country just below Sky Farm and there were two rooms available in the El Dorado, the same restaurant hotel where we had dinner with Diarmuid on the previous visit.

30 October: Sky Farm at 9 o'clock. Dunstan brought us to meet Prasanna, an Indian painter friend of his. For four hours we had a private showing of his paintings. These come from a mystical centre in himself and create a similar experience in the viewer. He had come from India some time ago with his wife. She had died and this experience had been so harrowing for him that it eventually led him to a space beyond it.

From here a series of paintings, which I found as powerful as Mark Rothko's but not as claustrophobic; there was a caesarian glimmer of hope pulsating from within, edging through to the surface as a crack through marble or a blade through cloth. Icons in a contemporary abstract style: 'Blessed be the Glory of the Lord in his dwelling-place.' Although Prasanna is not a Christian he has painted a series of faces of Christ. He wants these to be housed at Sky Farm.

We brought a Chinese takeaway back to the main house at Sky Farm. I listened to a tape of Denys Turner's 'The Darkness of God' on Meister Eckhart. Impressive tour de force. Fanny and I went to Mass in Sonoma and she cooked us dinner. I slept in the crow's nest on a sliver of styrofoam as a mattress. I kept dreaming I was on a slide over a cliff.

31 October: Sue Moon, who had written the account of Dunstan's life, and who had been here on our first visit, arrived with Dunstan's typewriter. We had lunch with pumpkin pie and watched a video, which was in the library, of Iris Murdoch in conversation with J. Krishnamurti in 1984. Seeing her on the video here was another confirming coincidence linking to many other threads. Dunstan wrote a will leaving Sky Farm to Glenstal as from now. This was witnessed and signed by Fanny and Sue. This is what Fanny had been working towards for the last two years. It combined with the happenings over the same period, sparked by her arrival in Glenstal, which resulted in Diarmuid staying at Sky Farm for three months and Dunstan arriving in Glenstal while Diarmuid was doing his live-in before joining our monastery last summer.

The atmosphere of this millennium year can best be conveyed through the miracle of our new library and its secret donor. The community had managed to be persuaded to go ahead with this library and Abbot Christopher had signed the contracts without a penny in the bank. Chuck Feeney and his family came to the opening of the new guest-house, 19 September. He said his board would meet 10 October. He would put this proposal to them himself.

So, when nothing came in October, I emphasised to Chuck that Hayes, our builders, were holding off any request for payment until the end of January, as a further incentive to persuade us to go ahead immediately. I gave him a full schedule of payments to be made. I was sure his bequest would come by the end of January. I had complete trust in Chuck Feeney as one of the people referred to in Joa's original identification of a trio in this area working towards renewal of the ancient Celtic spirit. He has changed the face of the earth in this Shannon region and with Ed Walsh helped to create the thriving University of Limerick.

6 December 1999 was the feastday of St Nicholas. Several coincidences made me certain of the divinity shaping our ends. The *Irish Times* of that same day – I have kept a copy – had front page headlines about the World Music Centre in the University of Limerick as well as commentary on the peace process in Northern Ireland (two of Chuck Feeney's many beneficiaries). Page 10 had a long article on 'The Real Father of Christmas' by Arminta Wallace with a picture of our icon of St Nicholas who appears 'In places as far apart as the icon chapel in Glenstal Abbey in Limerick and the Russian Orthodox cathedral in Helsinki.' But what was he doing in Antalya, a Turkish tourist resort in May? 'Well, far from being the last place on earth you'd expect to come across Santa Claus, the southern coast of Turkey is the original stomping ground of the real St Nicholas. In a beautifully lit reliquary in the Antalya Museum lie a few charred pieces of bone … of the third century bishop of the bustling Lycian port of Myra, now a sleepy town known as Demre.'

15 December Chuck was in Ireland on his way to Vietnam. We met in the Castletroy Park Hotel. He said he had my schedule of payment and not to worry.

At the end of January of the new millennium I was being hounded by everyone to contact Chuck and find out what the score was. I was reluctant. I knew the last thing he would want was a whining nagger in pursuit. But by March I was in despair. So I sent him a poem by fax.

Dear Chuck
we're stuck
without a buck
and several bills to pay
unless you bless
our neediness
this merry month of May
one monk
is sunk
must do a bunk

in total disarray!
I know
you're so
much on the go
its difficult to see
how you can pause
for every cause
so I address my plea
to one resort
that can't run short:
Ma Feeney's expandable meat loaf recipee!

The reference to Ma Feeney's meat loaf was about the menu which Chuck had produced for his own family and friends while they were staying at his hotel at Castletroy Park in Limerick.[28] It was his mother's way of coping with all the strays who inevitably populated her open-ended table. He said I would hear from him by 22 May and all my worries would be over.

I arranged for a community meeting on that Monday 22nd. We had to get a vote to put the community in debt for over a quarter of a million which we owed mostly to Hayes. Much grumbling and predictable criticism about this. We shouldn't have started without the money in the bank. I was responsible also the last time this happened and we were almost made bankrupt. But the vote was decisively in favour. I had no word from Chuck.

The day of Fr Bernard O'Dea's funeral, 25 May 2000, I got an email from Chuck's secretary, Bonnie Suchet: she wanted details of where to send the money. It would take about three weeks to transfer. St Nicholas had struck again.

22 October: To mark 250 years since Johann Sebastian Bach died, 28 July 1750, and Advent in the year of the new millennium, Ferens Szücs played Bach's six solo cello suites in Glenstal Abbey Church on 22 October, 26 November and 17 December, 2000. Bach believed that if he got his music right, God would be there. If Ferens got Bach's music right then God would be there also. These suites require only one performer and one instrument. The cello Ferens used was made at the time Bach was composing. Here we had the possibility of achieving real

presence and embedding this in the walls of our church. The Holy Spirit of music.

17 December: Today, Gaudete Sunday, we celebrate a certain kind of joy. The cello as lower-pitch instrument is particularly suited to this mood. Bach uses it in such a setting almost like the wood of the cross.

Today we sing at Vespers the Magnificat antiphon, *O Sapientia*:

O Wisdom, Sophia, Sapientia,

You come forth from the mouth of the Most High.

You fill the universe and hold all things together

in a way that is both gentle and strong.

O come, teach us the way of truth.

Bach's truth is in the spiritual quality of the music not in its external trappings. Pablo Casals advised his students to play a Bach Suite every day like a daily prayer. Music is time unfolding. Bach and his contemporaries had a concept of time and of music different from ours.

His music is self-contained perfection: 'It flows from one source, one seed, one principle. It does not contain any particular message, convey any creed. It is like the stars, the ocean, a waterfall. It is just there.'

In the cello suites we hear the intimacy of the soul as a solitary person meditating. This music does not call us out of the body, rather it calls to and speaks from the body's central axis, that place where we are most ourselves. It speaks the wisdom not of a God above us, but of the God within us. It is worship in spirit and in truth.

III

WALKABOUT

Three Years at the Beginning of the Millennium

Words of Joa Bolendas:

Commission for Mark & John (Abbreviated).

31.12.1999: It is no longer the Catholic Church alone which has the true faith, but a variety of Christian faiths are admissible/feasible.

12.01.2000: Now Johannine time begins. Fight for the Johannine. The Church is breaking up. Pray that what you have received from the Church shall be maintained.

15.01.2000: Clare of Assisi: Johannine theology transcends any of the existing churches. Freedom of spirit must be afforded to every person. This is the way of life lived with Christ, with God. Love and truth are the foundations on which faith with Christ is built. Structures/forms of Christian theology must live in the Holy Spirit. Spirit is always life! Hold these words in your heart.

03.06.2000: Pentecost 2000. The beginning of the new Johannine church. Pray each day for the new growth of the Church, of Christianity.

05.06.2000: I pray that all Christians be one! One Church!

The Church must work in its varied way at all times in the direction of personhood.

Pentecost must be alive with Christ for every christian. Spiritually you have experienced and prayed for the new steps of the Church. In a thousand years the Ten Commandments, the life of Christ, Pentecost, will still be valid as ways of life.

Advance in scientific knowledge brings new problems which Christians must help to resolve before God in prayer.

15.07.2000: Healing for Northern Ireland. Pray.

29.07.2000: Through Christ you will retrieve primordial energy.

With keenest purity in prayer you will influence, you will move: mountains, valleys, people.

Only God-centred people can work with this power.

23.09.2000: St Peter: Human beings must know that the one human creation gives way to the life of resurrection, the greater life of the spirit.

21.10.2000: A new scientific age opens. Nevertheless you must experience both the older era and the new.

Write these words down for John and Mark: Why must the Church remain. To renew itself. Remain thus preserved so that humanity can find life in it. Because only in this way can humanity remain connected with the original creation and with God the father, the Christ and the Holy Spirit. Humanity lives that superabundant life later on, and develops itself accordingly. This great wisdom must remain in tact here on earth, must be preserved by humanity.

(Further discussion with Joa Bolendas: The Church must remain. If you don't pray and if Christ is lost, union with heaven is lost and the development of humanity towards the greater life is lost. Humanity will devolve and lose its future.)

Mark and John have a commission from God to give back to humanity this life on earth, this life after death, the development of humanity in the hereafter. It is the church to come. The fundamental wisdom of the church must remain preserved.

What must remain intact for humanity?

For example: the essential teachings of Israel, the Ten Commandments, forgiveness, Christ, Mary, the Holy days: Christmas, Good Friday, Easter, Pentecost. Theology must always be founded in prayer.

27.10.2000: Humanity can not yet grasp the true meaning of life. Both the earthly and the spiritual live from energy that comes from God and the creation. God gave us Christ, the consummation of the incarnation. Move with Christ towards life. Through him, contact with the Holy Spirit.

Every atom of the earthly creation and the whole universe lives through spiritual impulses from God, for the most part from Christ. Try to build the church so that it gives even more life through Christ and the

Holy Spirit. You have experienced how atoms can change through prayer. But also how they can change through sin. Remember it was only three wise, far-seeing, men who searched out the cradle in Bethlehem.

2001:

Up to the new millennium I was leading this second life of the Holy Spirit on a part-time basis. Life as a secondary teacher, as principal of a school, however small, does not allow for too much leisure to be otherwise occupied. I finally got the freedom, the courage and the permission to devote myself entirely to the time of the Spirit. This 'walkabout' began in June of the year 2002, as far as I was concerned. I found out later that the journey had begun, from the Spirit's point of view, at least in 2001. This allowed, from the beginning of the new millennium, one year for each Person of the Trinity, the year 2003 being specifically the year of the Holy Spirit. A synoptic account of the first two calendar years, with a month by month description of the third, during which at least one happening of note per month occurred, will make up the penultimate chapter of this book.

This walkabout coincided with Gregory's appointment to teach theology in Rome; with Paul's going to London to study for an MA in musical theatre; with Miriam Mason, Joa Bolendas' grandniece, and her husband Stephan's decision to set out around the world to find the direction of the 'new consciousness' which is emerging. Diarmuid was studying theology in San Francisco. Nóirín had taken up residence in the lakeside cottage on Glenstal Abbey's grounds. She was attending our liturgies and doing a doctorate on 'theosony,' neologism for 'the sound of God.' This gave us ten months to work out what the next move should be. Fanny Howe and the Sky Farm connection were in the background.

Several communications from Joa Bolendas have suggested that this is the right thing for me to do at this time; that I am being guided by the Holy Spirit; that as I move various people will point out to me either the direction I should go, the people I should meet, the things I should examine, the places I should visit. I have been able to give carte blanche to the Holy Spirit to lead and guide. For my part, I agree to accept whatever invitations are issued, earn my keep, and go wherever the road seems to indicate.

Monks in early Celtic monasticism set off in a currach, throwing away the oars, and allowing the Spirit to guide their bark through the ebb and flow of water. I allow the Holy Spirit to prompt me to go anywhere in the world and use the internet to mediate the cheapest and most appropriate way of getting there. I also keep a record of what happens. Brian Lynch of The Columba Press has agreed to publish my findings and they have started a new publishing imprint for such maverick productions, suitably called the Currach Press. If something emerges from this time, which calls to be elaborated upon, that will be fine, I am ready to do whatever the Spirit indicates; if not, I am happy to return to Glenstal at the end of 2004. Walkabout involved the opposite of what was my monastic life for at least the thirty years previous to it. During that time I could have predicted where I would be and what I would be doing during every hour of every day from 6a.m. to 11p.m. The monastic horarium and the programme of a secondary school teacher leave little time for diversion.

Immediately after making this resolution a number of things happened:

The Glenstal Book of Prayer was Simon's idea spurred on by Fr Peter who ran the monastic shop. The Columba Press agreed to publish. At first, reluctant to print more than 2,000 copies, Simon pushed this to 4,000 saying we would be around for some time and visitors would buy the book in our shop over the years. These 4,000 copies were sold in the first week. By the end of the year 150,000 copies had been sold. It was a publishing phenomenon. Nobody could explain why such a book should sell, should become number one on the bestseller list in Ireland for a whole year. It was to do with the icons and Joa Bolendas' predictions. The icon of St Nicholas was on the dust jacket; Christ the Healer was on the first page inside. Bill Bolger, as always, did a neat job on the artistic design. But it was the icons themselves which provided the compulsion. It has been difficult to photograph the icon of Christ the Healer with integrity. A photograph taken by Muriel Shirey, friend of Jennifer Sleeman, who had come to the Sophia Conference, and who died a short time after this visit, was selected by Simon. He, Nóirín, Paul, Diarmuid, Gregory, and Vincent formed the committee putting together the liturgical shape and selection of prayers which make up the prayer book.

Saturday 26 May: Met Fanny Howe and Sue Moon in the Fairmont

Hotel, San Francisco. Fanny's *New Selected Poems* are up for a prestigious award in Toronto next month. Excellent reviews, comparing her to Emily Dickinson. We three drive to Sky Farm. Dinner in Simone Weil Library with Peter and Kate. Sleep in a wine vatt. In Sky Farm Fanny says 'the quality of silence is a thought silence.' Art and thinking should happen here.

Sunday 27 May: Meeting with Dunstan and Diarmuid at 9.00 on the future of Sky Farm. Dunstan recommends a book on Meister Eckhart called *Wandering Joy*. It is by Reiner Schürmann who was in Paris with me in 1968.[1] Dunstan paraphrases: Allowing God to give yourself back to yourself and *Gelassenheit* as allowing yourself to get out of your way.

Dunstan had signed a will in 1999 bequeathing Sky Farm to Glenstal Abbey. Since that date Abbot Christopher Dillon, Abbot President, Celestine Cullen, Fr Senan Furlong as well as Br Diarmuid Rooney (who had stayed there for three months retreat before entering Glenstal) and myself had visited.

There have been two meetings of the Glenstal community and several Seniorate meetings, at the last of which it was agreed that I should be the one to scout out the possibilities and try to discern the will of the Spirit.

Tom Jordan has been very helpful. He had put us in touch with some lawyer friends of his in Sonoma. From the point of view of the church and canon law it was suggested that Glenstal Abbey could not make a foundation in this diocese without the explicit invitation of the bishop. There had not been satisfactory or cordial relations between Dunstan and the diocesan authorities since he had established his hesychasterion on Sky Farm. It seems, therefore, that a traditional monastic foundation is not what is required in this instance.

At our meeting we agreed that there was already in existence a 'founding community' of Sky Farm which had gathered around the very need to keep it alive. These people numbered Nancy and Bruce Wales, whose generous financial support had enabled Dunstan to develop the place in the way it has emerged in terms of buildings and amenities. Then Peter and Kate who have lived in the house at the top end of Sky Farm for the last number of years and whose practical help and work have developed both that house and the whole property in ways that allow the daily rhythm of life and prayer to continue. Finally, there is the inspirational friendship of Fanny Howe and Sue Moon, which has given Dunstan the encouragement, help and support he needs, increasingly as he gets older, and which has forged links with Glenstal Abbey.

In other words, the kind of 'community' which will emerge here in the Sonoma Valley, need not be quite what Dunstan might have envisaged when he first decided to hand the property over to the monks of Glenstal Abbey. In fact, ecclesiastical empêchement and historical happenings would seem to point towards an alternative arrangement and one which takes cognisance of already existing structures and a providentially appointed community who are already in place. From these would be formed a board of management who would meet to decide future strategies and alignments.

I read for Dunstan from a paper given to me by Fr Vincent Ryan of Glenstal on St Romuald, feastday 18 June (my birthday) which I believed had been given for that purpose: 'On a wooded mountainside near Arezzo in Tuscany stands the ancient abbey of Camaldoli. The congregation comprises monks living in community and hermits whose lives are wholly devoted to prayer and contemplation. The latter live in a cluster of separate dwellings situated higher up on the slopes of the mountain. The purpose of the monastery is to prepare monks for the solitary life and later to support them in their solitary vocation. The founder of this unusual religious institute was the saint whose feast we celebrate today.

Born in Ravenna about 950, Romuald resolved to become a monk. It is said that this was partly as a result of his father killing a man in a duel; a way of doing penance and making reparation. His first experience of monastic life was in a conventional Benedictine monastery, but this did not satisfy his longing for a life of greater solitude. He was drawn to the eremitical ideal, but, recognizing the dangers of the solitary life without a rule and the support of a community, he devised a form of religious life which combined the eremetical with the cenobitical. It safeguarded and promoted the vocation of the hermit within the framework of an organised community following the Rule of St Benedict. The formula seems to have worked quite well. What kind of man was Romuald? There was a certain restlessness in his spiritual temperament. If the anchorite or hermit is one who is 'anchored' in one place, how was it that St Romuald was constantly on the move? Whatever the reason, his holy restlessness served the Church well since it suffused the benefits of the Camaldolese way of life. The monks were not only men of God but also exercised a civilising role by their contribution to scholarship and the arts. It was their observance that inspired another monk-hermit, St Bruno, to found, a century later, the Carthusian order.'

From the beginning of the Sky Farm story, which dates from the summer of 1997 on our horizon, (as it was in that summer that Fanny Howe, Sacha Abercorn, and Diarmuid Rooney arrived for the first time in Glenstal in June, July, and September respectively) John Hill and I connected this adventure with Joa Bolendas whose first volume of collected writings appeared also in that year.

Dunstan himself has always aligned his particular vision with the Indian painter, Prasanna, who lives and paints in a studio in Sonoma. The way he paints is the way Sky Farm should move forward, Dunstan seems to be saying.

It was in August 1999, the same year that Dunstan visited Glenstal, that we held the Sophia Conference at which Joa Bolendas was honoured. Her grandnephew Simon Mason was present and was returning directly to Switzerland after the conference. I asked him to ask Joa about Sky Farm, without giving too many details.

I went with Joa to church, Simon wrote back, I told her this monk had given you this land, trusting the Holy Spirit would guide you, and that you asked her for guidance. What should happen with the land, how shall the land be used? The words were:

'NO.' This monk would have to first grow into the new Johannine. Then a new church could develop here and thousands would benefit. If he stays spiritually as he is now, the earth will also quake here.'

Later there was an earthquake in the region and one of the buildings on Sky Farm was burnt down.

Visit to Prasanna and his painting of Sophia, the icon of the madonna burnt in the fire on Sky Farm. Dunstan did not accompany us. He had more or less forced Prasanna to paint a picture from a photograph of this icon. The painting was disturbingly subversive of the original, which I found significant in terms of the shift which must take place to sketch the icon of the future in and for Sky Farm. Dunstan had given him a precise figurative icon. Rumi says: 'We are afraid of non-existence but, on the other hand, non-existence is more afraid of God putting it into existence again.' Prasanna went on: 'Even though the forms here are concrete they lead us towards the formless because the concrete speaks to us about the source which is formless'. You have to look at the face until the eyes become details of the abstract. The model is indeed a limitation but there is 'Something outside that limitation which prompts me to work within that limitation.' Getting out of bed, putting on one's shoes and buttering the sky: that's more than enough contact with God for one day, says a poem of Hafis.

Tom Jordan drove us back the scenic route to San Francisco and down the Crooked Street. Outside our hotel is playing Athol Fugard's: *Master Harry and the Boys*, put on, it seemed, for our benefit.

Wednesday 30 May: Tom Hayes drove me to the airport. He was born in a small cottage at the end of the forty acres in Ballyneale, my old home. His father worked for my grandfather. Tom junior arrived in San Francisco at the age of 20. 'I came out here as soon as I heard about it.' Since then he has made good and is one of the pillars of Irish-American society here. Again, in the coincidences that are a theme to all of this, he rang me out of the blue the day before I set out on this trip to San Francisco.

San Diego, to Marianne McDonald's palace in Rancho Santa Fe. Swim in her pool. Peacocks. The neighbours are complaining of the noise. They make high pitched piercing screams through the night, especially if someone turns on a light in the house. No reason to complain, says Marianne, their mating season lasts only from March to September! Athol Fugard and Marianne meet me for dinner. Marianne is leaving for Ireland to receive an honorary doctorate from UCD. Athol's new play *Sorrows and Rejoicings* is off Broadway in May and is then on its way to South Africa. '(Theatre) is still the cornerstone of civilized morality in any society. Any society should nurture and nourish its theatre for all it's worth. It just goes to work on the moral matrix of a society in a way that the mass media can never do.' 'For me life has been an accumulation and discharging of appointments.' I had brought them *Vox de Nube* which has tracks by Nóirín singing Hildegaard. Athol's new play is about an event in Hildegaard's life. Bordeaux 1967 is our wine. Apricots plucked from trees in the garden, our fruit.

Thursday 31 May: Fanny Howe for lunch. I read proofs of her new book of poetry *Ash Grove*: beautiful but relentlessly on the sciatica groove. Walk on San Diego beach. Gentian blue. Sea lilacs. La Jolla Cove: more colonies of seals. 'Ecological reserve: No person shall disturb or take any plant, bird, mammal, fish, mollusk, crustacean or other marine life.'

2 June: Looking for Fanny's daughter's book *Caucasia* in BU bookstore. Found instead *Indivisible* by Fanny herself. 'There is a kind of story, God, that glides along under everything else that is happening, and this kind of story only jumps out into the light like a silver fish when it wants to see where it lives in relation to everything else.' (p.13) Written by 'an angel with an inkless pen' (p. 71).

'My religious friend came up behind me and put his arm across my shoulder ... My friend was tall, aristocratic in his gestures – that is, without greed. He said the holy spirit was everywhere if you paid attention. Not as a rewarded prayer but as an atmosphere that threw your body wide open. I said I hoped this was true. He was very intelligent and well-read. He had sacrificed intimacy and replaced it with intuition.'(p.8)

19 November: My book *The Haunted Inkwell* arrives on the same day as my Columbus poems published in *THE SHOp* a magazine of poetry.[2] The series is a sonnet redoublé comprising fourteen sonnets. Each end line is the same as the first line of the next sonnet. The last sonnet comprises the fourteen opening lines of all the preceding ones rearranged. I began the series in 1992 when I first went to America in the 500th year after Columbus sailed there for the first time. His journey became a symbol of my own. My mother had been American and made the same journey in reverse in the 1930s. Columbus (1451-1506) was an inspiration to two later contemporaries, Shakespeare (1564-1616) and St John of the Cross (1542-1591), for whom his sea voyages became imagery of the mystical life. Shakespeare in love was also master of the sonnet form. I believed that when this series was completed the last verse would fall into place. The Holy Spirit is in the inkwell, and would supply the last verse when the rest of the poem had been battered into shape. These sonnets were given to me as log-book of a journey made in this same spirit. I finished the sequence on the Feast of the

Epiphany in the year 2000. John and Hilary Wakeman had made reference to my book *Kissing the Dark* in their issue number 6, in the summer of 2001 and they asked me to write something for them on poetry. I wrote back to say that I had these 14 sonnets that they might find room for at some point. They said they would not have space for such a long sequence. Later however someone defaulted and they said they would go ahead and print. The coincidence of their issue number seven, Autumn/Winter 2001 arriving at the same time as my book *The Haunted Inkwell* which elaborates the role of the Holy Spirit in poetry and art confirmed my hunch. As did the further use of one of these sonnets by my sister-in-law, Mary Ryan (Hederman) as preamble to her book *Hope*[3] which appeared also this year. Possible proofs of the haunting which my book *The Haunted Inkwell* sought to detect.

In the summer of 2002 Miriam and Stephan came to Glenstal on their world tour in search of the next move in the evolution of human consciousness. They met Nóirín and we made together (with seven members of the Glenstal community) a recording of Joa's music in the new round room of the library. Miriam and Stephan remained on in Glenstal until John Hill arrived. He came with his cousin Edward Hamilton who had not been here before. John and I then drove to Barons Court to visit the white stone which Sacha has placed beside the log cabin on the grounds. Between the cabin and this white stone, which both John and Joa find significant, is an oak tree grown from an acorn found in Pushkinland, St Petersburg.

In 1986 during a weekend dedicated to commemorating Sacha's great great great grandfather, the Russian Poet Alexander Pushkin, people from across the broad spectrum of political and ideological perspective, both hard-line communists and those still loyal to the old Tsarist empire, came together. For one weekend poetry and art achieved what seventy years of politics and diplomacy could not. Would it be possible to transplant something of this spirit to the Irish context? Ireland and Russia hold much in common. Lands of the storyteller, they have vast repositories of myth, legend and fairytale, reservoirs of the symbolic. Such was the dream of this tree.

John Hill and I drove to Antrim where I was giving a talk at the John Hewitt summer school. John Hill spoke after my talk. He said that one of the most moving books he had ever read was *Lost in Translation* by Eva Hoffmann, one of the few survivors of the death camps in Germany. He turned round to find Eva Hoffmann herself sitting in the chair behind him. They had never met before. It was confirmation that we were in the right place on our travels.

10 August 2002: Fr Brendan Coffey and Br Luke Macnamara make solemn profession. The Abbot of Ligugé comes as guest with news of Saint Lambert des Bois a custom-built twelve-seater monastery complete with state-of-the-art conference centre available for occupation by a community, forty minutes by public transport from Paris. Abbot Celestine is responsible for its future.

Next came an unusual invitation, through Colin Morrison (theatre director) who had read *The Haunted Inkwell*, to address the cast of Marina Carr's new play, *Ariel*, for the Dublin Theatre Festival. I was also asked to write a blurb for the programme and be on a panel at the Abbey to discuss the play in October.

24 August: Met Martha McCarron at the Montrose Hotel. I had worked with her for some years doing 'Just a Thought' on radio. Back to her house, an old artisan cottage which she has refurbished with Tim Lehane, a well known radio personality at RTÉ. Exquisite garden. My tennis shoes disintegrate all over her kitchen. She drives me home in my socks. They want me to do six radio programmes on 'a monk views the 21st century' over the next weeks.

2 September: Gregory's book on the icons arrives on time for his feastday. In *The Glenstal Book of Icons* he combines scholarship in Byzantine studies, personal theological acumen, and prayerful meditation on each one of our icons. The photographs were taken by Valerie O'Sullivan, the design is again by Bill Bolger, and The Columba Press are unstinting in the lavishness of the production. 'In thanksgiving for the grace of Holy Thursday, 1980,' Gregory dedicates this work. Michael Kearney and his mother, Anne, stay the night. I show them the icon chapel and give her a key. Simon gives her one of Gregory's books. She and her family are close to the Healing Icon.

9 September: Addressed the cast of Marina Carr's play, *Ariel*, in the Abbey. Martha McCarron and Tim Lehane record this as part of the new series. End of September and beginning of October were given over to recording for 'Spirit Level' on RTÉ . We drove to Ballyneale, Ballingarry, Co Limerick where I grew up and we recorded a programme on

Knockfierna the mountain beside my old home where connection with the Holy Spirit began consciously for me.

Making these programmes made me understand, for the first time, the symbolic nature of history and geography and the use of coincidence to achieve the goals of the Spirit even when we are aware of neither the hijack on the original incident nor the target of the long-term goal. Invited to revisit and recount the events of my own life, I see patterns underlying the obverse side of the tapestry, invisible as we travel the paths of childhood for the first time. I became aware how haphazardly contingent were the events which caused me to appear on the planet in the first place.

Two examples: Paddy Sleeman, Simon's brother, who teaches in the Zoology Department at University College Cork, sent me a letter, 26/11/1994: 'I'm looking at historic rabies in Ireland using 19th century records from the Pasteur Insitute in Paris. I came across Daniel Hederman who was treated in 1892. You may be a relative? Or be familiar with this family?' The entry in their books reads: 'Daniel Hederman 32 ans, fermier, Ballinleena, Comté Limerick (Irlande). Mordu: 29 October, 1892.'

This was my grandfather, Daniel Hederman (1856-1948) bitten by a rabid dog which had previously attacked both his nephew and a boy working in the farmyard. Somehow, Daniel had heard of Louis Pasteur. He offered to take the boy with him to Paris but the parents refused to let him go. The boy died, my grandfather and his nephew survived. It was only in July 1885 that Pasteur tested his pioneering rabies treatment for the first time. In March 1886 he presented the results to the Academy of Sciences and the pasteur institute was inaugurated in 1888. Such vaccination, therefore, only became available four years before my grandfather was bitten. How he heard about it and had the courage and the means to make such a long voyage at that time are also remarkable.

Secondly, my father, John Hederman (1907-1984) was to marry a girl, whose sister had already married my uncle, living on the farm next door. It was an arranged match. Cattle might even have been exchanged! My mother, Josephine Mullaney (1907- 1987), came from Boston. She was studying at Trinity College, Dublin. Invited by my father's sister, Irene, the only girl in the family, to spend ten days on the farm at Ballyneale, my father fell in love and proposed to her. 'I know nothing about you,' she said. 'You know as much about me now as ever you will, so, make up your mind,' was his reply. Both agreed at 70 years of age that he was right! The other woman became a nun. Such chance occurrences allowed me to arrive on the planet on a farm in Co Limerick, Ireland in 1944.

Recording these radio programmes made me see in slow motion how incidents and events organized during these months of walkabout were strategically planted like symbolic bombs which would later explode into streams of significance. The exercise was helping me to understand the idiom of symbolic interpretation. The radio programmes were heard by many people which effected another kind of synchronicity (Letter L).

17 October: Afternoon with Abbé Jean-Pierre of Ligugé and Prieur Hughes in Saint Lambert-des-bois. Met Frère Jacques (resident Prieur of S Lambert-des-Bois). There was a letter on the table from Abbot Celestine telling him to close the place down in three months. On the wall was a copy of Christ and Abbot Menas, from the abbey of Bawit, one of the rare paintings on wood dating back to the sixth or seventh century and the only Coptic icon kept in the Louvre. It was a present to Frère Jacques from Taizé. This icon had been sent to all members of the cóiced by Ciarán for the new millennium.

27 October: Email from John Hill: 'I came back to Zürich and was presented with very interesting material from my clients and my own dreams, which seem to tell me that for the time being I am to keep my feet in Zürich. I did ask Joa about the monastery in France. She saw us quite content inside the house. But, all around it, she saw eyes of mistrust, even irritation. She does not know what that exactly means, but seems to imply that French soil might not be fertile ground for our endeavours.'

28 October: To Beauvais with Ryanair from Dublin for 1 euro. Stayed with Mary Hederman and Seán Dior at Desmesne de Guirot, about two hours drive from Bordeaux. Beautiful old manoir with lake. Huge fire. Marques de Riscal red wine, French cheese and baguettes until 2a.m. *La vie en rose.*

29 October: Beautiful day, almost like summer with autumnal hues. Breakfast in the conservatory overhung with majestic wysteria. Cazaboun – *historique et pittoresque*. Visibility so good we can see the

Pyrennees. Afternoon train ride to Marqueze: a preserved compound describing how local people lived in this country area in the nineteenth century. Thank God for the twenty-first century! This kind of 'community' would be death by claustrophobic asphyxiation.

31 October: To Cluny. Another beautiful day. *L'automne en Bourgogne*. Nine years ago Abbot Celestine met Benoit Dargent, architect, who was showing him and a group of abbots around Vézelay. Benoit told him about the first of these conferences which he was helping to organize at Lyons in 1993. Each conference asks the question: can beauty save the world? Celestine told him that he knew only one other person with such far-fetched ideas and gave him my address. I was going to Africa and so couldn't get there. Chris Kelly took Celestine's original fax to Ireland this summer and extended the same invitation to their fifth gathering. So, I am here. 100 people at La Maison de l'Europe to discover *'si la beauté pouvait sauver le monde'*. Each takes a different coloured card with a quotation on it. Mine is orange and has this from André Gence: *'L'artiste ne peut rien prévoir de son oeuvre car c'est en la créant qu'il découvre. Des qu'une expression artistique se fixe un but, elle n'est plus.'*

This lands me in a group of ten, working with Cécile Maudet on *'la parole'*. Attempt to incarnate gestural communication preceding word of mouth. She is a well known actress and the work-shop is about 'the word' in theatre. Asked to describe a recent experience of beauty I took 15 October, sitting in the Jardin des Tuileries, eating a jambon, emmenthal, tomate et salade baguette, surrounded by Paris, toujours égale à elle-même. I had been in that exact space, surrounded by those same pigeons, on the same seat, at the same time of year, eating the same sandwich, 35 years before. It was as if Paris provided a beauty which was a sacrament whereby to meet up again with myself at the age of 23 and recognise that I had, after all, kept some kind of tryst with myself in this city of Great Expectations. Dinner in Le Potin Gourmand. Followed by a play about Etty Hillesum played by Iris Aguettant and Cécile Maudet with Colin Dixon on the violin. Back to Gite No 629, about 20 minutes by car. Seven of us, three men and four women with three bedrooms and one bathroom! I share a room with Bernard. Marie-Claude and her husband Charles have driven from within sight of the twin towers of Maredsous. Christine Marsan, psychotherapeutic psychologist, big into

Analyse Transactionnelle, keeps the group on their toes, refuses to sleep
à trois with Fée and Nicole, and so sleeps in a camp bed in the living
room where we all have breakfast on top of her before departing in
whatever bagnole each morning. It is so uninviting and in-your-face that
you end up submerging yourself in it and find an unspoken connection
with people simply by inescapable proximity.

1 November: *La Toussaint.* Mass with the sisters of St Joseph of
Cluny. Music conducted by Eveline Causse. Sermon by André Gence.
Inspirational whisperings. Then a lecture by him, too much in the same
'charismatic' mode for my taste, without sufficiently convincing
discourse to connect the leaps from peak to peak, on *'La Charte du
Créateur'.* Exhortatory rhetoric, not however, *la beauté qui pourrait
sauver le monde.* Followed by *une promenade accompagnée* around
Cluny, where the largest number of medieval houses in the whole of
France still stand. Half the thirteenth-century houses in the country are
in Cluny. Dinner beside Olivier Fenoy, just out of hospital. He
summarises the story of this group and the book he is writing on how
beauty can save the world. Some of this is interesting and, more
importantly, connects with the present search. Up to now there were
singular voices in the desert hinting at a possibility: now the time has
come to establish forms. We are living at a time when the gossamer on
the hedgerows can be plucked from their sidelined tracery and woven
into the fabric to help create a better world. References to Maritain
weaken the prospect for me. And I sense that he is gathering up the
props after the play. He could spend the rest of his life lecturing on the
mirage that almost materialised. But he has creative energy and is hugely
likeable. *On verra.*

2 November: Interesting workshop. Shout a word (given by someone
else: *Liberté, trahison, victoire, guerre*, etc.) and then allow that word to
work its way into the emotional channels of your body, producing
whatever gestural reactions it may evoke until eventually it returns to your
mouth in a more embodied enunciation. Exploration of preverbal
acoustics and space. I give Cécile herself the word 'parole' itself to work
with. Her intestinal struggle with it is moving – *fruit de ses entrailles.*

Talk on *Cluny, un Souffle civilisateur* by Michel Bouillot. Cluny
survived as a monastery from 943 to the French Revolution. Guillaume
d'Aquitaine, named the pious, although he slaughtered most of his

family to eventually accede to the dukedom, invited the monks here to pray for his eternal salvation at the time of the break up of the empire of Charlemagne. He offered them anywhere they chose from his properties which were a quarter of the land of France, from Macon to the Pyrennees. The monks chose the nearest Mediterranean town outside Paris at the fortified center of a new Europe, la Bourgogne. 1000 years of civilising presence. Three abbots from 943-1109 spanned 150 years when male life expectancy averaged 33 years. Two novelties for the time: election rather than appointment of abbots and direct dependence on the Holy See at Rome. This broke the asphyxiating grip of the existing feudal system. Odo governed for 16 years; Mayeul for 40; Odilon for 55; Hugh for 60; and Peter the Venerable for 35 years. Their family ties put them in contact with all the European movers and shakers. 1109, at Hugh's death, there were 1,184 affiliated monasteries in Europe of which 883 were in France. The 450 monks of Cluny itself spent at least 7 hours a day in their church which was the largest in christendom (eventually superseded by St Peters in Rome). With them would have congregated 7 or 8 thousand worshippers. The heart of Cluny was the choir of the church which in turn became the heart of Europe. Around this space the whole town was clustered. It was a life of prayer inserted into the local community, all of which eventually prospered. The town became a place of palaces, which is why so many survive to this day. The market established around the cloister by the Abbot to prevent exploitation of the people by local landlords (fixed prices regulated by the monks) still exists. Medieval civilisation owes a whole artistry of life to Cluny: lives devoted to beauty, creativity, architecture, music, liturgy. All the great architectural discoveries of the period were in such monasteries, forced to provide adequate and dignified space for worship for so many people. The huge vaulted roofs acted as enhancing acoustic for the Latin chants. A processional liturgy – antisclerotic – had to be devised for such numbers who spent such lengthy hours in church. Everything was always new – the same could be said for their menus – *la gastronomie est sortie des monastères*. Cluny's success came from its discerning recruitment. Miraculous succession of saintly and talented abbots. The monks were ecumenical. They undertook the first translation of the Koran. Some were sent to Muslim countries where '*ils se fisent couper la tête, ce qui raccourcit, bien-sur, le dialogue.*' Cluny didn't invent; it used to the best purpose and highest quality whatever already existed, and transformed these. Cluny was an expression of civilisation in a certain form, the crowning symbol of which is probably the office of the Transfiguration composed by Peter the Venerable which might stand as spiritual equivalent to the later cathetrals in the gothic middle-ages.

There is an exaggerated version of the antagonism between the two local monastic communities of Cluny and Citeaux, mostly traceable to the venomous pen and theological terrorism of St Bernard. He was a Chevalier. His monks were reformers, young and vigorous. They separated themselves from the world and condemned the 'wordliness' of their ancient rivals at Cluny. Citeaux was a fortified citadel; the Cistercian rule forbade mingling with the local population, a fortiori with the city. In spite of any such understandable tensions between two opposing monastic spiritualities, there were 500 years of cooperation between the two monasteries.

This is what was relayed to me during my short stay in this inspirational place. In the aftermath of the French Revolution the monastery with its church were destroyed. Explosives at the time were insufficient to remove the foundations and the outline shapes still exist. Napoleon used the remaining infrastructures to stable his horses when the French army was on the march. Cluny today is embedded in the architectural remains of the monastery like a half-buried giant. The size of the church can be reconstructed in the imagination by standing at certain stragegic heights from which the massive outline can be viewed.

Afternoon session was a tri-partite discussion (in fact three monologues) with Iris Aguettant, Claire Fabre and Olivier Fenoy which tried to give an historical and philosophical underpinning to both the present congress and the nine year movement as a whole. Life becomes a liturgy which must be reinvented each day, developing our sensibility and creativity. This session was too long and monotonous to be effective.

Back to our ateliers. Describe a moment in your professional life which was really creative. Claire Fabre, who joined us, described the actual selection of Cluny as the site for this congress. She only knew which were the wrong places. Nothing had emerged as suitable until June of this year 2002. Then a series of co-incidences led to this choice and she knew Cluny was the place where it had to be. The conference itself was held four months later.

Buffet des Provinces et Soirée festive. Everyone brought something delectable from their region. It became a sumptuous banquet of cheeses, wines, vegetables, meats, oysters, and deserts etc.

We could select one of six *alteliers thématiques. 'Peut-on parler d'une spiritualité de la Beauté?'* was Iris Aguettant describing her spiritual and professional journey as an actress and proposing that those of us who might choose should accompany her for a weekend of dialogue where we would elucidate a theory of the theme. I demurred. I was cautious of the French obsession with confessional intimacy, pretty sure that the beauty which can save is created in private, and that under such circumstances, it suffices for one artist to create, to ensure that a whole world is improved. Later I walked with Iris to lunch and clarified my thoughts: I would not come to her weekend but did feel prompted to come to her production of *l'Alouette* by Anouilh in Paris next February, as this is about herself, as Joan of Arc, in another context. Cécile is her 'spiritual daughter' and plays the part of Joan in the play. Apart from this in depth dialogue which I recognise as given by the Holy Spirit and which I know happens by an almost jolting removal to another plane of communication, I had similar connection with: Olivier Fenoy, Philippe Riche (friend of Olivier), Marlene Tuininga ('Exile rather than Exodus' as the ultimate paradigm of Judaeo-Christian existence), Philippe Derudder (felt called to tell him not to abandon the commercial world altogether – to be like Cluny rather than Bernard at Citeaux); Bertrand, the newly-wed, Anièce, Brigitte Frénoy, Isabelle Desplats (her leaving the community and her dream of an interior cowl and monasticism of the heart), Véronique Feugère, Marie-Claire Grasset.

This network of artistic people has something similar to the Pushkin spirit which Sacha Abercorn has instigated in Ireland. They make up a virtual community with a secretariat at Palis (Aube) set up in 1999. They have had a number of conferences. One of these took place in Hungary about 'Artistic Education in Schools' in 2001.

I left with Chris Kelly, Yves Moisdon and Marie-Claire Grasset by car for Les Forges de Perreuil where Chris Kelly and his group have their Profil'Scene workshops and community. Roger from Togo interviews me with his sempiternal videocamera. I find myself telling him that I found in Cluny a new kind of monastic community without walls, arriving like a hive of bees to make honey from the invisible beauty around. Chris Kelly showed me around the decaying outhouses of the scenographic deserted village. TGV to Paris. Gare de Lyons – Big effect on my return there – ghosts and memories from my sojourn here in 1968.

12 November 2002: This morning as I wake up before 6a.m. a clear revelation is given to me. Glenstal must become the hub, the centre of a very much wider circle, spanning maybe Europe and even, perhaps, America – the Western World. Ambiguities will be ironed out in the wider frame. Goodness at the core is all that matters. Even in the school which can be widened somehow in quality and scope. There is a wider virtual community whether connected as separate entities in other organisms in California or Canada, or incorporated into Glenstal in houses around the property is not yet clear, but they will be part of the constellation. John Hill and Sacha are already not only involved but identified by Joa Bolendas as guardians of the Johannine, as it is being constituted. The picture which Ciarán had given me created by Deborah Pugh, which is above my bed in Louise's house, fell off its perch. It is called 'Ancient manuscript.' It is built on a series of very exact descending squares which resemble the remains of the church at Cluny, superimposed upon which are 'dyed and printed natural papers combined with flowers, feathers, leaves etc.' The music, feathers, leaves are in the centre as if scattered in the razed sanctuary. Around the outside of the square steps leading downwards are a series of texts written or printed in black and gold. The one on top seems to read 'Intercom'; the underneath reads 'Rudimenta Samatica'; on each of the sides the outside line is in gold, the inner line is some more ancient black print. One of the words in black is 'habundantissime' some of the golden words read 'petit qui vult.'

16 November: My brother, Ted, drives me to Belle-Isle, Co Fermanagh. I am the guest of James and Sacha Abercorn, lodged in the courtyard in the House of Lime. All the houses in the old Stables are named after trees. Beautiful day. Majestic setting. Charles Plunket and family live in the main house. He manages the estate. His mother and John Hill's were friends.

18 November: Rain/mist all day. Am writing a book on the Tarot cards. These preserve something of a symbolic capacity which our world has lost. Valentin Tomberg's book *Meditations on the Tarot* uses these

cards as a living tradition, giving access to the esoteric church of St John (the 'heart' of the Church), as distinct from the exoteric Church of St Peter (the 'head' of the Church). He holds that it was never the intention or the role of John to found a new Church, that was always Peter's charism. So the Johannine, as we are searching for it, is not something new. It already exists, has done so from the beginning, perhaps 'subsists in' is the way to describe how it is present today. Perfect conditions for writing and reading. The shape of the book continues to emerge.

19 November: Sacha comes at 11.30. She feels impelled to go into the desert in Arizona in February for 6 weeks. No plans, just go. Joe Jaworski says she must meet John Milton, an archaeologist of sacred places. He flies from Atlanta to Barons Court. Affirms the sacredness of the place and others such as Carrowkeale in Sligo. Suggests that there must be a seam of white stone at Barons Court. This they find some days later – a basin covered in moss.

22 November: Sacha picks me up at 2.30 and we drive to Sligo for fifteenth Anniversary of her Puskin Prize initiative in education. Ben Bulben visible all the way. Sligo Park Hotel has a profile view of Ben Bulben from the entrance to the town. Sacha's welcoming speech alludes to the appropriateness of this place for the fifteenth anniversary celebration of the Pushkin Prizes. Yeats and the White Stone of the imagination. Pushkin and his nurse. Yeats and Mary Battle. Sligo and Ben Bulben as crucibles of symbolic imagination. As each of the 42 participants register they put a red sticker on a map of Ireland indicating where they came from and so where the spirit of Pushkin has reached. This island map encircled with red dots represents the seedbed of fifteen years. Part of our reason for this conference was to see how to harvest this growth.

Sacha's summary described two previous visits to this site, with a Russian and an American (John Milton) 'site-diviner' both of whom confirmed the radiance of energy. She quoted the guide who had introduced us here and who was also a water diviner. When the Swedish archaeologist came to Carrowkeale and succeeeded in placing the sandstone rocks in their correct alignment, a black cloud gathered overhead and hailstones like golf balls fell on the spot. At exactly the same moment in his home place in Sweden a similar hail storm occurred.

When you play with energy and get it right, the Gods throw down fire.

Pushkin as a boy would listen to his nurse, Arina Rodiovnova, telling him stories of his native land, of giants and witches, lions and wolves, enchantments and bewitchments, the natural elements as portrayed through the Russian soil and soul. It seemed fitting to invoke the spirit of Pushkin in response to the needs of Ireland's children. The young boy and the wise woman, the psychopomp, suggested a model which might be adapted to the realm of education in the Western world, a model which would infuse learning with the thrill of inspiration.

This provided the basis from which the Pushkin Prizes in Ireland evolved. The project began in 1987 with eight schools, four Catholic and four Protestant, four from Northern Ireland, four from the Republic. Boys and girls between the ages of nine and twelve were prompted to write short stories or poems, to share their thoughts and feelings, to find a voice. Music, painting, sculpture and environmental awareness were added to the programme as the movement flourished and spread.

Fifteen years later the inspiration has spawned tiny centres of creativity throughout the whole island. The question is where do we go from here?

'We need to keep the good things and beware of the movement being hijacked, which can happen very subtley. The elusive magic of Pushkin must not be lost or diluted. However, we will not take the steps necessary if we continue simply in the register of adulation and appreciation for what has been. Staying put is inevitable demise. Everything must evolve organically, or die. At the same time we need a person/catalyst who will link the various schools, artists, organizations already on board and extend the network. Trying to connect with inspectorates, departments (both sides of the border) district and arts councils etc. Create places like Barons Court all over the island; give more and more teachers and pupils the Pushkin experience.' These were some of the comments of the participants.

Seamus Heaney gives a reading of his poems. All about forming the O of wonder from childhood to the wooden O of the phi beta kapa society auditorium in Harvard. The little o and its relationship to the big O of the world. In the ancient Celtic alphabet each letter designates a specific tree. The tree is the theme for Pushkin in 2003.

11 December 2002: Dorothy Walker's funeral. She had helped with *The Crane Bag*, written a book on Louis le Brocquy and another about *Modern Art in Ireland*, with a forward by Seamus Heaney. Louis and Anne le Brocquy and Marie Heaney were at the church. To the graveyard in Enniskerry, an hours drive in the funeral car with Dorothy's sister, Pauline. I said prayers over the grave where Dorothy is buried beside Robin, her husband. Dorothy had taught the whole country how to see beauty in difficult abstract art. She would teach us now how to do so in this difficult scene of death. Two horses are in the field beside. There had been white horses there when Robin was buried. Simon, her son, and I sign the register. Michan, Sarah, Corban and Ciannait are her other children. The beatific vision better be all its cracked up to be or Dorothy will give them hell! The undertaker drove me back to Louise's car. I drove to Glenstal in time for vespers.

15 December: ULG Centre at 12.15 *The Last*, a film by Stephen Benedict. Impressive symbolism: the last shoemaker in Dublin, making a perfect shoe for his bride on his revolving last. New multi-national businesses take over from personal artistic craftmanship. David Kelly gives a virtuoso performance. Cinema, too, can teach us symbolism.

18 December: After vespers (*O Adonai*) Simon and I meet Nóirín and Sacha in the icon chapel for a ceremony of light and darkness. Sacha declares herself ready to act as channel for this underground light if it wishes to emerge for others. What Nóirín is doing in the lakeside cottage here in Glenstal working on her doctorate is pioneering work Sacha feels. Glenstal is potentially a spiritual centre. Good energies between us four.

James Scanlon has completed a prayer-room in a shopping centre in Cork. He has made it like a prison cell, to capture people who wander in, slow them down. He wants texts (and music) on tape that will play continuously (from 9a.m. – 7p.m. the year round) and asks us to record these.

2003:

1 January (jasper): Ciarán gives me a tiny four-wood bird cage carved from bog oak, walnut, boxwood and cherry. Chuck and Helga Feeney come to Glenstal with her mother who is 99 years of age.

17 January: I am invited by Seán Conlan to address his group Excellence Ireland. After the meeting he tells me that I must meet

Bertrand Jouslin de Noray in Paris and attend the Summer Camp of the Imagination this summer in Maastricht, Holland.

21 January: In Dublin the so-called Millennium Spire is eventually completed and now stands 120 metres tall in the centre of O'Connell Street. This creation should be viewed as the spire of an underground cathedral encompassing the whole city of Dublin, and, perhaps, the whole country of Ireland. The underground cathedral, in my view, has been in process of excavation for quite some time and is now ripe for manifestation.

3 February (saphire): Very cold. Paris, France. Hotel St Cyr equidistant from Couvent de l'Annonciation and Theâtre de Village where *L'Alouette* is playing. The church and garden with statue of Jeanne D'Arc are beside. The play about Joan of Arc by Jean Anouilh was created in 1953. This anniversary production is directed by Iris Aguettant with Cécile Maudet starring as Jeanne. All the Cluny cast are present. The newly wed Anne-Louise de Ségogne, Francisco, Olivier Fenoy and Jan Contreras as the villain, looking like Anthony Hopkins in Silence of the Lambs, 'with an accent mix of Gestapo officer and Spanish Inquisitor' says Bertrand, who is with me in the audience. The end of the play has Jeanne dramatically burned on a pyre which looks like a space shuttle taking off from the stage. *'La vraie fin de l'histoire de Jeanne ... c'est l'alouette en plein ciel.'*

I think of Shakespeare's Sonnet 30:

> Yet in these thoughts myself almost despising,
> Haply I think on thee, and then my state
> (Like to the lark at break of day arising
> From sullen earth) sings hymns at heaven's gate.

'Mascarades! Cela, c'est l'histoire pour les enfants' Warwick comments in the play. News reports of the destruction of the American shuttle, Columbia, as it returns to earth. Its remains are scattered all over Texas. Another image of the dove (T. S. Eliot):

> The dove descending breaks the air
> With flame of incandescent terror.

5 February: No idea what all this is about until I awake this morning

and let it come. This is my third time in Paris since walkabout began. The third time in this third year of the millennium is the time of the Holy Spirit. We are under the sign of the dove. Vaughan Williams: The Lark (Paul Nash suggests) as music and the Columbia Shuttle. Sacha Abercorn is in Arizona where some of the debris of the shuttle has been scattered. All of these are connected to that image of the bird and the lizard in the San Clemente apse.

6 February: Bertrand Jouslin de Noray and I agreed to meet at the glass triangle in front of the Louvre. He is a 'changemaster' in Europe. 'Shifting paradigms: once you have actually moved from one world to another, then you know how to go. Otherwise you are always trying to include all the worlds you meet within your own.' We swop symbols. He brings me to see *Le Scribe Acroupi*, carved in limestone with eyes of ivory inserted into rock crystal sculpted between 2600-2350 BCE, found in the Nile valley at Sqqqara. I bring him to see Ciarán's icon: Christ and Abbot Menas, sixth-seventh century AD on painted wood from the abbey of Bawit. One of the rare paintings on wood dating back to the sixth or seventh century, the only Coptic icon in the Louvre. On the right, the bearded Christ is identified by a halo stamped with a Cross and by his name written in coptic, 'The Saviour'. He holds the book of the gospels and has his arm around the shoulders of the 'Abu' Menas, father superior of the monastery of Bawit. The holy man is represented as the equal of Christ. The simplicity of relationship comes from experience of many marvellous encounters. The two symbols are also linked: both belong to The Department of Egyptian Antiquities which displays the remains of the civilisations along the banks of the Nile from the time of Nagada, around 4000 before our time, up to the Christian era, around the XIth century A.D., with a large Coptic section.

Bertrand and I agree to meet with the changemasters of Europe in the Summer Camp of the Imagination at Maastricht in June 2003.

7 February: I meet with Guy Bedouelle for the first time in 30 years. This is reconnection not only with himself but with the community of Le Saulchoir with whom I stayed in Paris at the end of the 1960s. Such reconnection is essential in this year of the Holy Spirit.

15 February: Jennifer Sleeman with six others for the weekend in Glenstal. This group of seven represents a part of the new kind of community being formed by the Holy Spirit. Jennifer among others has

been responsible for persuading Clonakilty to become the first Fair Trade Town in Ireland.

24 February: Dallas, snow, sleet, hours late. Woman from Boston sitting beside me. She will never again fly with American Airlines. I wonder how they can be blamed for snow. No it's not that. In the East they know how to deal with snow. Here they have no idea. But this trauma did allow me to change my ticket for an extra day with no charge. On to Arizona. Big rainfalls. Sacha is there to meet me. I sense a change immediately. Everet our driver is hoping there will be a war. He is a captain in the marines. If called up he will automatically become a major in the greatest army the world has ever known and get $630 a month extra for life. He will get a medal for serving in three world wars – who has ever done that? He will be a legend in his own lifetime. The road is flooded on the way to Rex Ranch but no problem for this captain of the marines.

I am staying in an adobe house overlooking the mountains. Patti and Wayne Ross are running the ranch (Eleanor Roosevelt apparently liked 'scrambled eggs and brains for breakfast' so that is the menu in this contemplative centre also). Beautiful sunlight on the surrounding volcanic ridges. Purple cacti. Sacha has spent six days in the Chiricahua mountains of eastern Arizona near New Mexico on a native American 'sacred passage' organised by John Milton. Very cold time of the year. In a little yellow tent like a golden sun burst you lie with your back against the stone which generates heat, wisdom, energy. Sacha was born here and her mother brought her to the mountains when she was three months old. Connecting with the taproot, with the earth, in this way reestablishes a connection which sends back fruit in abundance. The tent becomes a yellow egg hatched by the earth. The desert somehow allows for something more universal than personal psychology to which one can give oneself in this way:[4]

> The spirit and the movements were those inimitable and unteachable Russian ones that 'uncle' had expected of her. As soon as she had struck her pose and smiled triumphantly, proudly, and with sly merriment, the fear that had at first seized Nicholai and the others that she might not do the right thing was at an end, and they were all already admiring her ... She did the right thing with such precision, such complete precision.

Are we to take it that a nation such as Russia may be held together by the unseen threads of a native sensibility? The question takes us to the heart of this book . . . from the folk embroidery of Natasha's shawl to the musical conventions of the peasant song.

27 February: Sacha's birthday. Important date with the number 27. We visit Mission San Xavier del Bac: 'White dove of the desert' (this church, Sacha later discovers, is also in the book *Churches* which I was given in Boston) on the Tohono O'odham American Indian Reservation.

28 February: Scott drives us to the airport. Even though Sadam Hussein agrees to destroy any weapons of mass destruction 'Bush will start the war to jumpstart the waning economy and get himself reelected'. At the airport, breakfast and sense of completion: 'Warriors don't venture into the unknown out of greed. Greed works only in the world of ordinary affairs. To venture into that terrifying loneliness of the unknown, one must have something greater than greed: love. One needs love for life, for intrigue, for mystery. One needs unquenchable curiosity and guts galore.'[5]

I fly to San Antonio. Surprise Liz at her arrival point from Boston. We are staying with her cousin Beverly Jarmon (visited by her sons Chris, Ty, Jim). Yet one more film of the Alamo in progress. The taxi driver tells me I could get a part. There were Irishmen fighting at the Alamo alongside John Wayne and Jim Bowie! I discover that the shop Yippy-I-O, where I bought cowboy boots second hand in 1992 in Boerne has been turned into a pewter shop. On Sunday at Mass with Beverly the readings are: 2 Cor 3: 1-6: 'written not in ink but in the Spirit of the living God.' And Hosea 2: 16; 21-22: 'I will lead her into the desert and speak to her heart. She shall respond there as in the days of her youth.'

March: (agate) 03/03/03. Thrice thrice three (27): Feastday of the Trinity par excellence. I wake in San Antonio, New Mexico, knowing I should be in Albuquerque. I go to the airport and haggle for a ticket. No problem. I fly there. In the Hyatt regency on the Plazza I email Miriam and Stephan who are touring somewhere in this region in their camper-van. They have no address, no phone, I have no idea where they are, no other possibility of reaching them. If you enter the larger hotels giving the impression that you are one of the guests staying there, it is possible to use their business facilities without charge. 'I shall walk through the main door of the Hyatt Regency Hotel on the Plazza in Albuquerque at 3p.m. and 4p.m. today. If you are there we shall meet, if not I'll be on my way.' My email went into orbit. Twenty minutes later at 3p.m. Miriam, Stephan and I were together outside the front door of the Hyatt Regency Hotel. They had parked their yellow all-purpose campomobile in the black marble awning. White-gloved porters ran at us from all sides to remove us from their five star ambiance: white trash destroying an image. Miriam and Stephan had been expecting a third person. (Three seemed *de rigueur* on this day of days 'where two or three are gathered in my name'.) They invite me to meditate with them at 3.33p.m. on the text of Jeremiah 33:3 'Call me and I shall answer. I will reveal to you great and hidden things you have not known.' We prayed together in silence in the old town quarter of Albuquerque. We stayed that night in The Centre for Action and Contemplation where Richard Rohr led us in silent prayer. I was in the room called after Jaegerstätter where I found a Gallen Priory Cross made in the Wild Goose Studio from a tenth-century carving on an Irish high cross: 'Humankind wrestles with energy of the unconscious while standing on reason.The linear base pattern wrestles with unrealised energy, the spiral uncoiling into serpents consuming four heads.'

Next day we were on the turquoise trail to Santa Fe, New Mexico. In the gothic chapel built for the Loretto sisters in 1878, designed *à la Sainte-Chapelle à Paris*, there is a stairway which supplied another dominant image of this journey. When the church was finished it was discovered that no provision had been made for access to the choir loft. Because of the height of the loft a conventional stairway would take up too much room in the building beneath. A ladder would have to be used or the whole choir loft reconstructed. The sisters made a novena to St Joseph. Legend has it that on the last day of the novena a grey-haired man with a donkey arrived. He worked for six to eight months with only a saw, a hammer and a T square. When he had finished his work he disappeared without payment.

The stairway is circular with 33 steps forming two complete turns of 360 degrees, without a central support. The railing which now exists was not part of the original construction but was added two years later. The wood is spliced in seven places on the inside, and in nine places on the outside, with each piece forming part of a perfect curve. Samples from the wood show an evergreen spruce but neither Engelmann nor Sitka which are native to New Mexico. The wood used by this carpenter has not yet been discovered anywhere, certainly not in this area. Climbing the stairs one can feel, according to Carl R. Albach, consulting engineer, 'a small amount of vertical movement, as if the two 360-degree turns were taken out of a large coiled spring.'

A week later in San Francisco Leah Buturain gave me a book called *The Mystic Spiral: Journey of the Soul*. And later again, in May, when lecturing at the Jung Institute, the first book I saw for sale in their shop was Aldo Carotenuto's *The Spiral Way, A Woman's Healing Journey*, which had on the cover Dore Hoyer, drawing by Johannes Richter, 1968, 'reproduced from Jill Purce's book *The Mystic Spiral: Journey of the Soul*'. Both books had this quotation from C. G. Jung: 'The way to the goal seems chaotic and interminable at first, and only gradually do the signs increase that it is leading anywhere. The way is not straight but appears to go round in circles. More accurate knowledge has proved it to go in spirals'. (*Psychology and Alchemy*). Aldo Carotenuto is the author of *A Secret Symmetry: Sabina Spielrein between Jung and Freud* (1983) which John Hill had recommended but which was out of print, and which I later found in the second hand bookshop beside The Stonleigh Hotel in Dallas, Texas. Spirals within mystic spirals. Each situation provides the hidden key to the next one if you have eyes to see. Miriam and Stephan conceived on All Saints Day on the beach in patmos and she is carrying their child, later born Adonia on 2 August 2003 at 12.55p.m. Pacific time.

Stephan André Josef Martineau was a hockey international of French Canadian origin. Working for his father with printing acid for cleaning in a printers shop he said to himself one day: 'I won't find it here.' He and his friend Mark, an Olympic swimmer, set off on a quest. Stephan found a place in Canada which he later bought and where he established a community called Morning Star. He planted trees to raise the money. He met Miriam at Taizé. They recently began a world-wide search for the next step in the evolution of consciousness.

The spiral stairway was a symbol of importance for the three of us as we celebrated Mardi Gras together in the Sangre de Cristo Mountains. Georgia O'Keeffe (1887-1996) introduced us to this countryside. Untitled skunk cabbage. 'Stieglitz wanted something to come out of America – something really important – and he felt you couldn't do that alone.' 'Singing has always seemed to me the most perfect means of expression ... it is so spontaneous ... Since I cannot sing, I paint.'

Miriam and Stephan drove me to Albuquerque airport. I spent the night on a seat in San Antonio Airport before heading to Dallas in the morning. Bobbie Sue was attending an Alpha programme. I joined her. Nicky Gumbel is the inspiration for this way of making Christianity relevant. (Later I come across tentative approbations from Christoph Schonbörn and Rowan Williams.) Mary Ann Perryman is now Mother of the Mistress of the Robes as her daughter Gretchen is in charge of the wardrobe for the Queens at the San Antonio fiesta. 'I want to practice my curtesy but first I have to see if I can stand up.' Describing help offered them by certain well-meaning but incompetent males (apart from Henry O'Shea who has supplied details on how to dress Queen Deirdre of the Sorrows): 'He's a few bricks shy of a load; his elevator doesn't go right to the top.' During the interval Mothers of the Mistresses wear T-Shirts with the logo: 'Inside every old person there is a young person wondering what the hell happened.'

Netta Blanchard who is constantly organising samovars of synchronicity has us all at an exhibition of paintings by a Northern Ireland Artist. One of his works includes a note from Colmán of our community about Croagh Patrick. And during the proceedings I am approached by a relation of Brother Matthew Corkery on his mother Carmel Mulcahy's side, whose son is going to Iraq. I give her a copy of the Glenstal prayer book.

And so to San Francisco. Staying at The French Café. Sue Moon drives us to Sky Farm. Her mother, we find, had started an artists' colony in this area. Sky Farm looks radiant: Californian poppies, wild calendulas. Bright orange, fresh green. Dunstan has become impatient with what he perceives as a reneging by Glenstal on previous promises to take over the place as a formal foundation by our monastery. He seems to have forgotten our later discussions and agreement about a community already present and in place. Sky Farm has now been offered by Dunstan to David Stendl-Rast. 'The hermits three' are on their way to take up residence. Dunstan was happy about this at the beginning, but now has second thoughts. He is going to take it back from them. We meet. After a long silence he gives a predictable lecture on hesychasm. Then he quotes Simone Weil: God comes; He knocks like a vulnerable beggar. If you do not respond he, like a vulnerable beggar, moves away. I take the book from him and repeat to him this quotation which he has just read to us. Then I say: 'This is my last time coming here.' I feel this sentence coming from another source. He says, 'Oh no, you must come again.' I ring Stanley Taschera, at Dunstan's request, renouncing our claim to the place. Dunstan is no longer falling into the grave. He is full of energy and looks like Burl Ives in *The Big Country*. He has to deal with Stendl-Rast and the hermits three. He is in contact with a blind lawyer in Sonoma and his dog.

Later I hear that Dunstan is in a retirement home in Sonoma. Stendl-Rast took the documents which he had signed and had Dunstan evicted. He said it was for his own good and the good of Sky Farm, that Dunstan was no longer able to make such decisions himself and certainly not able to manage the property. I find it a sad ending. Dunstan almost achieved something at Sky Farm in terms of the new consciousness but in the end he settled for the creature comforts of the caboose, as Stephan suggests Diarmuid might eventually do too!

Meeting with Jane Daggett Dillenberger. Kathleen Martinez (of the Milagro Beanfield War) drove us up up up to the appartment. Resplendent view over the Bay. Jane has written *The Religious Art of Andy Warhol*. Four scarlet and amber tulips open her apartment orgasmically. We meet under a rose of Sharon hibiscus. Schubert is playing in the background. There is almost a miniature Prasanna on the wall. It is also Martini time. Henry James and *The Golden Bowl* preside over our picnic. She will leave me her signed letter from him! She knew Cleo Webster, of course, years ago in Boston and phoned her later. Jane's birthday is also on 27 February. We agree to meet here again next year on that date. This meeting was bristling with synchronicity.

We find Catherine Ingram is talking at a bookstore downtown. *Passionate Presence*, her book and her theme. On the way to the bookstore a dove is crushed by an SUV.

Fanny on Martha's Vineyard. The island is the same size as Manhattan: When they arrived on Manhattan it must have looked like this! The question for us: How do you use the first model? There is no point reinventing the wheel. What should be discarded? She never felt heart to heart connection with that place (Sky Farm), she says. The way of thinking in poetry is spiral. 'Once two have met, their meeting can never be erased from history.The meeting may be minor, or major, in the emotional lives involved; but it has made an ineradicable place for itself in time.'

Wood's Hole, Buzzards' Bay.

Fanny's father died on 27 February.

Chez Liz. I meet Anne Emerson. Cleo Webster's Greek Orthodox father was The Rev Fr Vasilios Lambrides. She shows me *An Amulet of Greek Earth, Generations of Immigrant Folk Culture* by Helen Papanikolas, 2002. I see the film *The Russian Ark*. Coincidentally, Richard and Anne Kearney, Mícheál Ó Súilleabháin and I meet together for dinner chez Liz Shannon on this Saint Patrick's day, 2003.

Back in Glenstal, Frank Lawrence has sent on the missing piece of the mosaic: Hunting Gear. Shane Ordovas rejoins the community and changes his name to Joshua. Contact with Benedict on the anniversary of his death through Senan pointing out the twelve angels on his crucifix over the altar in our choir at Glenstal which mirrors the twelve doves on the cross in the San Clemente apse. The Wild Goose Studio, Kinsale produce a hand cast replica of this side of Benedict's cross this year.

Iffiok Idem Inyang, priest of the MSP in Nigeria makes a surprise visit to Glenstal having been part of a choir brought to Ireland by Mike Cowan to sing in Omagh. They also visited Sacha in Barons Court, where Simon joined the group. Iffiok brings Nigeria back onto the radar screen. He is about to study psychology in Italy.

My book on the Tarot cards arrives. This describes the resurrected life as a spiritual journey through 22 stages represented by the Major Arcana. I gave a summary of this in a talk to the community in March.

10 April (emerald) 2003: Anniversary day of the Icon Chapel. I had arranged to meet Sacha at the Merrion Hotel, Dublin. Neither of us had been aware of the date. When we meet in the foyer she has brought her key to the icon chapel to return it without any awareness of the anniversary. We go to the Paul Henry exhibition at the National Gallery of Ireland and to see the new millennium wing. Carmel Naughton's presence surrounds me in this building. A wedding box from Barons Court is on display in the fourteenth-century Italian section with very splendid exterior panels. This is like a trousseau chest for *The Wedding*

Dress, Fanny Howe's new book. We run into Ronnie O'Gorman and his daughter, on the street leading to Greene's bookshop. And later in Greystones we meet Pat Desmond who is walking with friends. Sacha and I discuss the distribution of the Pushkin Spirit throughout the whole country, and thinking of places equivalent to Barons Court and Glenstal which could become foyers of educational enrichment for the imagination both at the artistic and environmental level, I suggest Kilruddery where Louise and I used to go riding when we were based in Greystones. Sacha can't believe this idea. She knows the Meaths, Jack and Xenia, who have quite recently come to live in Kilruddery. We visit there and meet them both. Xenia has a Russian connection and was at finishing school with Sacha. The estate is perfect for Pushkin educational activity and even has a natural outdoor theatre.

Back to Louise and Risteard's where we find on the internet two copies of *Chiron* by Melanie Reinhart and discover that the original Eden might have been between the Tigris and Euphrates rivers which must be modern day Iraq. That night we see the film *Frida*. This biography of the Mexican painter Frida Kahlo (1907-1954) had been recommended to me by Caroline Rose Hunt. The symbolism of art conquering oppression, the Mexican artist in 'Gringolandia,' the woman artist in a gallery of men, one link between two worlds. In her Self-portrait on the Borderline between Mexico and the United States there is an electricity generator standing on North American soil which draws its energy from the roots of a Mexican plant, which it then supplies to the socket on the pedestal on which she is standing. The story becomes linked with the Francis Bacon studio through the Trotsky connection. A similar connection between two worlds is generated in the icon chapel. Frida paints butterflies on the plaster cast surrounding her limbs and torso after the fateful accident which made her whole body a prisoner to pain for life.

14 April: Trinity College. I meet Brendan Kennelly coincidentally, and he gives me the brochure about the new library building which someone else has just handed him, he promises to send me his latest book *Martial Arts*, and helps me to find the portrait of Berkeley beside the dining hall.

17 April: Holy Thursday. I am billed to give a talk on education to a seminar at Dublin City University. Marie Louise O'Donnell has

organised this. Fergal Flood, Feargal Quinn and Fintan O'Toole are the other speakers. Every one at the conference gets a free copy of the *Irish Independent*. I try to get a copy of *The Irish Times* to see what Fintan O'Toole has to say this morning. No copy to be had for love or money. Eventually they find a copy in some obscure corner and secrete it to me. It is fifty years since the discovery of the double helix of DNA, I see. The conference takes place in the new Helix theatre. This is rubbing my nose in the imagery. Helix is the word for a spiral in Greek. Education = creating a spiral movement out of the prison of our DNA. This is also what Holy Week is about, developing that passageway.

19 April: Holy Saturday this year. Nóirín sings the Exultet at the Easter vigil. She has no recollection of doing so. She felt she had lost her voice. But some power in the unconscious took over and it became the voice of theosony in person.

May 2003: (onyx) In Switzerland, lecturing at the Jung Institute. John Hill brought me to see Joa Bolendas. She told me that my real business was in Russia; that I should go there and find a very important and ancient book which risked being destroyed or lost in an earthquake or some other disaster; I should bring it back to Glenstal and keep it safely until the time came to return it to Russia.

John Hill then took me on the Holy Spirit tour: First Einsiedeln and then the house of Bruder Klaus. We visited the valley of the Middle Ages where Nicolas of Flue lived and prayed. We spent a long time down at the hermitage, absorbing that spiritual landscape which naturally carves itself out of the mountain like a deep green spiral. In the church there we both became silent for an indefinite period. It was prayer within the green spiral of these mountains surrounding an untouched valley at the centre of Europe.

Simon Mason and I visit Stadelhofen, the belly of the whale, designed by Argentinian architect, Gallatrava. Also the Chagall windows at Fraumünster in Zurich.

14 May: Second time in the Hugh Lane Gallery for Anne Madden's exhibition: *A Space of Time*. Icons of the Holy Spirit: 12 panels of doves. Hopkins, the Windhover, Anne says. The San Clemente crucifix in flight, from gold to lapis lazuli in the icon spectrum. Also present at the opening of this exhibition is one of the George Mitchell Scholars 2003, Emily Mark, doing an M.Litt in the History of Art at Trinity.

June: (carnelian) A new bridge across the River Liffey officially opened on Bloomsday 2003. This 'James Joyce Bridge' links Ellis Quay on the north of the river to Ushers Island, where the actual house of 'The Dead' in *Dubliners* is situated. The two main parabolic arches of the bridge were constructed, we read,[6] by joining the sections of thick walled tubes together with connecting fishplates to create two continuous, tilted, tied arches as the support spans for this unique steel structure. In a similar way, the two main parabolic arches of *Ulysses* are the journeys of Stephen and Bloom through the streets of Dublin on the original Bloomsday. This is one of the flying buttresses of the underground cathedral.

8 July: (chrysolite) In Maastricht, Holland, for a week with the change masters of Europe on their summer camp of the imagination. Maastricht is the ancient town where the Romans built a bridge across the river (Meuse/Maas). It is surrounded by several countries, all of whom it perceived to be enemies at some moment in the past. The whole town is built on paranoia. From the early roman ruins to the medieval walls and parapets, it speaks of defensiveness and constant attack from the outside. Every window is a slit, every balustrade is designed to pour boiling oil or whatever on the advancing marauders. It is a barricaded and impregnable citadel at a critical junction of Europe.

Recently they built a conference centre outside the city. This is round, open and with windows to every side. It is such a successful environment for meetings that it was selected to host the signing of the Maastricht Treaty which was an important step in the integration of the European Community. This was where we held our meeting. At a round table every person had a microphone which could be switched on if you wished to intervene. There were also headphones which could be used to translate whatever was being said into your own language. One of the group attending our meeting was developing a technology whereby each participant could press a button on the desk in front which would register on a large screen above, approval or disapproval of what was being said while the speaker was making his or her intervention.

This meeting was about symbolism. Louk Hollands gave me his personal copy of *Python, A Study of Delphic Myth and its Origins*. We sang Beatles songs on all festive occasions. Everyone in the group seemed to know them, young and old from whatever nationality. Shoji

Shiba of the University of Tsukuba in Japan gave a talk which provided a key. He introduced the book *Who Says Elephants Can't Dance, Inside IBM's Historic Turnaround* by Louis V. Gerstner, which claims that this turnaround was achieved by understanding and transforming symbols within the company.

Frank Verheggen one of the main organisers of the event remembered that there had been a meeting of the health section of this group, The European Society of Quality and Healthcare, at the University of Limerick. They had come to Glenstal for Vespers, had met William and Luke of our community.

Frank Steer and Michael Webster were impressive representatives from England. Seán Conlan, Mary Morrissey and Bridget McAdam O'Connell and myself represented Ireland. Sylvie Hendrick organised with elegance and panache, and of the French delegation Marie de Franssu (distant relative of Racine) and I had connection. She later visited Glenstal for a weekend.

August: (beryl) Gregory is giving seven talks on Kenosis and Transfiguration to the community during the annual retreat. I give two talks. These are based on what I have learned from walkabout so far: the household which is a Benedictine monastery should be one whose every rule, ritual, custom and practice must be examined and reexamined to ensure that it is promoting freedom and joy of life rather than prejudice, intolerance, elitism, discrimination, competition, domination, alienation. We have to examine the symbols which consciously or unconsciously describe us lest they betray us and the basic truth which we are or we should be about. If this is the house of God, the place where his glory dwells, where we are called to live, not just any kind of life, but life at its fullest, then every aspect of this place, every thing we do, eat, say, wear, build, plan, accomplish should promote that life. If the habit we wear speaks of death rather than life then throw it away, design one that speaks of being alive. I'm not saying that it does or it does not, I am saying that we are the ones who are responsible for the monastery as a sign of resurrection, of life as it was meant to be. And if we are not advertisements for that life and if every rite we perform, reading we read, song that we sing, clothing that we wear, is not signifying that life, then we are betraying the reason why we are here, and it is no wonder that we may die out because no one else wants to come and join us.

Leaving the symbolism of Mountains and Mitres in the first of my talks I moved forward in the second to Fortresses and Fountains. We live in a fortress. We inherited it. Outside the window at this moment a fountain plays. This one was designed by Benedict Tutty. In Maastricht I learned what a whole town built on paranoia can look like. Our monastery could easily give the same impression to an outsider.

The fortress or the fountain, these are two conflicting symbols. The transfiguration, it seems to me, which was the inspiration of Cluny, symbolises a monasticism which is open to the world around it. Like the fountain outside, it is a centre perforated with openings which allow the water to spray in every direction around it. The castle which we inherited is a fortress on a mountain. It speaks of defensiveness, it keeps out the world, it encloses its members in a circle of protected insulation. It seems to me that whatever about the past, Glenstal in the future should be a monastery of the transfiguration, where all the resurrected energy which accrues to us should be poured out on all those who come to us and all those who live and work around and about us.

All the creativity which we have been given and have developed should become a spiritual centre from which and in which a spirituality of resurrected life can be imparted and shared by an ever-increasing number in a series of circles emanating from our liturgy.

September: (topaz) 2003 being the year of the Holy Spirit, Third Person of the Trinity, September was the ninth month of that third year of the new millennium. Telling Senan about the Church of the Transfiguration as something round and tentlike, as in the drawings James Scanlon had given me and framed, he mentioned Liam McCormick's church at Burt, Co Donegal. I had met Liam's widow, Joy, at Barons Court and later in the Shelbourne hotel, where she was trying to get me interested in her husband's work. This church at Burt was also the illustration chosen by Austin Flannery to illustrate a review he asked me to do of Richard Hurley's book on Irish church architecture. I looked up this book for Senan to find a picture of the McCormick church and came across a photograph on page 99 of the Church of the Irish Martyrs designed by Eamon Hedderman, a name similar to my own, which I pointed out to Senan. Senan then went to a funeral in Donegal and passed by the McCormick church on the way which he visited without planning to do so. Four days later I was in the Stillorgan

Shopping Centre when a man approached me and said he was Eamon Hedderman who wanted to make himself known to me. He later wrote (8/9/03) enclosing 'some images of our recent work, which strives to create hope' and suggesting that 'there are perhaps areas where we might have common interests in the "liturgical health" of the church, the renewal of which I fear has lost its vitality.'

Biscantorat: Sounds of the Spirit. This recording took place on Friday 19 September 2003, the anniversary in 1883 of the first balloon launched into the air with live creatures on board – a sheep, a rooster and a duck.

27 September (3x3x3) 2003 twelve of us met to listen to what had been recorded. This was the day that Nóirín ní Riain finished her doctorate thesis on theosony: the sound of God. Our recording was a manifestation of her work. Wherever two or three are gathered in my name, I am singing through them.

The title of the CD is a word describing an ancient proverb used by Saints Ambrose and Augustine that singing means praying twice (*Bis orat qui cantat*). The twelve of us who met together in the round stone chapter room to hear what had been recorded expected to be in varied disagreement. We reached immediate and unprecedented consensus about the order, the content and the nature of the CD which is the result. Everything here has been given by a presence other than the people who recorded it.

John O'Donohue had finished writing his book on *Divine Beauty*. 'The beauty of God is reachable for everyone and can be awakened in all dimensions of our experience' (DB 222). 'It is vital to provide an atmosphere whereby the deeper levels of what is happening can emerge and be engaged' (DB 203). 'If you attend reverently and listen tenderly, you will be given the words that are needed. It is as if these words make a raft to carry the persons over to the further shore' (DB 204). 'The experience of the beautiful … is the invocation of a potentially whole and holy order of things'. Such 'invocation' is liturgical. It makes present what is otherwise invisible because 'beauty is so quietly woven through our ordinary days that we hardly notice it' (DB 12). This CD celebrates his work. Where is Divine Beauty to be heard? 'Anywhere: in prayer, family, front line, hospital, brothel or prison, anywhere care comes alive, God is present'(DB 225).

The words I speak on this recording were given to me by the author of this book also. 'On this recording you hear sounds, voices, music. Latin chants, Irish songs, English hymns. Voices singing alone, voices singing together, voices in harmony. Whose are these voices? They belong to no one in particular. They have been given by and to another. These are not professional singers; nor is this a commercial enterprise. The voices you hear are singing with each other but beyond themselves. The Spirit blows where it chooses, and you hear the sound of it, but you do not know where it comes from or where it goes (John 3:8).

Sineád (Marie Bernadette) O'Connor had reached a turning-point. She was searching for voice in religious music. She followed the Spirit to Glenstal Abbey where Nóirín Ní Riain was in residence completing her doctorate on this topic, an articulation of what she has been singing all her life. Rather than talk about it they decided to do it.

Nóirín's two sons, Eoin and Micheál, with some of the boys from the Glenstal Abbey School Choir make up the remainder of the prayer group who celebrated with twelve monks of Glenstal Abbey. We stand in a circle. We breathe a column of air moving upwards, formed by our singing. The song gives shape and colour to the pillar of sound. Each one of us releases ownership, unties the anchor from our hearts, opens the window and lets the songbird free. This upward-flowing energy is the Holy Spirit. *Sounds of the Spirit* take us where the Spirit moves.

'The Spirit and the Bride say come'.

'Enter their courts with songs of praise'.

October: Russia, (chrysoprase) St Petersburg. You have to see The Russian Ark (2002) directed by Aleksandr Sokurov, shot in a single 96-minute take, on High Definition digtal video, to glimpse the kind of breakneck tour of one Russian city which we were privileged to make this autumn. The film weaves through 33 rooms of the Hermitage at St. Petersburg, and past 2,000 actors and extras, following Russian history of the past 300 years. It was a prelude to and preview of this October tour of St Petersburg in its tricentenniel year.

The city was built by Peter the Great in 1703 to establish the European direction of Russia and himself as master of the Baltic shores. Local mythology claims that he constructed the city in the sky and then found a site where the Neva river enters the Baltic Sea. In fact the city was built upon bones! One of the many magnificent churches that are scattered between the hundreds of palaces is appropriately called the Cathedral of the Spilt Blood. Thousands of Swedish prisoners of war died in the construction of the foundations on a marsh. Dostoievsky describes it as a city monster crawling out of the swamps. Built on water with imported stone it is like some magic city out of a Russian fairy tale, suspended between sea and sky. The gulf of Finland is fifty miles off. There is greenery for only two months of the year. A gloomy atmosphere pervades the astounding architectural beauty of its facades. There are 600 palaces open to every kind of access. These are neither castles nor fortresses, they are wide open and hospitable. The Russians are unafraid. There are always parties with huge numbers of guests in every palace. It is all formally elegant and European in front: the city of Tchaikovsky's Swan Lake, Pushkin's Bronze Horseman, the early Akhmatova; but behind all that, down the back alleys, it is the city of Dostoievsky. In 1712 it became the capital of Russia.

We are here at Sacha's invitation to celebrate her Pushkin movement and its connections with Russia. Alexander Pushkin (born in 1795) died from wounds received fighting a duel (January 27th 1837). He was, in person, the beginning of literature in Russian. Gogol tells us that he was 'an extraordinary and perhaps unique manifestation of the Russian Spirit and a prophetic one which will eventually save Europe.' 'Pushkin died in the full development of his powers, and undoubtedly carried to his grave a certain great mystery ... and now we must solve this mystery without him.'

Anna Achmatova (1889 - 1966) Josef Brodsky's muse, also presides in this city of artists. The Queen of Spades. Soviet critics attacked her as symbol of the old regime. Stalin never read a line of her poetry but condemned it and her.

'I will stand and howl under the Kremlin towers.'

In her preface to 'Requiem' she wrote, 1 April 1957, 'In the fearful years of the Yezhov terror I spent seventeen months in prison queues in Leningrad. One day somebody 'identified' me. Beside me, in the queue, there was a woman with blue lips. She had, of course, never heard of me; but she suddenly came out of that trance so common to us all and whispered in my ear (everybody spoke in whispers there): 'Can you describe this?' And I said: 'Yes, I can.' And then something like the shadow of a smile crossed what had once been her face.'[7]

Marinsky Theatre for a performance of *La Sylphide* – not the greatest ballet – but a visit backstage during the interval to see the theatre and meet the cast was Hollywood stuff. As Putin comes from St Petersburg it gets lots of subvention to reconstruct this unreal, artificial, abstract, foreign city (in the words of some more traditional Muscovites) mostly for tourism. There are always tourists: for the ballet, the snow, the white nights of summer. We saw the chapel where the eventually slaughtered family of Nicholas and Alexandra spent their last days; the room where Pushkin died after the duel; the rooms where Anna Achmatova was kept as a political prisoner; the places where Rasputin was poisoned, shot and eventually drowned; and finally the hermitage for which Catherine the Great plundered the libraries and art galleries of Europe to decorate the Winter Palace where she liked to be alone. If you spend one minute examining each of the treasures in this endless museum it will take nine years of your life.

As in the rest of Europe, this year was milder than others in Russia. Snows only began to fall at the end of our stay. On the last day in the airport one of the poets in our group, Joan Newmann, told me she had had a dream: the book I was meant to find and bring out of Russia was the one I was now about to write!

21/22 October: Nóirín is awarded her doctorate. 'The work could be described as a phenomenology of hearing as the basis for human interconnectedness including our relationship with God. It describes the human ear as the most fundamental layer of human being: the membrane which allows access to all that is beyond ourselves and, therefore, one of the most privileged inlets to God.

Physiologically, the ear is our most characteristic organ. We are 'all ears' not just as a manner of speaking but as an existential reality. Our bodies are, to an extent, incarnations of our ears. Our enveloping skin is an aural membrane. We hear with the soles of our feet. The ear never sleeps. Like the heart it is ever awake, our ever vigilant insomniac. As such it is our most sensitive burglar alarm: capable of registering even the most unobtrusive presences.

The writer being herself a professional singer of mostly sacred songs has provided as accurate an account as possible of what happens when the event of singing occurs within the human frame. The accomplishment of 'song as existence,' in the words of the poet Rainer

Maria Rilke, has been documented here in as far as such introspection, observation, analysis, and the verbal recording of a spontaneous reality are possible.'

1 November: (*jacinth*)Marie de Franssu visits for the weekend. She hears during her stay a voice from outside: 'Glenstal very beautiful but needs the feminine.'

28-30 November 2003: I am in the Portmarnock Hotel in Dublin with a group called 'Encounter' established by the British and Irish governments in 1983 to 'contribute to the improvement of relations between our peoples in the interest of peace, reconciliation and stability.' We discuss inter-relationships between England, Scotland, Wales, Northern Ireland and the Republic. It is the weekend of the Northern Ireland elections where the DUP and Sinn Féin top the polls as unionist and nationalist representatives respectively. Many are on their mobiles during the breaks but there is no mention of this situation during official proceedings.

Circa forty-five present at round-table discussion led by Joint chairs: Sir David Blatherwick former British Ambassador to Ireland and Egypt, & Vice-Chair: Dorothea Melvin (Director, Cultures of Ireland (Dublin), and organised by: Salters Sterling (formerly Academic Secretary of Trinity College, Dublin).

Of the twenty participants listed from Ireland, North (6) and South (14), seven were affiliated with Trinity College Dublin. Introductory speakers included: Callum G. Brown, author of *The Death of Christian Britain*, Richard Dawkins of Oxford University, some of whose well known books include *The Selfish Gene* and *The Blind Watchmaker*, Shirley Williams, (*God and Caesar, Personal Reflections on Politics and Religion*) who founded the now-defunct SDP (Social Democratic Party) were among the speakers. Malachi O'Doherty, commentator and journalist, widely known in Northern Ireland for his column in the *Belfast Telegraph*, and for his work with the BBC was also listed as an official speaker. His book *The Trouble with Guns: Republican strategy and the IRA* was published in 1998. His new book, *I was a Teenage Catholic*, was published this year. Rev Dr Alan Billings, Minister in the Church of England, politician and BBC broadcaster and Sr Helena O'Donoghue, Provincial Leader of the Mercy Sisters of Ireland made up the rest of the programme. Breda O'Brien of *The Irish Times* was raporteur and the after dinner speaker was playwright Tom Kilroy.

The title of the 'encounter' was 'Post-Christian Society' and the majority of this gathering seemed to agree that religion was an undermining anachronism in a twenty-first century Ireland. It was a salutary swipe at most presuppositions underpinning this book. 'The general assumption was that Ireland had begun to experience a similar diminution of religious belief and practice within the Christian tradition, though not necessarily to the same degree as had been experienced in Britain over a somewhat longer period.' For Callum Brown, committed agnostic and post-modernist, 'significant numbers of people no longer interpret reality using a religious ... framework.' Baroness Shirley Williams, House of Lords, Westminster, attributed this decline to a loss of the Wordsworth factor: domestic comfort lessened exposure to the awesome power of nature; a prevailing lack of respect; the failure of organised religion to address the needs of women.

Areas of consensus were limited between a polarisation of the minority who identified themselves as believers and a majority who were atheist, agnostic or post-modern. The question was asked as to whether decline in church attendance automatically created a post-christian society? It could mean mutation into a less institutional form of Christianity. Helena O'Donoghue describes this as a more christian society where each person of whatever race, creed or background should feel at home. 'It was emphasised that Western Europe is an anomaly in world terms, and that the US is perhaps the second most religious country in the world, the first being India.'[8]

10 December (amethyst): In the Hugh Lane Gallery for the third time this year at the launch of Sacha Abercorn's book of prose poems, *Feather from the Firebird*, published by Joan and Kate Newmann in their Summer Palace Press. At this launch Sacha brought me back the book on Russian Theology[9] which Gregory had lent me at least a year ago. Its flyleaf says: 'Cover illustration: tableau (1926) by Natalia Goncharova for the ballet *The Firebird*.'

> The Russian school of modern Orthodox theology has made an immense but under-valued contribution to Christian thought. Neglected in Western Theology and viewed with suspicion by some other schools of Orthodox theology, its greatest thinkers have laid the foundations for a new ecumenism and a recovery of the cosmic

dimension of Christianity. This ground-breaking study … examines the creative ideas they devised or adapted, including the 'humanity of God,' sophiology, pan-humanity, and prophetic ecumenism.

There was a train ticket inside the book 'Dublin-Limerick' of exactly the same day two years ago 10/12/2001 – when Gregory had given me the book.

I had in my pocket an exactly similar ticket dated for today: 10/12/2003. Two things dawned: the first ticket was the time of the beginning of the walkabout. Also, this book on Russian theology was an important part of 'the book' to be taken out of Russia and returned there at a later time.

During the launch Kate and Joan Newmann asked me to be the main speaker. I imagine they were expecting someone else to turn up who would do this. Normally I would have been upset about such short notice. This time I knew that it was part of the 'walkabout contract' and that the words would be given. They were as follows:

'Like a shaman or wise woman of the tribe, Sacha Abercorn has journeyed for us to the land of far below, the deepest pit, the bottom of the pool, and has emerged as *sophiaphore* (bearer of wisdom) bringing with her pearls of insight contained in the pages of this book. 54 prose-poems, one painting, one photograph, a feather from the firebird for my father: 'Silent Tears' for each year of a single lifetime.

'Earlier this year Sacha returned to the desert where she had been born. Travelling deep into the Chiricahua mountains in February and remaining there in solitude in a small yellow tent, she reached beyond the limits of merely personal history. She tapped the rock beneath which opened and let her in. This hazardous quest at a freezing time of year, the time of her birthday, required courage. One of the instruction sheets recommends a small aerosol spray for use in case of visits from bears. Snakes also seek shelter in warm yellow tents on the mountainside. Even the most hardened traveller needs a steely nerve. But the time in the Chiricahuas, the final movement of a 25 year search, repaid the effort made. The rocky earth gave way and allowed this stubborn daughter access to the secret depths of being.

'Pearls are fashioned by the irritation caused between the hardened outer shell and the sensitive skin. Usually some grain, some sand, comes in between. These tiny individual pearls make up the necklace of a lifetime. Each one captures, as in a snapshot epiphany, some moment of the past which traces the history of a depth of bruising. Pointillage of birthmarks; 'scar tissue impacted with time'; the tapestry is now complete. Each one of these prose-poems on a page is more than poetry. These are drops of blood spilt delicately one by one. But it is not enough simply to bleed. If blood is to be fashioned into art, Yeats reminds us, it must be packed with ice or salt. Reticence and accuracy require that not a word more than necessary appear in print.

'Each page describes a shuddering moment of arrest as each tree-ring marks the texture and the climate of a year's growth in a single tree. We are grateful for this exercise, this painstaking self-expression. It is what Sacha has been urging all the children and the teachers of the Pushkin movement to undertake for themselves in their own lives: to find their own voice however tremulous and allow it to sound out like a bell. Now she has accomplished this great task in herself, for herself and for all of us. We have the proof between the covers of this book.

'You only know that the bell, which has been created from the molten ore, poured into the shape you fashioned in the earth, rings true when you hang it in its place and strike it like a gong. Every one of these bells rings true: a xylophone of love. This is more than poetry, this is life, distilled in sparkling crystals. Take and read, it will bring you into contact with your own.'

At the end of December I got a phonecall from Chuck Feeney. He asked me how the year had been. Hopeful, I said. 'I wonder if we have been living on the same planet, he said, or where on earth you have been hiding yourself?' He invited me to dinner on the first day of the new year with his wife Helga and her mother, who would be entering her 100th year, and I agreed to tell him why I had found this year so hopeful.

New Year's Eve 2003

Dear Chuck,
You ask me to write down what I found so hopeful about 2003. Despite all the ostensible disaster around the world it has been my privilege to 'walkabout' in the Holy Spirit during this year. I have been to a different country almost every month searching for signs

of a new consciousness trying to emerge in our world. This is, in my understanding, the Holy Spirit using people to incarnate the way forward for the evolutionary appetite of humanity.

The millennium spire in Dublin which was only finished this year should be viewed as 'the spire of an underground cathedral' in the words of the architect. This allows Ireland to go underground spiritually and examine the unconscious world from which most of our troubles spring.

I had told you previously how, on my journeys in the past, some places (one outside Paris, one in Sonoma Valley, California, for example) had presented themselves as possible places where this Spirit might be ready to make a move. In August of 2003 it became clear to me, and to others here, that Glenstal Abbey was indeed the place where the Spirit was anxious and ready to make a move.

Yesterday, 30/12/2003 we had the first meeting of GASP (Glenstal Abbey Spiritual Programme) which will be planned in 2004 and come into being in 2005. It will help to make of this whole Shannon area a 'fifth province' which will give life, hope, and meaning to the world we step into in this promising millennium.

The work that you, Ed Walsh, Brendan O'Regan, Mícheál Ó Suilleabháin and so many others have done in this part of the country and of the world will be rounded off in a way that makes this region a centre of healing, meeting, understanding and peace. Already we are hoping to combine with the Castletroy Park Hotel, so conveniently situated, to form a reachable triangle between UL and ourselves, for meetings with academics, business people, counsellors, doctors, explorers, financiers, government agents, historians, internationalists, jurists, king-makers, negotiators, oceanographers, philosophers, quantum physicists, regulators, scientists, trend-setters, urban planners, visionaries, writers etc. in whatever alphabet of achievement you care to elaborate.

The Glenstal community will expand to include an outer ring of people engaged in formulating a philosophy of life which will provide sustenance for a new generation.

For the last 27 years I have been keeping a log-book of the wonders which have happened in this Shannon region and in the last 3 years I have been allowed to give all my time and attention to the shape of the future which this privileged part of the world can now offer as a new culture for the universe. This year, already beginning today, is for planning; next year, 2005 is for implementation. This year I am writing a book *Walkabout: Life as Holy Spirit* which will describe why and how all this has happened and can happen.

Even if the world looks war and violence weary, it is still true to say that the Spirit breathes and that the various sparks of inspiration can ignite and begin a healthy conflagration.'

2004:

The truth is that I did not know when exactly the 'walkabout' was meant to end. I knew it was to become a book but had no idea of the publication date. I also felt that it should be the seventh book I write. 2004 seemed to be the year for writing it down. However, things kept on happening which seemed necessary to include. I had already published in this year 2004 a book about dialogue in the Roman Catholic Church which appeared in March.[10] This gave me leeway to postpone publication of this walkabout until 2005.

24 January 2004: Fanny Howe and I take a January Bloomsday walk around Dublin. Seamus and Marie Heaney brought out the blue Russian cups and saucers from St Petersburg at 191 Strand Road for our morning visit to them. Seamus drove us in his second hand Merc. to the Francis Bacon Studio. We passed the Millennium spire and walked over the Halfpenny Bridge to Templebar. We took in both the Gresham and Shelbourne hotels with a marathon through various art galleries. The Rembrandt in the National Gallery had gone to Boston where Fanny had just come from. The wedding chest had gone home to Barons Court. Carravaggio's betrayal was all that was left, and rumour has it as a fake! All the straying ends of this walkabout seemed to meet in the new gallery shop under the millennium wing of the National Gallery.

15 February: Took a tiny red aeroplane from Fort Lauderdale with provisions for a month to the island of Eleuthera in the Bahamas. Another country to add to the Walkabout. Staying with the Abercorns in Hamilton House on Windemere. We stop at a sea port on the way to buy pieces of freshly fished grouper. Staying on the island also are Lee and Julie Folger who are next door neighbours in Washington to former

ambassador to Ireland William H. G. Fitzgerald. On a six-mile beach in front of the house Sacha and I rescue a starfish. Gospel of Thomas provides this quotation: 'If you bring forth what is within you what you bring forth will save you; if you do not bring forth what is within you what you do not bring forth will destroy you.'

16 March: Email from John Hill:

I spent the day with John O'Donohue. I took him on the Holy Spirit tour. First Einsiedeln and there we met -by chance- exactly the right person, who was at his lecture the night before. She showed him some of the wonders of the monastery's baroque library. We arrived late at the house of Bruder Klaus and it was closed. To our surprise a man appeared and gave us the key to enter. In the main room of the family we both became aware of the saint's presence and remained silent for an indefinite period of time. John spent a very long time down at the hermitage, absorbing that spiritual landscape. Later we talked about the silence, the river, the mountains in that untouched vale of the Middle Ages. He plans to return and write about it.

April 03/04/04: In the offices of Dublin Public Libraries at Wood Quay, Tim Pat Coogan, Marie Heaney and I are asked to talk with assembled readers of our various books. The guest speaker of the afternoon is Salley Vickers. Louise has asked me to get her latest book signed. Otherwise I would probably not have stayed to hear her speak in the afternoon as our assignments were in the morning. Her talk was about writing as an exercise of the unconscious. I met her briefly. An aspect of the unconscious symbolism of the journey was vividly pointed out to me by her words and when I discovered a day later 04/04/04 that the title of her second novel was *Instances of the number 3*.

April 04/04/04: *Burial at Thebes*, Heaney's translation of *Antigone* at The Abbey. Fanny Howe had intended to come and asked Paul Keegan, poetry editor for Faber & Faber, to get me a ticket. My second time at The Abbey during this Walkabout. *Ariel* and *Antigone*. I was three times in Paris during this Walkabout, the third time in 2003 when *L'Alouette* made up the third in these theatrical instances of three.

It was only now, a year-and-a-half later, that I understood some of the resonances of Marina Carr's *Ariel* in the Abbey which had been taken off after a short time (2 October – 9 November 2002) because it did not achieve the kind of immediate box office popularity which allows such plays a more extended run.

In the book of the icons which I had circulated to the Cóiced and others at the end of 1996, I had noted in my diary for 16 December:

So, what is happening? I am not sure myself. I know that it is happening, that I am committed to it and that it has elements already present which I can recognise. These last pages will enumerate these.

The first comes through *Anecdotes of Destiny* by Isak Dinesen, given to me by Ciarán. This is the book in which the story of 'Babette's Feast' appeared. The first story is called 'The Diver' in which a young Mohammedan theology student fails to reach the absolute when he tries to fly, but reaches it instead when he becomes a diver. This states the theme of the whole volume of stories and the theme of this new vision of theology which the icon chapel incarnates.

The story 'Tempests' is a counterpoint to Shakespeare's play of the same name. Ariel in Shakespeare's play is the spiritual principle as opposed to Caliban, the fleshly one. The character in the story who is trying to cast Shakespeare's play is finding it difficult to choose a suitable Ariel. 'It is a revelation that he finally finds "the most exquisite Ariel the world has ever known" in a girl of his company whom no one but a man of genius would have recognised as Ariel. So moved is he, we are told, that he forgets Ariel is male. But that is the point. It is because the girl Malli is still all potentiality, because she has not yet discovered her body, has not yet been born as a woman, that she is right for an epicene spirit like Ariel.'

Add this to the first story and you find that it is impossible to reach the absolute by trying to fly, by being trained as an Ariel. Only the divers, those who descend into their bodies, cross the threshold of existence as human beings. Most remain, in a psychological and spiritual sense, Ariel. To cross from the ethereal, epicine atmosphere above the orbit of the earth means to fall, to descend into hell. This is not a question of happiness, it is a matter of life or death. Ariel existence is non-existence: unable to reconcile spirit and flesh we remain, whether angelic or diabolic, spirit; we operate along the single line of the Ariel force.

The passage from the Bible which falls open in the story comes from Isaiah, 29: 'Woe to Ariel, to Ariel! ... And thou shalt be brought down, and thou shalt speak out of the ground ... and thy voice shall be as of one that hath a familiar spirit, out of the ground, and thy speech shall whisper out of the dust!'

Thomas Mann is quoted by Robert Langbaum in his book on Isak Dinesen: 'Freud ... will, I make no doubt at all, be honoured as the path-finder towards a humanism of the future, which we dimly divine and which will have experienced much that the earlier humanism knew not of. It will be a humanism standing in a different relation to the powers of the lower world, the unconscious, the id: a relation bolder, freer, blither, productive of a riper art than any possible in our neurotic, fear-ridden, hate-ridden world.'

Marina Carr will also be hailed as such a path-finder at some future time. Her play had been specifically pointed out to me during the time of this walkabout and I was forced to articulate some immediate reactions to it by a letter from Brian Jackson (7/10/02) inviting me to participate in a panel discussion, chaired by Justice Adrian Hardiman of the Supreme Court along with Ivana Bacik, Edith Hall, Melissa Sihra, on the theme Justice, Vengeance and Myth. This discussion took place after the matinee performance of Ariel on Saturday 12 October, 2002.

The first connection I made was with the most popular notion of Ariel which is the washing powder advertised endlessly and ubiquitously on radio and TV ads. The danger with this play is that we take it at face value, get caught up in the soap. Ariel as automatic powder with biological action. This pack contains 75 scoops. Shock effect could land us in a riot of laughs. To get the most out of it, please measure according to the soil levels of your own wash, and the water hardness in your area. ('I think at certain times in your life you can be visited by presences, and the temperature at which they visit you depends on what state you're in yourself' Marina Carr herself says about her play).

('There are two types of playwrights: there are prose writers of the theatre and there are poets of the theatre' again quoting Marina Carr.)

The language in the play is powerful, at times like blood spouting from a jugular slashed at the neck. ('If left to my own devices I'd still be talking like a midlander. It's a very rich language. It's a language of metaphor and a lot of story-telling. People think you're straining for effect sometimes when you're just reporting what you've heard. The best lines I've ever written are things I've heard and I've just written them down'.)

It is a deep and a difficult journey and yet this play is expected to jostle and compete with popular entertainment and sporting fixtures in order to remain for any length of time on our consumerist radar screens. There should be a place where such plays are available continually and relentlessly to bring us towards those depths from which they spring. Perhaps the most poignant introduction to at least one of the harrowing themes should come from Sylvia Plath's collection *Ariel* and, probably, her most famous poem:

Daddy

So daddy, I'm finally through.
The black telephone's off at the root,
The voices just can't worm through.

If I've killed one man, I've killed two –
The vampire who said he was you
And drank my blood for a year,
Seven years, if you want to know.
Daddy, you can lie back now.

There's a stake in your fat black heart
And the villagers never liked you.
They are dancing and stamping on you.
They always *knew* it was you.
Daddy, daddy, you bastard, I'm through.

Burial at Thebes began well. Ritual, music, ballet-like movement. The Heaney word-score powerful and tender. But then the Abbey Centenary Celebratory Performance takes over and it becomes a spectacle. For Creon read George W. Bush who by the end of the play is transformed into Saddam Hussein. No interval. Implausible nemesis in too short a time. Words were lost: sent scurrying 'to skirl above my head.' 'There was no meaning to them. I knew by the whirl of wings/ And the rips and spits of blood the birds were mad.' The audience should have been condemned like Antigone to 'a rock vault'. We should have been shut inside stone tombs to listen to the words alone.

> Stone of my wedding chamber, stone of my tomb,
> Stone of my prison roof and prison floor,
> Behind you and beyond you stand the dead.

Instead of honouring the music of this word-score, the Abbey chose to celebrate its centenary with a spectacle ending in gory climax: Creon carrying Haemon in batiks of blood. Melodrama. Saddam and sons Bushwhacked. 'Was I going to humour you, or honour Gods?' Antigone askes Creon scornfully. Except for the chorus, Barry McGovern and Garrett Keogh, honouring the poetry, the rest was outsized to the point of bathos. It was commissioning the Nobel Laureate to translate Antigone into circus music for the centenary. What I understood from both these visits is that the search for another venue for the Abbey theatre should result in a second kind of Abbey connected with the main setting of the National Theatre where such plays are celebrated in liturgical fashion and in a contemplative setting.

18 April 2004: Email from John Hill:
Dear Mark,

Easter Greetings!
My cousin Patricia and her daughter and grandchildren stayed with us for the Easter week. They are all good people and something important happened, which I would like to share.
Of course I brought them on the Holy Ghost tour to Einsiedeln, Bruder Klaus and Joa Bolendas. These women asked Joa about the future of Ireland, and it seems their questions activated Joa's connection to God and Ireland.
Today Bruder Klaus conveyed the following message to Joa Ireland will be a spiritual centre of culture for Europe and America.

This will take place over the next 100 years. Work on it!

Joa asked: What is culture?

Br Klaus: Life energy, learning.

Religion is important. Psychology and some philosophy.

Let three candles burn.

Later Joa said that she saw Mark, John, a young priest or monk, John O'Donohue, and two or three others in this work. She sends you greetings and 'sees' that in time you will know what to do.

Joa also wondered why she did not get this message when you were here, but it seems now is the time for it.

So let us keep in touch and see what happens next.

Love at this time of resurrection.

In 1999 John Hannon commissioned me to compose a poem on love for the new millennium. I had been writing a book called *Manikon Eros* which I began in 1972 and finished for publication in 2000. Peter O'Meara visited me with his father Basil at this time. He had been an actor since he left the school here in 1988. I had seen him in several productions on stage including *The Crucible* and *The Colleen Bawn*. He had just finished playing Edmund to Sir Nigel Hawthorne's King Lear at The Royal Shakespeare Company. I had never seen him so down in himself. He was questioning the whole energy which had driven him to a career in acting. I gave him the typescript of *Manikon Eros*. He was the first person to read the finished version. I believed that it had been written for him in a certain sense, that if he understood it, it would 'cure' him. The book was a distillation of what I had 'found' in my own life and it had been given to me by the Holy Spirit.

Christmas 2003 there was a phone message from LA. Peter O'Meara at some ungodly hour of the morning over there. He left a number but I couldn't reach him. Then came an invitation to his wedding at Zihuatanejo in Mexico for Saturday 29 May 2004. I went to the television room, clicked on Sky Movies and there he was in a series called *Peacemakers*, playing the role of Dr Larimer Finch, riding a horse beside a moving train and leaping onto the roof of a carriage thwarting some villain of evil intent and rescuing a damsel in distress. I knew then that I should be at the wedding, and that its location was a humourous way of indicating that this was my last port of call. The book I had written through all those years was also to be published in America the following month. John Jones of The Crossroad Publishing Company had worked on the original text and had improved it considerably, mostly by simplifying sentences which I had made unnecessarily complicated. The new title was *Love Impatient, Love Unkind*. At first I thought my original title was better. But I now think that The Holy Spirit works through many different 'handlers' and that the eventual product is no one's direct responsibility but, thirty years later, the nearest approximation to what this Holy Spirit originally had in mind. This 2004 version becomes, therefore, the definitive edition.[11]

I was not surprised, therefore, when Peter O'Meara's parents asked me to go to the wedding and paid for my ticket. His father, Basil, could not travel as he had a dangerous heart condition. Kayla Alpert, Peter's bride to be, is Jewish. The ceremony was to be both Christian and Jewish and I was to be co-president with Richard Hiller, a lawyer from New York. This wedding was symbol of another theme of this book: the essential unity of the judeo-christian tradition. Richard Hiller devised with the bride and groom a ritual which had elements from many traditions. It was a moving ceremony for all who were fortunate enough to be present in this beautiful corner of the world.

I performed for the first time the poem I had written for the millennium as a new song of love. It became the canticle for the exchange of rings between these two representative persons. The wedding ceremony took place on the terrace of La Quinta Troppo overlooking the Ocean. My walkabout in The Holy Spirit from A-Z (Albuquerque to Zihuatanejo) had come to an end.

Villanelle for a Wedding

I am the Bridegroom, Love, you are the bride
Mountains of cinnamon surround our wedding bed
Love me until the wild world's tears are dried

Set me like a seal, my love replied
Priests in the temple of the body take this bread
You are the bridegroom, love, I am the bride

Even when now and then our worlds collide
Passion flowers striped and peonies blood red
Love me until the wild world's tears are dried

Nothing can break this bond once we decide
To weave it round our hearts with scarlet thread
I am the bridegroom, love, you are the bride

Strolling through gardens where love was denied
Old age won't find these sap-filled branches dead
Love me until the wild world's tears are dried

Bodies inside a tomb identified
As man and woman intertwined, they said
I am the bridegroom, love, you are the bride
Love me until the wild world's tears are dried

IV

MOSAIC OF TIME AND SPACE

Last Part of the Jig-Saw:
Signs of the Times

The San Clemente mosaic was the bigger picture: what Judeochristianity was meant to be. An icon also of how to get this back on track. The various details represent different aspects of the salvage operation. The mystery is expressed in symbolic form, the only language capable of providing such glimpses. Otherwise mystery is impenetrable.

St Paul uses much of the terminology of a mystery religion when introducing the essence of Christianity. *Mysterion* (the hidden mystery), is the eternal counsel (wisdom, *sophia*) hidden in God (Eph, 3:9) before ever the world came to be (1 Cor 2:7). Paul himself as steward of the mystery must be acquainted with these secrets. The gift of a prophet is to penetrate the mysteries of God (1 Cor 2:10; 4:1; 13:2). *Mysterion* is connected with *Kerygma* (the proclaimed message) as the Father is manifested by the Son, who is an epistle (from the Greek *epi* + *stellein*, meaning 'to send') from God. Paul describes the Christians of Corinth as, in themselves, a letter of Christ 'prepared by us, written not with ink but with the Spirit of the living God, not on tablets of stone but on human hearts' (II Cor 3:3). Christ is the living icon of the Father; we are the living icons of the Son, written by the Holy Spirit. All knowledge of God is a mystery both in the way it is communicated and the way it is received. No human agency has proprietory claims, production control, or distribution rights in this regard. The way a mystery is handed on is itself a mystery.

Gnosticism was one of the first heresies with which Christianity had to contend, and from which it had to differentiate itself. It is understandable that every attempt was made to rid the newly established mystery religion of all connection with, all ambiguous terminology redolent of, the circumambient cults which threatened to invade, dilute or dissipate the originality which Christianity incorporated into its liturgy and sacraments. However, the bitterness and intensity of the struggle between gnosticism and early Christianity were owing to their proximity rather than their difference; were caused by the similarity which threatened to absorb, rather than any heterogeneity which might define them as contradictory opposites.

Whatever the dangers of misinterpretation or of identification with alien religions, Christianity remains essentially a mystery religion. And this means that its substance, its secret core, can never become comprehensively enshrined in any work of human hands of whatever variety or intricacy. Christ came on earth to reveal the mystery of that life which is lived eternally by the three persons of the Trinity. He replaced one mystery with another mystery. The only reality more mysterious than the three persons in one God is the reality of the person in human form. And this is the basis of our religion, the mystery on which it is founded. When Pilate asked Jesus: 'What is truth?' The answer was silence. The truth, in person, was standing in front of him. No more accurate or comprehensive embodiment of truth could have been present to Pilate or to anyone else. The person is the only reliable expression of truth. Jesus Christ never wrote anything down himself. The only recorded account of his writing was with his finger in the sand. So, any account of his life or his teaching is second hand. And all such accounts display inconsistencies and irreconcilable disagreements.

The resurrection of Jesus Christ, which is the essential mystery upon which any faith in Christianity is based, was an unwitnessed event. No human person was present. Witnesses have testified to having seen his empty tomb; others claim to have met Jesus Christ in his resurrected humanity after the event; but no one knows how or when his body was brought back to life. No one was present to see this happening.

Tradition for Christianity is the process whereby the mystery of Jesus Christ, the revelation of God's love in person, is transmitted by his followers. These followers are now organized into an official body called the church. However, the truth which they transmit is ultimately derived from an oral preaching by the original bearers of this truth (which is no more and no less than privileged contact with Jesus Christ as the Risen Lord in person) passed on in many different ways through the ever-present agency of the Holy Spirit. The Holy Spirit is the mystery of tradition in person.

Tradition in itself is silence and every word of revelation has a margin of silence. Certain nuggets hewn from this great silence have come down to us in both the Scriptures and Liturgical tradition but as Ignatius of Antioch says (Ephesians 15:2) 'The person who possesses in truth the word of Jesus can hear also its silence.' If all the great silence of tradition had become scripture, St John tells us, 'then the world itself would not be able to contain the books that would have to be written' (John 21:25). This silence is our turning towards the great abyss of divine love towards which every scrap of revelation every detail of tradition points.

'Do this in memory of me.' Christ is remembered after 2000 years in a series of cultic actions which are known to the faithful as the Liturgy. Art can also express most fruitfully the 'length and the breadth' of Divine Revelation, its 'height and its depth.' The apse of San Clemente does this majestically. Although its details are borrowed from myriad sources, its overall design depicts the mystery of Christianity as this is accomplished in the liturgical action on the altar underneath.

Behold the vineyard of the Lord. The vine as vast acanthus springs from the ground watered by the blood flowing from the side of Christ opened on the cross. This is a fourth or fifth century cross as new 'Tree of Life' originally planted on the hill of paradise, from which a river divided into four (Phison, Gehon, Tigris, Euphrates) flows through paradise and into the whole world (Genesis 2:10-14).

The workings of the Trinity in the economy of universal salvation are symbolically represented. The hand of God, the Father, (holding a wreath of victory) can be seen with the monogram of Christ, the Son (X + P = CH + R of our alphabet), and the alpha and omega – enclosed in an elliptical disc (*clipeus*) – all signify victory. Twelve doves on the arms of the cross indicate the vivifying power of God, the Holy Spirit, Lord and Giver of Life. They also symbolise twelve fruits of that same Spirit.

The Cross of Christ, Second Person of the Trinity, is the central motif: axis of the universe it draws everything to its centre. It is tree of life and also vine 'whence flows abundance of sweet wine – red with the red of blood' (Venantius Fortunatus, 535-600). 'Let us liken the Church of Christ to this vine' reads the inscription underneath.

Early Christian art drew upon secular tradition not only for such monograms as the *chi rho*, but also when translating visually the verbal imagery of the Bible. Vines, grapes and wine-making, for instance, had long been associated with Dionysos or Bacchus, Graeco-Roman God of wine, who died, was buried and rose again.[1]

Two aspects of this particular church in Rome revealed themselves to be important to this search: its being founded upon a very much more ancient religious site and its borrowing of imagery and symbolism from cultures flanking it on every side. Judeochristianity is rooted in the soil from which we all come; its flowers are the flowers of the fields; its fruits are the fruits of the earth.

On the lower rim there are twelve lambs taking up another scriptural image to represent the apostles, with Christ, as Lamb of God, at the centre. These form a procession passing between two cities: Bethlehem and Jerusalem marking the horizontal history of both the church and the historical Jesus, birth to death, cradle to cross; House of Bread (Bethlehem) to Heavenly Jerusalem.

And now one of the seven angels carried me off in a trance to a great mountain high up and there showed me the holy city of Jerusalem. The angel showed me too a river whose waters give life. On either side of the river grows the tree that gives life, bearing its fruit twelvefold, one yield for each month (Rev.21-22).

G. K. Chesterton describes the San Clemente apse in words reproduced in most official guide literature at the site:

Here is an older type of symbolism in which the real nature of the triumph of Christian things is traced in mosaic in the apse of the ancient church of San Clemente, one of the most remarkable and yet one of the most Roman of churches. The old decoration of the apse expresses the idea with a symmetry that is almost startling. The apse is a half moon of gold on the usual pattern; but at the top there is a cloud out of which comes the hand of God above the crucifix. It does not merely bless it or even merely rest on it. It seems to take the cross as if by the cross-hilt and thrust it like a sword into the earth below. Yet in one sense it is the very reverse of a sword, since its touch is not death but life; life springing and sprouting and shooting into the air, that the world may have life, and that it may have it more abundantly. It is impossible to say too much of the fruitful violence of this effect. It is not the normal groping of roots and branches. It is more like the blood of the earth spurting instantly from its arteries at the first wound. The living shoots go swirling away into space covering the whole background with their gyres and eddies; as if to lasso the stars. This antique design does really achieve what so many Futurist experiments or crazy jazz decorations have attempted; to make a dynamic diagram and to express suddenness in a pattern.

The very disproportion between the long loops and circles sprawling everywhere and the slender cross at whose touch they have leapt into life, emphasises with energy the power of that magic wand. Curled inside each of the circles, as in something that is at once a nest and a new and separate world, is a bird, to express the universal birth of life; and each bird is different in species or colour.

No one but a madman could stand before it and say that our faith is anti-vital or a creed of death. And there is one last touch, which has already been remarked by many; that the face of the Crucified, which in most images is naturally tragic, is in this case radiant and like the sun at noon; or like the words that have no need to be written here in any motto or inscription: 'I am the Resurrection and the Life.'[2]

What can such symbolism and imagery mean for us today? W. B. Yeats puts it succinctly:

> I wished for a world where I could discover this tradition perpetually, and not in pictures and in poems only, but in tiles round the chimney-piece and in the hangings that kept out the draught. I had even created a dogma: 'Because those imaginary people are created out of the deepest instinct of man, to be his measure and his norm, whatever I can imagine those mouths speaking may be the nearest I can go to truth.' When I listened they seemed always to speak of one thing only: they, their loves, every incident of their lives, were steeped in the supernatural.[3]

This last quotation is an introduction to the theme and methodology of this walkabout: Having been through the history of it as unconscious and instinctual sleepwalker it is now necessary to interpret these signs of the times. However, to be able to listen to what they say we have to reintroduce ourselves to a mythic way of thinking.

Nestlings: Emblems
Education + Pushkin

Essential to the work of the Holy Spirit is an education of the imagination, an education in the reading of symbols, the signs of the times. It is clear that in this area Ireland could become, yet again, an oasis in the desert. During this walkabout several initiatives in this regard were highlighted, most especially the initiative known as The Pushkin Prizes.

Several books were also forced upon me, in particular *Orality and Literacy* by Walter J. Ong.[4] Homo Sapiens has been on earth perhaps 50,000 years. Writing, in the strict sense of the word, the technology which has shaped and powered the intellectual activity of modern humanity, was a very late development in human history. The first script, or true writing, that we know, was developed among the Sumerians in Mesoppotamia around 3500 BC. The statue which Bertrand Jouslin de Noray showed me in the Louvre: *Le Scribe Acroupi*, sculpted between 2600 – 2350 BCE and found in the Nile valley at Sqqqara, must be one of the earlier confirmations of such scribes and their activity.

Writing is a preemptive and imperialist activity, locking words into a visual field forever. Written words are residue. Oral tradition has no such residue or deposit. Reading and writing also detach and isolate us. Sight isolates, sound incorporates. Vision comes to a human being from one direction at a time: to look at a room or a landscape, I must move my eyes around from one part to another. When I hear, however, I gather sound simultaneously from every direction at once: I am at the centre of my auditory world, which envelops me, establishing me at a kind of core of sensation and existence. For oral cultures, the cosmos is an ongoing event with man at its center. Man is the *umbilicus mundi*, the navel of the world. Only after print and the extensive experience with maps that print made possible would human beings, when they thought about the cosmos or universe or 'world', think primarily of something laid out before their eyes, as in a modern printed atlas, a vast surface or assemblage of surfaces. Vision presents surfaces ready to be 'explored'. Television introduces every one of those surfaces into our living-rooms.

The technology of writing may not be immediately apparent to us. But writing has always involved some external implements: goose quills, 'Pen knife,' (we still use the word for the instrument for paring these), hollow bovine inkhorns. Paper, manufactured in China in the second century BC, and diffused by Arabs to the Middle East by the eighth century of the Christian era, was first manufactured in Europe only in the twelfth century. Europe came late to this technology. But once it came it did so with a vengeance. Writing leads to printing and both spawn computer technology. The three technologies follow each other. Writing is the most drastic invention of the three. It initiates what printing and computers continue, 'the reduction of dynamic sound to quiescent space' (Ong p.82).

It was only those marginalised from our education system who stumbled upon the alternative and who, in many cases, thereby became what we have termed great artists or geniuses of one kind or another. W. B. Yeats is a case in point. John Carey, reviewing Roy Foster's biography of Yeats, asks: 'Was he, you find yourself blasphemously wondering, really that intelligent?' and he lists the usual proofs of intellectual backwardness: 'He was substandard at school ... He never learnt to spell: even as a grown man, simple monosyllables foxed him ... His gullibility was fathomless. Mysticism and magic, to which he was introduced by the half-batty George Russell, occupied much of his waking and sleeping life. He believed he conversed with old Celtic gods and a copious ragbag of other supernaturals.'[5] What this critic fails to recognise is that there are different kinds of intelligence. Yeats's intelligence was essentially mythic. Such intelligence weaves its way through symbols and has a very different perspective on the universe to that of the scientist, for instance.

In Western European philosophy we were introduced by Auguste Compte to the idea that human intelligence had developed from a primitive mythic stage, through a medieval mataphysical stage, right up to the scientific rationalism which has so marked and transformed our world. This development was linear and rendered all stages that preceded it obsolete.

There is no such evolutionary progress in a linear module, which casts off the previous in an advance towards the present, as a rocket might detach itself from the parts that launch it. Mythic intelligence is an essential kind of human understanding and it is to our great impoverishment that our educational systems and our academic leaders treat it with such contempt.

It is difficult for us to step outside the spaceship and recognize just how programmed we are. Much in the same way that we recognize the overwhelming extent to which we are dependent upon electricity only when there is a power cut, we have to exercise our imagination almost violently to recognize the extent to which we are automised clones of an infrastructural grid called 'Common Sense.' We are able to symbolise but this faculty is erased by our learning the three Rs. As A. N. Whitehead puts it: 'The seventeenth century produced a scheme of scientific thought framed by mathematicians for the use of mathematicians'.[6]

Civilised societies of the twentieth century democratised the languages of reading and writing. These became the fundamental currency in the West. They also became the criteria for 'intelligence.'

People of Western Europe in the twentieth century were not only able to read and write more or less instinctively, they translated everything that presented itself to them into this narrow network. We read music, art, cinema, life and love. Everything we do is a story, an alphabet, a grammar, a plot, a chapter, a closed book, a best seller. We read and we write our lives. My diary is my day translated into linear modules of coherent literacy.

While on Walkabout the nearest approximation to such alternative education, emphasising imagination and giving symbolism its crucial place was shown to be Sacha Abercorn's Pushkin initiative. Learning a new kind of alphabet involves recognition of at least some of the following:

One of the capacities which children have naturally and in abundance is imagination. It should be our most cherished heritage, our most carefully cultivated natural energy. And yet, the story of our educational history over the years has been of neglect and devaluation of this faculty. 'Teach these boys and girls nothing but facts,' we learned from Mr Gradgrind 150 years ago,[7] and we have been obeying this command ever since. If there are weapons of mass destruction hidden in our midst, one of these must surely be the education system we have put in place.

We refuse to listen to the poets who tell us that facts are important only to those who have never really lived. We have neglected the three-ringed circus of the imagination where children's flights of fancy are given free rein.

We have borrowed our education systems from armies, conquerors, mathematicians, technologists. These should provide only one half of what education might mean, if even that much. The Industrial revolution, the scientific revolution, the technological revolution, the cybernetic revolution: these have transformed our lives and we are grateful to them. We know also that they need young hands to keep them going, to make them work, to maintain the infrastructure of our Western World. But there is more to life than science; there is more to science than technology. That more is an inner garden of the imagination to which we should be given access, in which we should be allowed to cultivate, and where we should actively be encouraged to dwell for at least some part of our days and lives.

Other important realities have been allowed to crowd imagination out. Children are afforded no time for pondering, no space for inner or outer exploration, no opportunity for dreaming. Every minute of every day is filled with learning: core subjects of the curriculum, homework, cramming, examinations, points awarded for examinations – they have no time to be children. We have all grown up before we were allowed to know what was happening. We must carve out effective spaces in the educational curriculum for imagination. Many of our greatest writers are those who were tried and found wanting, even sometimes rejected, by the official system.

Finland or Hungary can act as examples of small countries with an exceptional flowering of musical genius. They have learned from their experience of such riches and have put in place educational oportunities for musical talent which are the envy of their neighbours.

The Pushkin movement has the right ingredients to fire the imagination, awaken the senses and encourage self-expression. It inspires confidence and engenders enthusiasm, spontaneity, fun; it provokes curiosity, and instils motivation at the same time as providing a task-oriented self-discipline. Nothing focuses the attention more than accomplishing a worthwhile creative task.

There has been huge and unanimous affirmation of its achievement from schools, both teachers and children, ungainsayably aware of the creative energy it unleashed in people's personal lives both teachers and pupils alike. Teachers at both ends of the spectrum were impressed: those who have been in the classroom for years and who reconnected with their own creative voice, and student teachers from training colleges, who found themselves inspired.

The essential energy of such a model should become central to the way every child learns in the classroom. Creativity must become the central motivating and coordinating energy in every school. This does not mean trying to establish an alternative or parallel system of education. It means injecting into established educational systems a transforming element. Such a spirit needs to pervade the perhaps necessarily monolithic structures of most educational systems. What is proposed is the amalgamation of the best in both realities. Without the magic of creativity education is without spark or zest. Our educational system needs to harness and make provision for imaginative energy. If it does not do so creativity is quenched. We can produce very clever, very efficient, very obedient automatons, but the essential spark of imagination is missing. If we succeed in flooding the already existing structures with imaginative life, every aspect and every part of how and what we learn could be enhanced.

The Hand of God: The Holy Spirit.

The most important lesson of this journey was familiarity with, insight into, experience of, day to day working of the Holy Spirit. The title of this book is *Walkabout: Life as Holy Spirit*. This is ambiguous. It could mean that I regard myself as the Holy Spirit in Person; it could mean that life itself is the Holy Spirit. The answer is very nearly both, if understood accurately. The mystery of the Holy Spirit is so intimate and so subtle that it can easily be misunderstood and certainly has been distorted. Most of what the Roman Catholic Church has described as mariology, the truth about the mother of God, is, in fact, pneumatology, the truth about the Holy Spirit, as Third Person of the Trinity. As

Bulgakov says '(T)he revelation of the Third Hypostasis ... has already happened in the Mother of God.'[8] When Gerard Manley Hopkins writes a poem about 'The Blessed Virgin compared to the Air we Breathe,' it seems to me that he is actually writing about the Holy Spirit. 'Wild air, world-mothering air,/Nestling me everywhere' that is the Holy Spirit. 'I say that we are wound/With mercy round and round/ As if with air:' that too is the Holy Spirit. We 'are meant to share/ Her life as life does air.'

The Second Person of the Trinity became incarnate in a particular human body with an historical identity, Jesus of Nazareth. The Holy Spirit, on the other hand, becomes ensouled in the person of each and every one of us so that we too become, each in our turn, mother of God. All the mysteries which christianity has celebrated so specifically in terms of Mary the Mother of God are applicable in every detail to each one of us. And these mysteries happened from the beginning of time. Through the Spirit, with the Spirit, in the Spirit, the mystical body of the communion of saints is personalised allowing Christ to play 'in ten thousand places, / lovely in limbs, and lovely in eyes not his/ To the father through the features of men's faces' (Hopkins).

We have to recognise that the Holy Spirit was at work in the world from the very beginning, as indeed was the Word of God as Second Person of the Trinity. The three Persons of the Trinity have all been involved from the outset in the specific roles which each assumes in the economy of salvation. But somehow, the Western Church managed to convince itself that the work of the Spirit really only began after the Ascension of Jesus and His sending of the same Spirit at Pentecost. This in turn led to an impounding of the Spirit of God within the precincts of the one holy catholic and apostolic church which took over all manifestation of the Holy Spirit and every initiative of divine trinitarian energy in our world.

And, of course this is ludicrous and one wonders how anyone could have been allowed to perpetrate or, indeed, believe it. The Holy Spirit has always been at work everywhere in the world. Everywhere, that is, where persons of good will were ready and willing to become spokespersons for that same Spirit, to unite their unique personhood with the Divine Personhood of Third Person of the Trinity. Incarnation of the Son happens through assumption of flesh-and-blood humanity;

impregnation by the Spirit happens wherever a human person allows entry to their person by the self-effacing Spirit. It happened with Mary, who is pre-Christian, just as it happened to Abraham, Isaiah, John the Baptist, Anna, Miriam and Elizabeth. Christians have been mesmerised by the invasive surgury achieved so dramatically by the Second Person of the Trinity. We have sometimes lost sight of the more long-term and widespread homoeopathy which has been from the beginning, and will be to the end of time, the prerogative of the Third Person of the Trinity. The two arms of the Father have been truncated and foreshortened to the human hands of the Son. There is much more to the divine plan for salvation of the world than a thirty-three year life history of one Jewish man, even though he is God in human form. The Holy Spirit was at work before, during and after that plenipotentiary moment of Divine Self-Revelation. The Trinitarian plan involves both Persons working together in really distinct idioms, while, at the same time, in complete harmony and complementarity. The Son works centrifugally from the heartbeat of the Trinity outwards to the ends of the earth. The Holy Spirit works centripetally from the margins of the unknown world to the epicentre which is secretly sought by every heart in the history of humanity. The reason for this apparent divergence of mission is the ungainsayable mystery of human freedom which even the Persons of the Trinity must respect. The inspiration of the Spirit leads those who truly seek God towards the still point of the turning world situated incontrovertibly 'in' Christ. But not a Christ triumphantly arrayed in the garments and the customs of one particular culture. Rather a naked Christ stripped of every vestige of ethnical identity; a zero Christ who has emptied himself to the point of death where He can become completely one with our common humanity; a post-christian Christ, leaving us Himself as the greatest blessing ever bestowed on our humanity, nothingness in Person. Leaving us to find out who we really are. 'Christ is nothing' Kierkegaard whispers, 'never forget it, Christianity'. The cross of Christ is a vortex fed by radiating quadrants from the four corners of the world. The word 'universe' means turned into one. There are prophetic priests working all over the planet to burrow their way towards this one vertical escape route.

Everything about the life of Jesus Christ is encompassed in a web woven by the Holy Spirit. His birth, His baptism, His hour of triumph, were the Holy Spirit impregnating the womb, breathing on the waters, lifting Him up. At his death Jesus 'crying out in a loud voice, yielded up his spirit'[8] or, in another account of the same event, breathed his last having cried out in a loud voice 'Father, into your hands I commend my spirit'[9] quoting from psalm 30 verse 6. These scriptures, also written under the inspiration of the Holy Spirit, are recognising that at this axial moment in the history of the Holy Trinity's rescue operation of the world, the man Jesus had emptied himself so completely that there was nothing left in him to prevent complete inspiration of the Holy Spirit. At this moment, like every other human person who achieves such perfect alignment of their spirit with the will of God, the spirit of Jesus and the Holy Spirit become fully one and thus can be proclaimed 'my' spirit.

Earlier in another paradigmatic manifestation which is the feast of the Epiphany, the three magi, wise men, priests and prophets from the so-called pagan world, where the Holy Spirit is always at work, are led to the recognition of the incarnation of the second Person of the Trinity by a star in the firmament and are told how not to return home, to their previous religiosity, by a warning in a dream.[10] Stars and dreams of the Holy Spirit.

In the Hebrew Testament, the Holy Spirit inspired Melchisedek, pagan priest, to seek out and bless Abraham. And this same Melchisedek is representative of the everpresent priesthood of the so-called 'Pagans.' Even before the levitical priesthood was established, this priest from nowhere was anointed by the Holy Spirit. His pneumatic priesthood is invoked in Psalm 109 as guarantor of all others: 'A prince from the day of your birth on the holy mountains; from the womb before the dawn I begot you. The Lord has sworn an oath he will not change: "You are a priest forever, a priest like Melchisedek of old."'

The Epistle to the Hebrews devotes a whole chapter to explaining that Jesus Christ is in fact a second Melchisedek, 'who is a priest not by virtue of a law about physical descent, but by the power of an indestructible life'. This indestructible life is the Holy Spirit in Person. And the pagan priest anointed by that same Spirit is invoked even in the Canon of the Roman Catholic Mass: 'Look with favour on these offerings and accept them as once you accepted the sacrifice of your servant Abel, the sacrifice of Abraham, our father in faith, and the bread and wine offered by your priest, Melchisedech'. We cannot but gaze in wonder at the portrait of this priest-king Melchizedek emerging from the darkness of paganism to bless Abraham and offer him gifts of bread and wine prefiguring the eucharist.[12] In the meeting of Abraham with Melchizedek we see an encounter, through the Holy Spirit, of two equally valid priesthoods, one inside the church, one outside. 'And Mel-chiz'edek king of Salem brought out bread and wine; he was priest of God Most High. And he blessed him and said, "Blessed be Abram by God Most High, maker of heaven and earth; and blessed be God Most High, who has delivered your enemies into your hand!" And Abram gave him a tenth of everything.' (Genesis: 14: 18-20)

Giving tithes in the context of the Hebrew Bible puts the receiver in a higher class or order to the donor: 'See how great this man was to whom Abraham the patriarch gave a tenth of the spoils! And those descendants of Levi who receive the priestly office have a commandment in the law to take tithes from the people, that is, from their brothers, though these also are descended from Abraham. But this man who does not have his descent from them received tithes from Abraham and blessed him who had the promises. It is beyond dispute that the inferior is blessed by the superior. In the one case tithes are received by mortal men, but in the other case, by one of whom it is testified that he lives. One might even say that Levi himself, who receives tithes, paid tithes through Abraham, for he was still in the loins of his ancestor when Melchizedek met him.' (Hebrews 7: 4-10).

The Holy Spirit is the Person, in cooperation with the person of the Virgin Mary, who gave birth to Jesus. The Holy Spirit later raised Him from the dead, because S/he is Lord and Giver of Life, who placed Him at the right hand of the Father. This same Holy Spirit works now in the world in every religion and wherever S/he wills. As the wind blows where it will and as the sun shines on every person on the planet so the presence of the Lord, the giver of life, is sempiternally with us. The suggestion that the Holy Spirit is confined to the Roman Catholic Church or, indeed, any other particular denomination or restricted community, is not simply heresy it is ultimately sin against the Spirit.

In certain vocabularies about the inner workings of the Blessed Trinity, about which others prefer to remain silent, it is the Son who is 'generated' and therefore, in our human order, it is the Son who is born; but following this selfsame economy of trinitarian personhood the Spirit 'proceeds' from the Father and this is an endless and ubiquitous procession which can inspire any particular person or persons on the planet willing to cooperate with the energy of this invisible and lifegiving Spirit. Christ was born, Christ has died, Christ has left the planet in Person. The Spirit was never born, never died and will never leave the planet until every single person has been shepherded into the one holy catholic and apostolic plan of salvation which all three persons of the trinity have been trying to implement, while at all times respecting the infuriatingly unpredictable free will of each and every human being. This was, and is, the unimaginably generous gameplan from the outset.

During the time of walkabout I found myself being used by the Holy Spirit on various occasions when I was asked to speak, especially when and where I did not have time myself to prepare what I thought should be said. 'Do not worry about how you are to speak or what you are to say; for what you are to say will be given to you at that time; for it is not you who speak, but the Spirit of your Father speaking through you' (Matthew: 10, 16-23).

Two such occasions I have recorded verbatim: when we opened the new guesthouse (19/09/1999) and when 'Feather from the Firebird' was launched (10/12/2003). The third was the most important. Not only did it allow me to speak with the breathing of the Holy Spirit but the substance of what I would say described such breathing itself. It provides, therefore, the most elaborate phenomenology and the most appropriate ending to this particular pericope. It was the time we made a recording with Nóirín Ní Riain and Sineád O'Connor. I was asked to write three spoken pieces to be recorded. Most especially on this occasion I recognised that what I said was about and through the Holy Spirit.

JUBILATE DEO OMNIS TERRA

Jubilation comes from the Latin for a wild shout. In more ancient Hebrew it describes a ram's horn turned into a trumpet. It celebrates a fallow patch, a place apart, a sacred space: time standing still in apprehension.

We too stand in a circle. We breathe into a column of air moving upwards, formed by our singing together. The song gives shape and colour to the pillar of sound as it moves between us and upwards, sculpting it into a pagoda, carving arabesques, decorating it with bright porcelain and sharp enamel. Tower of ivory, house of gold. This is vertical breathing: up and down. This is our cathedral of the moment which we share with you. Such is prayer as impulse towards the spiral. Different from our ordinary horizonal breathing: in and out, which we do every minute of our lives, even in our sleep, to survive. Singing, as prayer, is attaching our voices to this upwardly moving column. The breath from our deepest selves dances with the music as an agile and intimate partner. Each one of us releases ownership, unties the anchor from our hearts, opens the window and lets the songbird free. Once outside it changes direction and joins the current flowing upwards. This upward-flowing energy is the Holy Spirit infusing us with resurrected life: life moving upwards and forever. Song is existence as existence was meant to be. Learn to forget for a while another kind of passionate singing. It will end. Join your voice to a deeper flow, allow your mouth to be opened wide by the energy of a different more distant music, spread it wide over the scale and surface, the subtlety of the Spirit's sound. Crush yourself willingly into the turning groove. Learn the words and the music off by heart so the singing becomes part of your bloodstream. Let it carry you upwards to wherever the Spirit is anxious to take you. 'The Spirit and the Bride say come'. 'Enter their courts with songs of praise'.

The Eagle in the Apse

The pagan roots of religion have been important infrastructures to this presiding apse of San Clemente. The ecumenical openness essential to Judeochristianity are its authentic and identifiable fruits. Anything less than the whole of humanity is too narrow a base for the Church of Christ, the communion in the Holy Spirit.

> Then I saw in the right hand of the one seated on the throne a scroll written on the inside and on the back, sealed with seven seals.
>
> And no one in heaven or on earth or under the earth was able to open the scroll or to look into it.
>
> Then I saw between the throne and the four living creatures and among the elders a Lamb standing as if it had been slaughtered, having seven horns and seven eyes, which are the seven spirits of God sent out into all the earth.[13]

We are not talking about founding a new church. We are presenting Christianity as a mystery religion revealed most perfectly in Jesus Christ but elaborated and developed from the beginning until the end of time by the Holy Spirit. The One Holy Catholic and Apostolic Church founded by Jesus Christ has had many shapes and manifestations, but in itself it is the Holy Spirit and thereby unidentifiable with any human or earthly manifestation.

In 2003 I was writing a book on the Tarot cards as medieval symbolism depicting the mystery of the Trinity. My book uses the *Tarot de Marseilles* as a pretext for teaching a living tradition, namely the esoteric church of St John (the 'heart' of the Church), as distinct from the exoteric Church of St Peter (the 'head' of the Church). It was never the intention or the role of John to found a new Church, that was always Peter's charism.[14] St Augustine says something similar:[15]

> The Church knows two lives which have been laid down and commended to her by God. One is through faith, the other through vision. The apostle Peter personifies the first life, John the second. The first has no place except on earth; it lasts only to the end of the present age and comes to an end in the next world. The second life has no end in the age to come, and its perfection is delayed until the end of the present age. And so Peter is told: Follow me,' while it is said of John: 'If it is my will that he remain until I come, what is that to you? You are to follow me.' To preserve the still and secret heart

of the next life, John the Evangelist rested on Christ's breast:
sublime knowledge proclaimed by John concerning the trinity and
unity of the whole godhead, which in his kingdom we shall see face
to face, but now, until the Lord comes, we must behold in a glass
darkly. It was not only John who drank: the Lord himself has spread
John's gospel throughout the world, so that according to each one's
capacity all people may drink it.'

The essential mystery of the church is magisterially suzerain, untameably
free. This mystery was best understood by the beloved disciple who
then, under the guidance of the Holy Spirit, found the words most
appropriate to expressing it in language available to our understanding.
However, even he recognised that his words were poor and trembling
substitutes and that his efforts recorded only a fraction of the reality he
sought to convey. 'This is the disciple who testifies to these things and
who wrote them down. We know that his testimony is true. Jesus did
many other things as well. If every one of them were written down, I
suppose that even the whole world would not have room for the books
that would be written.'[16]

Each incarnation of the Spirit is creative adoption and adaptation of
shapes and forms of the places and times in which we live. When the
Spirit and the bride say come, they say it in a language quite other than
the commands of presiding officers. Theirs is a world of freedom, of
growth and of love; its government and structures derive from its inner
identity of well-being and self-esteem. Artists are the natural forgers of
such shapes and forms. St John is the consummate artist of agape. This
new life inspires creative cooperation with its concomitent asceticism of
purposeful achievement. It prompts us to go further because we feel, we
embody, the tangible reality which such effort has produced in us so far.
The litmus test is life which is difficult to mistake for anything less. The
inner glow of energy which has landed, made its home, and penetrated
to the quick, is difficult to simulate, impossible to mistake.

Such life breathes its own asceticism. Discipline comes naturally
from the joy of such accomplishment; the effort required for any
worthwhile achievement. Ethics emerge as realisation of genuine
growth, muscular development of being, more and more life in the
Spirit. These are 'commandments' appropriated in lived actuality, woven

organically into the fibre of my being. Life and love produce their own fruit. Wherever I feel them reaching into the depths of my despair, I automatically open myself and throw away the keys. This is what is meant by rising from the dead. We simply let go of whatever is holding us back, whatever ballast we cling to out of insecurity or habit. We let ourselves rise with the swell.

Emblem of the Peacock as Symbol of Resurrected Life.

The golden glow suffusing the apse symbolises resurrected life, the life to which each and every one of us is called. Not some supernatural state acceded to after we die and are separated from our bodily existence here on earth, but resurrection of the body as we now experience it, superabundance of life as we live it from morning to evening all the days of our existence on this planet and beyond. Resurrection is not some all-powerful divine act, some magic. It is the visible, tangible effect of divine love on and in human being.

The way we are by our human birth conflicts with the way we could be by resurrection. Such is the cross of human existence. Biology fashions us in ways that militate against resurrection. Birth, marriage, death, are the horizontal way. The physical mechanism of heredity results in the imitation, voluntary or involuntary, of a ready-made model, instinctual conformity to our DNA. Instead of the accomplishment of original and creative being, we prefer to live like ants or bees with an in-built code of behaviour, a blue-print for conducting ourselves. Naturally we are human; potentially we are gods.

Biological life is flat and circular: tramlines round the earthly city constructed by human hands; time as birth, growth, decay, death. This is chonological time, chronological life. Resurrected life is time as *kairos* not *chronos*. Event replaces cycles. We have to set our watches and our hearts to awaken and be ready for ecstasy. Ecstasy means standing outside (*ex – stasis*) the time which is measured in minutes and in hours. It is the time difference between slavery in Egypt and freedom as Exodus, meaning 'path out of' – escape route from – the vicious circle of ourselves.

The human machine functions normally according to a determined programme. Our natural inclination is to go round in circles. We have to stop this clock by breaking out of the linear, horizontal and circular tendency. We have this naturally circular propensity because we are children of the serpent. We crawl along the ground. In mesazoic times the planet was dominated by serpents. We are their descendants. To counteract our serpentine habits and to prevent the circle from being an eternally repeated error, we have to develop within us the urge upwards towards the spiral. The spiral is the beginning of resurrection, the movement upwards which transforms the flat and inflexible roundabout into a way upwards and out.

Resurrection means standing up straight and tall, not lying down or crawling on our hands and knees. We must develop a back bone if we are to live our lives in the rhythm of resurrection rather than as spineless crustacians. Resurrection means calcifying without ossifying the spinal column. The tree as growth upwards and outwards is the model for such spiral growth. Every tree ring contains a weather report for the year that we survived as we moved upwards. This is asceticism of achieved spontaneity rather than asceticism of punitive discipline to borrow a useful distinction of Charles Davis.

We are made of dust and earth, they tell us, vessels of clay, pots thrown by the almighty potter. And all this to suggest that we should remain lying on the ground that gave birth to us. But if we are earthenware, so are the Pyramids, the Grand Canyon, the Cathedral at Chartres. It is not an insult: it is a possibility. Humility, which comes from the Latin word for earth (*humus*) means realising fully who we are. It does not mean settling for the lowest common denominator in ourselves. The effect of divine love in us shatters such moulds, makes us capable of real love. We have to do for ourselves what God has already done for Himself in our regard: break out of our natural mode of being and ensure that our nature no longer determines the limits of our personhood.

It is not a question of either/or, of choosing this world or the next world, of choosing God or creation, of being either human or divine. It is a question of both/and. What is proposed is not exclusion, denial, mortification, destruction of some particular element of what we are now, in order to develop some hybrid variation of ourselves, grafted onto the stem at a point above those areas which we intend to bypass or eliminate. The evolution which we must achieve will be a transformation and elevation of the whole human being to a level where the imperatives of biological reproduction, instinctual self-preservation, grasping survival tactics will not be as pressing or overpowering, but where the vocation to love will be more specifically human, more personal, more total. It is a question of becoming fully human. We become a new creation, entering new ways of being.

Resurrection is an art form. It is living, acting, doing miraculously, as opposed to 'naturally'. Loving our enemies, forgiving our persecutors, giving away what holds us in thrall, these are so unnatural that they seem almost miraculous. They are not. They are another way of being in the world. The world and we ourselves are to be understood neither as organisms nor mechanisms, but as works of art. The miracle is to create the possibility of everlasting life within every second of our existence. Being rather than having sounds like a cliché but living it is resurrected life. Turning water into wine means turning life into eternal life.

Scripture has at least two Greek words for life: *zoe* and *bios*. The first is life that vivifies, the second is life as inherited. Bios passes horizontally from generation to generation. Zoe is life from elsewhere, vertical connection as opposed to horizontal, if we talk of these in spatial terms. Bios, as in 'biology,' is the horizontal movement of serpent life as it is passed from one generation to the next. Resurrected living, Zoe, is a form of love. True strength, true power, true generosity, are the energy of resurrected life which is every second at our disposal, but we have to connect with it creatively, discerningly. We can choose, at each moment, between life and life, bios and zoe, ordinary or superabundant life. If we allow the second kind of life to inform our nature it leads us, as from now, to resurrection, life lived to the full and forever.

Science has shown us that matter is energy at base. Sooner or later we will know that resurrection is a way of energising ourselves, a question of consciousness. We have to move ourselves from the biological to the resurrected mode. This does not just happen, it is done (it is created). It is an art work – a truth that enters the world through human being. We either continue to live naturally or we begin, at each moment, to live creatively. That is the meaning of miracle: stretching nature beyond itself. Evolution suggests, biology confirms, that we are the only species on earth which can bend itself towards whatever it chooses to become. We are architects of our future selves, and of our own future as planet. We can become whatever we choose to become.

Naturally, we are beings-towards-death. To become resurrected we must like the ancient Vikings, build ourselves a ship of death. We can adapt ourselves to this inevitable eventuality, death, not as an end, but as transformation to another way of being, by a number of body building exercises. It is almost as if the next stage in our evolution is to sprout wings, to fly. Not as aeroplanes or as birds, mechanically or organically, but as human beings called to live in some corporeal dimension for ever and ever. It is a question of consciousness. We achieve such flight in the spiral of the third eye, radiant brow of intentionality. It happens through the energy of desire. *Amor transit in conditionem objecti*, the medieval mystics held: love passes into the idiom of the loved one. We train ourselves, like astronauts to live in the strange atmosphere beyond the orbit of our earth.

This becomes essentially a modification of our breathing. We have to train ourselves to the habit of vertical breathing (up-down) as contrasted with horizonal breathing (in-out). The experience of singing is one of such breathing. We allow the air expelled from our lungs to attach itself to an upward moving volume as a chain latches into sprockets. Such breathing can connect to upward heart movement also in efforts to reach higher in prayer as impulse towards the spiral.

Death in its terminal stage effects an abrupt passage from horizontal to vertical respiration. To those who have learnt vertical respiration all through their lifetime and have exercised their bodies in such breathing techniques, death will be a negotiable arc rather than an abrupt unwelcome and angular jerk - emergence rather than emergency. Such respiration is what St Paul calls 'freedom in God'. It is a new way of breathing. 'This breathing of the air is an ability. By a divine breath-like infusion, the Holy Spirit makes the soul capable of breathing God in the same circulation of love which the Father breathes in the Son and the Son in the Father. We must not think it impossible that the soul is capable of so sublime an activity as this breathing in God.'17 In the inhalation of such a breath, death itself is breathing one's last in love. Death comes as kiss of the eternal one.

Bird and Lizard

This last card which I received and the final image in the right hand corner of the apse describes vertical and horizontal movement. Both are necessary to create the spiral movement of resurrected life, either on its own induces postures of imbalance. Russia has been, from the beginning of this story, a symbolic as well as geographical and political lynchpin. The icons which were seen in vision in 1976 came from Russia, and were heralded in by Saint Nicholas, patron of Russia. The opening of the icon chapel occurred 1,000 years after Christianity came to Russia towards the end of the so-called Cold War between the Soviet Union and the United States of America. *Peristroika* as a word and as an attitude entered the vocabulary of the Western World.

However, at a symbolic level, the signs of this Walkabout were pointing towards a grave imbalance represented by the bird descending vertically and the red lizard moving horizontally. The result of what happened between Russia and America was that one moved up too high and the other descended too low. Capitalism gained too heady a victory, communism suffered too comprehensive a defeat. A redress of this balance, both economically and symbolically is needed to create the spiral.

Events such as the Columbia shuttle disaster and the sinking of the Kursk submarine were signs of the times which spelt out the vertical movement of the dove and the horizontal levelling of the lizard in ungainsayably graphic design. I was in Paris watching *L'Alouette*, Sacha Abercorn was in Arizona as the remains of the Columbia shuttle were scattered all over that part of America. Sacha had also been in the icon chapel while Miriam was singing in the sanctuary above. Something of an earthing is required so that some middle voice can sound.

Later in October 2003 while we were in Saint Petersburg miners were trapped underground in Novoshakhtinsk, a scattering of crumbling Soviet-era collieries near the Ukrainian border about 1,000 km (600 miles) south of Moscow. A giant underground lake burst into the shaft. A week later eleven miners were found alive and brought to the surface.

As these miners were lifted from one shaft, a methane blast rocked another in Russia's Far East, killing five. These accidents capped a long string of mining disasters in the dense network of antiquated and loss-making collieries, some dating back to the years of Josef Stalin's mass industrialization drive in the 1920s or earlier.

In the Novoshakhtinsk mine, rescuers had to cut what they called a 'tunnel of hope' through solid rock from the adjacent shaft toward a tiny air pocket where the miners found refuge from the surging lake. Crews lowered an underwater video camera – the same model used during the futile bid to rescue the 118 crew members of the Kursk submarine – into the shaft. Russia must be put back on its feet both economically and symbolically. There has to be some alternative to unquestioned hegemony of the market economy. Single model totalitarianism must be eschewed in any and every domain if movement towards the spiral is to be achieved.

The Underground Basilica, Icon Chapel, Cathedral

San Clemente was built on the remains of a very much older basilica constructed over or beside the temple of an Eastern Mystery religion, Mithraism, which held sway for at least 2,000 years before Christianity made its appearance.

The religion of the Romans always developed within the framework of their politics. In the third century AD the worship of Mithras had spread widely within the Roman Empire. Interest in Eastern deities was encouraged by kinship between Roman emperors and the Syrian dynasty. Mystery cults established a personal relationship with the god of one's choice. The later search for a monotheistic religion stimulated by philosophical doctrines of the time, led to an all-embracing cult of the unvanquished Sun-god. Aurelian built a large temple to the Sun in the Campus Martius. The anniversary of the Sun-god's birth was 25 December. The influence of the Mithraic cult was at its height during this period and it might have reigned supreme. Renan in his book on Marcus Aurelius suggests that, had Christianity been halted in the early stages, the world might have become Mithraic.

The battle at the Milvian Bridge on the Tiber (AD 312) was decisive not only for Constantine but also for Mithras. Constantine planted the cross on Roman soil. Christianity began to develop within the framework of Roman politics. The second half of the fourth century was decisive for the struggle between Christianity and paganism. Julian, named the Apostate because he abandoned Christianity and declared himself for Mithras, was the last emperor to profess this faith. His life was cut short by an arrow during an expedition against the Persian King Shapur. After his death in 363 AD a period of comparative tolerance set in, cut short by an edict of the Emperor Gratian in AD 382. The altar of Victory was removed from the Senate, and state support for the upkeep of the Roman cult was withdrawn. Gratian in AD 379 was the first emperor to refuse the title *Pontifex Maximus*. Theodosius became the spiritual son of the forceful Christian bishop Ambrose of Milan. Edicts of February 391 forbade pagan worship in Rome and visits to pagan temples.

Around this time our Mithraic site beneath San Clemente was acquired by Christian clergy. A church, mentioned by St Jerome in 390, was built to the memory of the third pope after Peter, St Clement. His basilica survived until about 1100. It was razed and a somewhat smaller replica, which is the present San Clemente, was built on the same site. The remodelling would have been done in the twelfth or thirteenth centuries. The exact date of the apse is disputed. Motifs of the fourth and fifth century suggest that the present mosaic is a reproduction of one originally in the abandoned basilica below.

Walkabout in the Holy Spirit has led, through the construction of an icon chapel underneath the church at Glenstal Abbey to the realisation that such a symbolic structure lies underneath the world as we inhabit it, and that this reality must be brought to light. Ireland, for instance, has to excavate and provide access to such an underground cathedral and thereby become both a paradigm and an example to other peoples and countries around the world who must do likewise, if humanity is to find the underground that links us all, the cathedral to which we can eventually come to celebrate our unity.

Dublin the capital city of Ireland, or *Duibh linn*, as the name is written in the ancient annals, means a black pool. The name has psychological resonances. Many explorers of the twentieth century have pioneered ways into an underground darkness of the unconscious. On this walkabout, Dublin assumed a symbolical significance in this regard. In 2003, the so-called Millennium Spire was eventually completed and now stands 120 metres tall in the centre of O'Connell Street. The architect, Ian Ritchie, says that this creation should be viewed as the spire of an underground cathedral encompassing the whole city of Dublin, and, perhaps, the whole country of Ireland.

James Joyce who was foremost among such pioneers of the undergound cathedral made the city of Dublin the basic geography of his works. Walkable Dublin of Joyce's *Ulysses* has almost expanded and diluted itself to extinction. Southwards it has spread to the foothills, northwards it falls into the sea, westwards it transgresses the boundaries of itself as a county and embraces much of Meath and Kildare. Dublin of Joyce's day would be equivalent to 'inner city' Dublin today. This 'inner' city which Joyce made famous has, however, recently developed a number of symbolic outer features which suggest that its inhabitants are at last becoming aware of the directions in which he was pointing and the areas his works undertook to investigate. The Dublin of Joyce's imagination was essentially a place of trams. Nelson's Pillar to Kingstown

(Dún Laoghaire); Phoenix Park to Donnybrook; Glasnevin cemetery to Dolphin's Barn; Drumcondra to Kingsbridge Station. Half way through this particular millennium (1904-2004) the whole system was scrapped. Dublin became tramless for 50 years. The Bloomsday centenary of 2004 coincides with the reintroduction of two new tramlines: Sandyford to St Stephen's Green, Tallaght to Connolly Station, suggesting that the city has readjusted itself to at least two determined lines of peregrination.

Dubliners, Joyce's book of short stories, describes the paralysis of his native city owing to monolithic infrastructures of politics and religion which caused entrapment in alcoholism, sexual repression, poverty. Joyce left Dublin in 1904 frustrated by such oppression. He called *Dubliners* a 'chapter in the moral history of my country,' an attempt to galvanise the creative energy which would help his fellow citizens to 'revolt against the dull inelegance' of the city. These dubliners were refusing to examine the darkness underpinning the veneer of their shabby respectability, the sewage system underpinning the surface topography. Bridges had to be designed which would allow access to this underground and, as yet, unexplored, world.

A new bridge across the River Liffey was officially opened on Bloomsday 2003. This 'James Joyce Bridge' links Ellis Quay on the north of the river to Ushers Island, where the actual house of 'The Dead' in *Dubliners* is situated. Costing €9 million, the bridge was designed by Santiago Calatrava Vallas. Its steelwork was manufactured by Harland and Wolff, the makers of the Titanic, in Belfast, Northern Ireland. It was one of the last works of this most famous shipyard which has since closed down. The bridge itself took six months longer than anticipated to construct because of its unusual design, which incorporates splayed steel arches, with a concrete deck suspended from high-tensile hangers. Finished in gleaming white, it provides not only a most elegant sculptured connection between the teeming city and the house of 'The Dead' but also twin pedestrianised walkways and viewing areas on each side of a central four-lane section carrying road traffic. It allows for Bloomsday pilgrims to walk across the waters of 'anna livia plurabelle' accomplishing their own odyssey from paralysis to flexibility. The engineers tell us that 'the main arch steelwork was formed on a large hydraulic press (thought to be the largest horizontal open press in the world).' The same might be said for the press on which the original works of Joyce were printed. And the purpose of his works were also: 'to produce complex multi-axis bends as specified for this uniquely designed structure.' Both presses helped 'to develop the bend geometry' which was unique. The technical term used by the bridgebuilders to describe their method of achieving such 'multi-axis bends' is 'cold forming.' 'Cold forming' was selected as opposed to 'Induction bending' as the most efficient method of production, 'owing to the three dimensional curvature of this unique bridge.' This again describes symbolically the difference between what Joyce was proposing artistically as liberation from what he was leaving behind him in Dublin. Induction bending is education as propaganda and party line; cold forming is education as liberation of the unique form of each individual person: 'reflecting from his own individual person life unlivable,' processing the various 'scalds and burns and blisters, impetiginous sores and pustules' through 'cold forming' in 'the slow fires of consciousness' (FW 613).

The two main parabolic arches of the bridge were constructed, we read,[18] by joining the sections of thick walled tubes together with connecting fishplates to create two continuous, tilted, tied arches as the support spans for this unique steel structure. In a similar way, the two main parabolic arches of Ulysses are the journeys of Stephen and Bloom through the streets of Dublin on the original Bloomsday. 'In Ulysses, I have recorded, simultaneously, what a man says, sees, thinks, and what such saying, seeing and thinking does, to what you Freudians call the subconscious – but as for psychoanalysis, it's neither more nor less than blackmail.'[19] Joyce had developed his own twin tramlines for his tour of the inner and the outer city.

The Millennium Spire stands 120 metres tall in the centre of O'Connell Street. Made of rolled stainless steel its base is three metres in diameter set in black Kilkenny marble. Unadorned, pellucid, assured, it moves upwards without trappings, ideology or 'isms' of whatever kind. The architect, Ian Ritchie, won the competition for this project and described how 'the monument will be constructed in celebration of Ireland's confident future in the third millennium'. His website also quotes him as saying that 'ignorance, fear and the inability to take risks are the common ingredients of a non-creative environment.' This could be a distillation of the wisdom of Joyce's *Dubliners*. The jaunty bronze statue of the artist on North Earl Street seems to be squinting up in approval.

Joyce defended the orthodoxy of humanity in opposition to all neat geometrical orthodoxies applied from other sources. Refusal to accept and come to terms with the humanity which is our lot as sons and daughters of men and women is the ultimate source of paralysis. The words with which he ends *A Portrait of the Artist as a Young Man* may well be taking flesh three generations later: 'I go to encounter for the millionth time the reality of experience and to forge in the smithy of my soul the uncreated conscience of my race'. At the time he was alone in his heroic struggle during, for instance, the eighteen years that it took him to complete his final work.

The reason why he had to use the style he eventually forged for himself in *Finnegans Wake* is because 'one great part of every human existence is passed in a state which cannot be rendered sensible by the use of wideawake language, cut-and-dry grammar and go-ahead plot' as he explained to Ezra Pound.[20] He dismissed psychoanalysis because its symbolism was mechanical, but this was surely because, as Ellmann suggests, he 'was close to the new psychoanalysis at so many points that he always disavowed any interest in it'. He was in fact working along the same lines himself at an artistic level and was disdainful of the plodding scientists who were tapping the same sources in a much less direct and revealing way. Cold form rather than heated induction: Art was the only appropriate medium for Joyce. Medicine and science were half measures which were even less satisfactory than the religion which he had rejected.

What is it that all these people were discovering? The answer is an inner continent, the discovery of which had greater significance and repercussion than the discovery of the 'New World' by Europeans in the fifteenth century. The difference between Joyce and the psychoanalysts, for instance, was that he was discovering as an artist and therefore sought to express this reality in all its originality, subtlety and polyvalence, whereas they, as scientists sought to conquer it by reducing it to the machinery available to their limited fields of competence. Joyce described *Finnegans Wake* as written 'to suit the esthetic of the dream, where the forms prolong and multiply themselves, where the visions pass from the trivial to the apocalyptic, where the brain uses the roots of vocables to make others from them which will be capable of naming its phantasms, its allergies, its illusions'.[21] The 'new conscience' which Joyce was forging in the smithy of his soul was not the rational ordering of life borrowed from Aristotelian or Thomistic principles, it was a totally different understanding of human reality.

Apart from the spire of this cathedral and the bridge as flying buttress over the river, a most impressive sacristy has emerged in the shape and design of the Francis Bacon Studio. John Edwards, heir to the estate of the artist Francis Bacon (1909-92), bequeathed his studio and its contents at Reece Mews, London, to the Hugh Lane Municipal Gallery of Modern Art. This was the first public Gallery of modern art in these islands. It opened in 1908. Conservator Mary McGrath, directed the relocation of the studio, which had remained unaltered since the time of the artist's death. John Edwards described it as a dump. It was reopened on 22 May 2001 after being dismantled and shipped from London. More than 7,000 items, including books, floor and roof timbers, tubes of paint, a dressing gown and discarded boxes of champagne, feature in the recreation of the artist's habitat. Even the dust which had accumulated there was swept up and scattered over the Dublin display. Standard archaeological techniques of excavating and recording a site layer by layer provided an effective means of copying the chaotic contents of the studio down to the smallest detail. 'About that original hen. (A)n iceclad shiverer, merest of bantlings observed a cold fowl behaviourising strangely on that fatal midden or chip factory or comicalbottomed copsjute (dump for short) afterwards changed into the orangery when in the course of deeper demolition unexpectedly one bushman's holiday its limon threw up a few spontaneous fragments of orangepeel, the last remains of an outdoor meal by some unknown sunseeker or placehider *illico* way back in his mistridden past' (FW 110). Dear dirty Dublin, the dumpheap of the world, can become in this 21st century, with the help of certain gifted artists, the way forward towards a better world.

Bacon says that 'the texture of a painting seems to come immediately onto the nervous system'[22] that 'the mystery of fact is conveyed by an image being made out of non-rational marks ... that there is a coagulation of non-representional marks which have led to making up this very great image'. The way he works is by making 'involuntary marks on the canvas which may suggest much deeper ways by which you can trap the fact that you are obsessed by.[23] He is aware of an a-causal principle, which he calls chance or accident, which is the ultimate source of his work. 'One knows that by some accidental brushmarks suddenly appearance comes in with such vividness that no accepted way of doing it would have brought about. I'm always trying through chance or accident to find a way by which appearance can be there but remade out of other shapes . To me the mystery of painting today is how can appearance be made. I know it can be illustrated, I know it can be photographed. But how can this thing be made so that you catch the mystery of appearance within the mystery of making?'[24]

From the sacristy of the cathedral I was led into the crypt. Since 1998 Lorcan Walshe, a Dublin artist, has been resurrecting Celtic and pre Celtic artefacts, working in the National Museum at Collins Barracks for three months each year over a four year period. This National Museum of Ireland was opened in 1890 and was the result of the merging of several Irish Collections. It contains artefacts and masterpieces dating from 2000 BC to the twentieth century. The archaeological collections consist of the National Treasury (which includes the Ardagh Chalice, Tara Brooch and Cross of Cong), the Ór – Ireland's Gold exhibition which features the finest collection of Prehistoric gold artefacts in Europe. Prehistoric Ireland, an exhibition whose main purpose is to introduce the visitor to the everyday material culture of the time. Viking Age Ireland, focuses on Irish Archaelogy from 800–1200 AD. 'What child of a strandlooper but keepy little Kevin in the despondful surrounding of such sneezing cold would ever have trouved up on a strate that was called strete a motive for future saintity by euchring the finding of the Ardagh chalice by another heily innocent and beachwalker whilst trying with pious clamour to wheedle Tipperaw raw raw reeraw puteters out of Now Sealand in spignt of the patchpurple of the massacre, a dual a duel to die to day, goddam and biggod, sticks and stanks, of most of the Jacobiters' (FW 110-111).

The museum houses a collection of ancient objects as diverse as Bronze Age containers, Stone Age spirals, Medieval chalices, croziers, reliquaries, bells. Lorcan Walshe's art is a ritual whereby the spirit of these ancient objects is made present to us today. In his drawings he works past the surface detail and captures the essence of the artefacts and the sensibility of the craftsperson who created them. More than that, he shows that the original inspiration for such work was a religious one, that reverence is what imbued each craft with the artistic genius now incarnated in the objects themselves. Through his painstaking representation of the works themselves he makes manifest the aura which radiates from each artefact as a kind of phosphorescence. Yet, the manifestation occurs, not in the attempt to paint or to draw any such phosphorescence, but rather in attention to the exact representation of the object itself. In 1995 in Denmark in one of the oldest pottery studios in Europe, he understood the possibility of inhabiting and transcribing the space between the fingers of a potter and the shape of the bowl being turned.

Such painstaking painterly stalking of the artefact is not just recording in the sense that if the objects were stolen or if they were destroyed by fire or in an earthquake we would have a representative file of what had been there. More than that, these entrapments of the Spirit, dream-catchers, make present in a real way the originality of the instruments or vessels. Such art is anamnesis so accurately accomplished that it evokes the epiclesis which is the Spirit reinvigorating the work. 'You should understand this as a monk,' Lorcan suggests to me, 'Artists of old believed that God would be encompassed within their works as in a tabernacle or a reliquary. What they may have failed to notice is that God was actually present in the making and that this presence is still inscribed in whatever they made.' Anamnesis and epiclesis are technical terms in Greek for the precise way in which liturgy makes present actions from the past which are salvific and eternal. Art of this kind is sacramental in this way. It makes present The Spirit in some original manifestation of the past: in a crozier, a reliquary, a bell.

'I believe that these drawings can cure you' the artist says of his representations of medieval reliquaries. Medieval artists and craftspeople believed that they were encircling and embossing a piece of the Divine inside the reliquaries and shrines they were fashioning. Sometimes one work of this kind took up a whole lifetime, maybe two lifetimes. Now that the relic has been removed and the shell left on the beach, Lorcan Walshe can see that the imprint of the Divine is left in the artefact through the reverence which informed the making. Reverence, for him, is what makes craft into art. The Holy Spirit, as *Digitus Dei*, God's finger, hovers over the attentive fingers of the artisan. That original breath within the breathing finger can be traced in dedicated archaeological probing today. It means going beyond the detail, beyond the seduction of effect. Most representation of so-called Celtic art focuses on the copy-book detail of The Book of Kells, for instance, and crowds us out with festoonery of foliage and curlicues, awash with heavy duty gold ink. Such Celtic decorators can't see the wood for the trees. Taking an arial view of the medieval forest shows a major shift in human consciousness similar to the one which occurred in chronological sequence throughout the first part of the twentieth century: the dialectic between figurative and abstract rendidition. Within essentially functional art (all these croziers, vessels, reliquaries and bells were being used for very specific purposes), appears a quality of abstraction which bespeaks the mystery of another presence, a greater purpose. This medieval craftmanship is simultaneously representational and abstract and rides like an expert windsurfer the cusp of both. There is a human presence, the fingerprints of persons, detectable in the work of art.

After many months of observation and familiarisation with the contents of the National Museum, Lorcan still was an outsider, an orphan looking through the window of an elegant home, an archeologist peering through the peep-hole of an unexcavated tomb. Then he saw the bells and these became his point of entry. Bells have personality. Their shape is as a human torso. The upper part is even referred to as a shoulder. These shapes belong to any time in the history of humanity. And their purpose is to sound. But as they stand in their silent stillness waiting to be moved into sounding, they hold within their weight and shape, their poised heaviness, a figurative abstraction which is beyond themselves and which remains like an aching possibility radiating from their contained musculature. Lorcan Walshe, like Iris Murdoch in her novel of the same name, has excavated for us The Bell of an underground cathedral. In his studio there is a painting on the end wall of 'The Black Bell of St Patrick.'

Cornucopia

The Horn of Plenty: Glenstal and the future. Erexit cornu salutis.

The future is an evolutionary process instigated by the Holy Spirit, implemented by ourselves. Those who climb mountains to survey the horizon and plan the next step, are pioneers: artists, scientists, entrepreneurs. Sometimes it takes a hundred years before the rest of us hear the message and find the trail they have reconnoitered. Mostly they are ridiculed, misunderstood, reviled.

There has to be a place where such inspiration can be received, distilled, distributed more universally and expeditiously to allow the evolutionary purpose of the planet to keep pace with contemporaneity. Otherwise we are always playing catch-up, or clear-up, after disasters accruing from having made the wrong move. The Spirit can only travel at our pace. There is, there has to be, a constant regrouping, reformulation of strategy, performance of running repairs on a continually sabotaged rescue operation. Some bulwark has to be built which can shore up the gameplan already accomplished and provide a runway for the next series of test flights.

Monasteries should provide such places. In Russia, for instance, 200 kilometres south of Moscow, Optina Pustyn, the last great monastery of hermits connecting Russia with Byzantium, came to be regarded as a spiritual centre. All the great writers of the nineteenth century – Gogol, Dostoievsky and Tolstoy among them – went there in search of the 'Russian soul'. Unless we dwell poetically on this earth, we are strangers here, and abuse our environment. Such dwelling requires obedience to the earth, humility, stability: an established and yet an open space.

Monasteries should be dwelling-places, with listening ears for the world around, essential parts of any society, providing touchstones for our deeper selves, for nature, for God. *Ausculta*, the Latin word for 'Listen' is the first word in the Rule of Benedict, written down in the fifth century. Monasteries should act as beehives of the invisible, making honey which can be tasted, out of otherwise unavailable nectar hidden in flowers designed to conceal. Monasteries are like breweries distilling wisdom from many sources, searching out new perspectives: ways of hearing, seeing, touching invisible life.

Seamus Heaney provides a compelling image in a poem of his own which he quoted when receiving the Nobel Prize for literature in 1995:[25]

The annals say: when the monks of Clonmacnoise
Were all at prayers inside the oratory
A ship appeared above them in the air.

The anchor dragged along behind so deep
It hooked itself into the altar rails
And then, as the big hull rocked to a standstill,

A crewman shinned and grappled down the rope
And struggled to release it. But in vain.
'This man can't bear our life here and will drown,'

The abbot said, 'unless we help him.' So
They did, the freed ship sailed, and the man climbed back
Out of the marvellous as he had known it.

The poet is struggling with two dimensions which must receive equal attention if our passage to the future is to be rooted and on course. All the success in the world will be sawdust and tinsel unless our connections with the depths of our own reality and that of the marvellous are maintained. Monks and artists can and must play a role in such essential maintenance.

About the Clonmacnoise spaceship Heaney says: 'I take it to be pure story. It has the entrancement of a narrative that's mysterious and absolute. It needs no explanation but even so, you could read it as a text about the necessity of being in two places at the one time, on the ground with the fatherly earthiness, but also keeping your mind open and being able to go up with the kite, on the magic carpet too, and live in the world of fantasy. To live in either world entirely and resolutely, and not to shift, is risky. For your wholeness you need to inhabit both worlds.'[26]

Another poem by Seamus Heaney called 'The Forge'[27] describes the way in which we approach the door into the dark of the future. Somewhere near the centre of this forge there is an anvil which he describes as an altar 'set there immoveable' on which real iron can be beaten out and the shape and music of the future sketched. If we are to establish a future which can house us adequately we too have to find such an altar. Forging the future requires the right kind of relationship with the true Spirit of the living God. Without this, the future will be shortsighted, cramped, and incomplete.

Two presences are required to ensure that the form of the future is genuinely ours. Those who know about culture and understand its length and breadth, its height and depth, must combine with the genuinely contemplative to ensure that a dynamic equivalence is maintained between what we are now and what we shall become in the future. The line of history must connect itself with the well of hope. Two kinds of explorer must listen for the footsteps of the other:

> But what is that clinking in the darkness?
> Maybe we shall know each other better
> When the tunnels meet beneath the mountain.[28]

Our future is spliced through the rope dangling between monastery and mountaineer.

What has become apparent to me after 27 years of sporadic intervention followed by three years of intensive concentration, is that this monastery of ours, Glenstal Abbey in Limerick, is being offered first refusal – and everything always depends upon the willingness of those who are approached – on establishing a triune Community of the Holy Spirit in and around the present structure of the monastic community here as it now exists. Having travelled around the world looking for manifestations of the Holy Spirit, an understanding similar to one recorded by W .B. Yeats eventually dawned. 'Then one day I understood quite suddenly that I was seeking something unchanging and unmixed and always outside myself, a stone or an Elixir that was always out of reach, and that I myself was the fleeting thing that held out its hand'[29]

(W. B. Yeats EI 272). Monastic life is not a club, a consortium, a cabal, a corporation. Its identity does not come from some agreement between members, a circle formed around the periphery by like-minded people holding hands. As a circle its circumference is formed by the radius of each particular person on the periphery connected to the centre. Its identity comes from the resurrected life of each monk radiating outwards. In another sentence from W. B. Yeats: 'I had not learned what sweetness, what rhythmic movement, there is in those who have become the joy that is themselves.'[30] Resurrected life does not come in cohorts. It happens to each person coming into direct and energising relationship with the Person of the Risen One, the energy of the Spirit of Life.

But the introduction to such life can be mediated, an atmosphere can be created, a congenial setting can be marked out. And so, a monastery can be established as a school in the service of such abundant life. The outer rim would comprise professional people, some married, some not, men and women who are interested in living the liturgical life of the core community and some of whom will be involved in the active life and professional engagements of the Abbey as a whole. The inmost circle forms the contemplative liturgical core: those who undertake to live the full schedule of Trinitarian life here on earth. In between these two there will be accommodation and space for a third party who might want to live with us for a certain time, at their own rhythm and to the extent that they find appropriate. This last group might be artists, business people, consultants, doctors, entertainers, families, general practitioners, historians, iconographers, journalists, knights of the road, liturgists, musicians, novelists, OAPs, painters, quantum physicists, ramblers, scientists, teenagers, university students, visitors, writers, etc. whose interest in being in such an environment might be temporary and even sometimes quite tangential to the purpose of the whole.

Glenstal Abbey could establish a spiritual centre which would offer initiation (G.A.S.P. = Glenstal Abbey Spiritual Programme) into a way of life which aligns the whole person, body, mind and spirit, with the universe as a whole, with those who are in it, and with the Three Persons of the Trinity who have invited each one of us to share in their life. A team of mentors and spiritual explorers would provide an advertised round of lectures, seminars, work-shops and courses covering most aspects of what is essentially a new culture: an alternative way of using the senses, developing underemployed creativity, and sharpening spiritual awareness. This would not be the usual university course, although we might seek recognition in some official accreditation from whichever third level institute is willing to so provide without influencing the content, texture, rhythm and ethos of the programme. It would be life-enhancing education for the whole person and could include modules about art, cinema, literature, liturgy, music, philosophy, psychology, theology, etc.

Such an ambiance requires appropriate space and atmosphere for creative expression of varied kinds and at many levels. Theatres and studios, amenities and facilities for many kinds of artistic endeavour should be available not necessarily within the precincts of the centre itself but certainly within easy and accessible reach of it. Many such places already exist and could be developed in adjacent locations.

Whenever it is feasible a new church of the Holy Spirit should be built, along the lines of the conference centre designed for Berne in Switzerland by Mario Botta for the millennium, circular and tentlike, where every person in attendance would be fully part of the liturgical celebration. The nomadic quality suggested by a tent describes its descent from on high to meet foundations laid on earth, as well as allowing it to be moved to wherever the Spirit might next choose to pitch it.

Taking our cue from Cluny, Glenstal could provide many people with an element and an atmosphere allowing them to breathe spiritually.

> If you came this way in may time, you would find the hedges
> White again, in May, with voluptuary sweetness.
>
>   There are other places
> Which are also the world's end, some at the sea jaws,
> Or over a dark lake, in a desert or a city –
> But this is the nearest, in place and time.

There are other places,[31] of course. But the Spirit seems to be saying that at this moment and as things are, Glenstal Abbey is the nearest in place and time. We have a naturally beautiful and appropriate place imbued with liturgical time.

This is not a new idea. In my experience and understanding it goes back to 1976. In this community at Glenstal it is especially connected, for me, with Benedict Tutty whose legacy remains permanent in our midst. Those of us who did not know him personally are still permeated by his energy and presence as we pass his works of art: these are not simply artifacts or décor, they are a language which Benedict in his gifted and often frustrated way spent his life trying to teach both this community and the wider church in Ireland how to speak. This language was one which came naturally to him and it was only towards the end of his life that he understood that the rest of us were not being perverse, stubborn or obtuse but that we were actually blind, deaf and dumb. And one of the reasons why he could see in this way was because his so-called education was foreshortened, he was a lay-brother and bypassed by default the educational system which has taught the rest of us to reach third level literacy and numeracy with a corresponding deficiency in what might be termed symbolic vision. We can no longer read what Vatican II named, after the terminology of M-D Chenu, I imagine, 'the signs of the times'.

Most people educated of the twentieth century are blind and deaf to the symbolism of liturgy, the 'divine beauty' of nature, the language of art. Western European civilisation has long ago sold its birthright for a mess of pottage. Our birthright is the mystery of life hidden in the symbols from the beginning of time; the mess of pottage is a world constructed by scientific technology. Science and technology are both wonderful and essential but without the other dimension they become 'a dry weary land without water.'

Monks should provide for a world that has become blind, deaf and dumb to the language of symbolism, a secret garden where such insight can be retrieved. We should be able to pour that trickle of water on the palm of the hand which allowed Anne Sullivan, imaginative, patient and inspired educator, to teach Hellen Keller, born blind, deaf and dumb, how to retrieve her sensibility, her humanity, her personality, her spirituality.

On 3 March 1887 Anne arrived at the house in Tuscumbia and for the first time met Helen Keller. Anne immediately started teaching Helen to finger spell. Although Helen could repeat these finger movements she could not quite understand what they meant. Anne and Helen moved into a small cottage on the land of the main house. After a month of Anne's teaching, what the people of the time called a 'miracle' occurred.

Helen had until now not yet fully understood the meaning of words. When Anne led her to the water pump on 5 April 1887, all that was about to change. As Anne pumped the water over Helen's hand , Anne spelled out the word water in the girl's free hand. Something about this explained the meaning of words within Helen, and Anne could immediately see in her face that she finally understood.

Helen later recounted the incident:

'We walked down the path to the well-house, attracted by the fragrance of the honey-suckle with which it was covered. Someone was drawing water and my teacher placed my hand under the spout. As the cool stream gushed over one hand she spelled into the other the word water, first slowly, then rapidly. I stood still, my whole attention fixed upon the motions of her fingers. Suddenly I felt a misty consciousness as of something forgotten, a thrill of returning thought, and somehow the mystery of language was revealed to me.'

Monks must first of all learn for themselves the language of symbolism, the language of liturgy, the language of the saving mysteries of Jesus Christ, made real for us on a daily basis through the power of the Holy Spirit. The *digitus Dei* (finger of God, as the Holy Spirit is named) spells out 'the word' for us as the water of life is poured on the other hand. The Holy Spirit writes on our palms, as blind deaf and dumb people, also through the medium of sound. 'I was dumb, silent and still ... He put a new song into my mouth' (Psalms 38:3;39:4).

Gifts of place, time and culture have been lavished upon us as providential sources from which to offer 'the running streams' for which many, if not every soul is gasping. And once we ourselves have learned and are living from this mystery, we too can provide 'small cottages on the land of the main house' which will allow as many people as possible to have, or to gain, access to these mysteries.

This means initiating people, starting with ourselves, to a new culture, a new alphabet, which is really the very old culture, the very ancient language of liturgy. But a language and a culture which help us to become fully alive, with that fullness of life which the Trinity have always wished to share with us: resurrected life, the life of love with God.

Glenstal would become like Clonmacnoise in Seamus Heaney's poem. A place where the abbot and the community help the artist to anchor the altar. The monastery becomes a place where artists can hope to tie whatever kite they happen to be flying to a firm and stable anchor. The monastery as silent hub of a fireworks display which art and culture are called to scatter into the night: flare-pathed runways where the future can land.

Such revelation is possible only from the ambiance and tranquility of a place where liturgical life is permanent and constant, and where, to quote Alexander Solzenitsyn: people have the time, the atmosphere and the opportunity 'to survey, as from a great height, the whole tortuous errant flow of history; and yet at the same time, like people completely immersed in it, they can see every pebble in its depths.'[32]

Providentially, it seems to me, the Holy Spirit has gathered together in this beautiful and sacred place, the people and the competences, the genius and the generosity, which could allow provision of a well organised and effective oasis in an ever-expanding spiritual desert. Ireland, as a small island off the edge of Europe, is a place where the Johannine church could become manifest. The signs are that this is already happening. While the official, institutional churches are in disarray, the secret work of the Holy Spirit, never dependent upon any structures made by human hands, is bearing fruit. As Uisneach was the spiritual centre, distinct from Tara the political centre, in Ireland of the five provinces, so, Glenstal Abbey can become a hub of the Johannine Church, that spiritual tradition which underlies and supersedes all institutional embodiment. As such it would become focal point to a network of other such centres spreading, whether consciously or unconsciously, the influence of the Holy Spirit in the world of the 21st century.

July 2004 presented itself as month of inauguration and gradual emergence of some shape.

I send an invitation to the Glenstal community which I call 'Invitatory': 'On this auspicious weekend of (9-11 July 2004) feastday of St Benedict, patron of Europe, and the golden jubilee of ordination of three, indeed five, of our community, G—P may be launched. This will not be organised by us specifically but may take place of its own accord. Our role is to facilitate, watch out for, and record. Certain people have already turned up, consciously or unconsciously, others will be prompted to do so. Each of these may have been sent for this purpose. Fanny Howe, John O'Donohue, Nóirín Ní Riain, and Shane

Leyden are among those who have already been prompted to present themselves during this time, others are appearing more haphazardly over the horizons, and the full complement of presence will only become apparent as each occasion takes place.'

11/07/04. Meeting in the library. Anthony Keane warns that the openness and emptiness of Glenstal could be compromised by encrustation, impedimenta, heavy sewage, camp followers. The Crane Bag should remain our model: full when the great sea swelled, empty when the sea ebbed. We do not want to end up with an asylum or an old folks home. We must respect the empty space, so rare a commodity.' Others present suggest that we need oxygen, that outsiders, especially the feminine presence, have something life-giving to offer the present all-male monasticism. Women can provide the other half of the otherwise irretrievably deprived human person.

I offer Cluny as a model. Radiating its spirituality throughout Europe for 1,000 years. An open energy as opposed to fortress monasticism.

Others point to both the strengths and weaknesses of Cluny: selfcontained and focused. The cosmos as sacramental. Its obvious weaknesses led to its destruction after the French Revolution. Even then, there were theological and sociological imbalances which would have brought implosion from internal combustion. Also, Gregory suggests, irradiation becomes problematical if the source, the core of the community, is not involved in the dialogue which generates it. He sees a double dialogue of the deaf going on in Glenstal: Official monasticism versus spiritual exploration. Cuthbert feels that the Spirit is moving in the direction of this meeting. He felt as if something pentecostal was present at the community meeting where the idea of G.A.S.P. was proposed. Something of the spirit of the upper room, an unusual consensus and positive energy around the community.

John O'Donohue affirms that we have here in Glenstal a very privileged place. 'There is a silence, a rhythm and a life here which is palpable from the moment you come through the gates. And it is being tended.' I ask him if this is a property of the place itself or if it is dependent upon the monastery and/or the community. 'The community is the custodian of this presence,' he feels. However, there must surely be complicit connivance between the spirit of the place and the people who happen to turn up here. 'When people begin life in a new place they drill for water. No matter how far down, water has to be found for survival. Prayer is like a drilling into the ethos of a place. It is essentially the space opened up by and through the full fervour of the contemplative risk. This shelters the sanctuary of essence, which is rare, and always endangered from inside and outside. It needs protection. Glenstal should be, in the most precise sense, a centre of excellence, although this particular phrase has been bandied about in compromising ways. At the heart of this contemplative abyss there has to be a certain clarity. Its centre, as he sees it, is the eucharist.'

Our discussion is an old polarity between identity and relevance. Institution seeks to preserve identity sometimes to the exclusion of everything and everyone and the eventual asphyxiation of itself; the desire to be relevant can dissipate to the point of dissolution whatever was worth preserving in the first place. There is no theology in Ireland, so recent disarray in the institutional church and the consequent abandonment of all forms and structures mean that the population of the country have gone into freeflow. It is sad now to see so much hunger and spiritual need bypassing the gates of plenty in favour of the most arbitrary forms of consumerist 'spirituality' or psychotherapy.

Institution can kill. At the same time structures are necessary. These are like the bones scattered in the valley which the Spirit can assemble and breathe into life. Gregory prefers the word 'form'. John O'Donohue agrees. Contemplatives can survive on the form itself. People need such things to be incarnate in what Nóirín then identifies as a 'culture': a way of seeing, hearing, touching, tasting what is otherwise transcendent and unavailable to our senses. All this can be, in Gregory's image, like flocks of birds, beautiful in flight but then they disappear without trace. How do we make the birds stay, salvage something permanent from their flight-patterns. This image makes Fanny Howe think of children. She sees the necessity to preserve something of tradition, the structures, the institution. She gave the example of orphanages in America. Recent scandals in the institutions caused people to overreact and put all the children into fosterage. With disastrous consequences. Untold misery can prevail in isolated and scattered locations; much less so when people are at least aware of the place where the children are gathered. It is better to critique and improve the traditional ways of doing things than to abandon them altogether and try to reinvent the wheel.

There is, however, an intransigence about the current structure which is difficult to soften or transform. There has to evolve a creative dialogue which will allow something new to enter in, a leavening of the batch. Gregory again favours the idea of 'form' as the flexible third term between structure and relevance. He takes our liturgy as an example. It was a frozen tridentine block from Maredsous and is even still waiting to be liberated. Fortunately the imperatives of post-Vatican II participation etc. did not allow it to be diluted or whittled away. Perhaps it was stubbornness or even stupidity which prevented us from abandoning the Gregorian chant, for instance, which now, with hindsight must be viewed as an endangered species, a treasure which it has been almost miraculous for us to have maintained.

Contemplatives must preserve both the integrity of their loyalty to the invisible while at the same time working towards the emergence of the visible in the culture, the nature, the liturgy of the monastery as a place of worship. Such threshholds, where the very pores are kept open between the visible and the invisible, are essential to both a people and a culture, without them both perish in the reductive monotony of materialism. The very reality and location of Glenstal seems to have invited us here this weekend to get a handle on both the complexity and the lyricism of this question.

John O'Donohue gives us the following which we recognise as a final prayer and blessing for the meeting:

HOPI ELDERS SPEAK

You have been telling the people that this is the Eleventh Hour.
Now you must go back and tell the people that this is The Hour.
There are things to be considered.
Where are you living?
What are you doing?
What are your relationships?
Are you in right relation?
Where is your water?
Know your garden.
It is time to speak your truth.

Create your community.

Be good to each other.

And do not look outside yourself for the leader.

This could be a good time!

There is a river flowing very fast.

It is so great and swift that there are those who will be afraid.

They will try to hold on to the shore.

They will feel they are being torn apart, and they will suffer greatly.

Know the river has its destination.

The elders say we must let go of the shore,

Push off into the middle of the river.

Keep our eyes open and our heads above the water.

See who is in there with us and celebrate.

At this time in history we are to take nothing personally,

Least of all ourselves.

For the moment that we do,

Our spiritual growth and journey comes to a halt.

The time of the lone wolf is over.

Gather yourselves.

Banish the word 'struggle' from your attitude and vocabulary.

All that we do now must be done in a sacred manner and in celebration.

We are the ones we've been waiting for.

Later Fanny Howe sends this reaction: 'I am thinking instead about G-P and how important it is to get the name of it right. The beauty of that morning meeting was that the vocabulary and imagery for the dream were taking place at an unconscious language level, the way a poem is formed, but communally. The language we ultimately choose for any experience in life is what gives it form and trajectory. The birds in the Wisdom of Solomon.'

11/07/04: Three monks, Celestine Cullen, Mark and Philip Tierney, celebrated their fiftieth anniversary of ordination to the priesthood during mass at midday. They were five at the time of their ordination, Gerard and Bede having died in the meantime. Another Cóiced.

16/07/04: Chuck Feeney's last hurrah party at the Castletroy Park Hotel which he has sold after thirteen years. Champagne reception and buffet meal are expansive and lavish as always. Nostalgic reunion. Helga's mother had died this year before her 100th birthday. The last time I was here for dinner with her was on the first day of this year. Walburga Flaiz was born in 1904, the year of Bloomsday. Arlene Fitzpatrick and Ursula Healy, Chuck's sisters, are also present. Arlene says that the Icon Chapel has kept her alive. She too was suffering from cancer. Musicians from the World Music Centre play. Micheál Ó Suilleabháin introduces Seán óg Graham, button accordian player. Jazz musicians talk about 'swing' as the element which makes their music live. Irish traditional musicians talk of 'lift.' Lift is what makes the music fully alive. We were shown what 'lift' means, both when Seán óg played and when he danced accompanied by Matt Bashford on the uileann pipes. These pipes are bellows blown. Their name could come from the 'angle' at which they are held under the elbow to accomplish the music. As in resurrection it concerns vertical breathing. The bellows pumps the air through a 'chanter' in the centre fitted with three regulators.

During dinner I tell Stephanie and Ed Walsh about my recent journeys and about the hidden symbolic language which I am trying to read and resurrect. Ed Walsh asks me what the symbolic meaning of this event is.

Number 4 is symbolic of wholeness. The geometric equivalent is the square. There are 4 points of the compass, four winds, four corners of the earth. He, Brendan O'Regan, Chuck Feeney and Micheál Ó Suilleabháin are the four pillars of wisdom on which an impressive edifice rests and whereby a whole region is permeated with 'lift.' However, the meaning of these four quartets is in the centre, the centre which is about to emerge. The most important person is the fifth person who has inspired this whole development programme. The Holy Spirit makes up the Cóiced and is about to unearth a temple at the centre of the Fifth Province, which is the Shannon region. The acordian player is symbol of resurrected life – 'lift' is exactly what resurrection means: his music and his dancing were the body risen from the dead. He would not have been here without the World Music Centre in UL, which would not have been here without the University established by Ed Walsh, who head-hunted Micheál from University College Cork. The music department would not have been there without the Concert Hall, the Concert Hall would not have been there without Chuck Feeney, neither would most of the buildings at the university, and, for that matter, most of the campuses all over Ireland. And Chuck Feeney would probably not have been here without the miracle of Shannon Airport and its surrounding development which was attributable to the vision and management skills of Brendan O'Regan. These are the builders of the infrastructure of what is about to happen.

Ed Walsh and Brendan O'Regan give moving tributes to Chuck Feeney. But Paul Hannon, puts his finger on the real issue when he describes Chuck as a saint. He doesn't say it in any maudlin or psychophantic way, but with humour and almost as a surprise to himself. The truth is that there is inspiration here from another source and this source is eager to meet in person. God has been made manifest by allowing Chuck to act like God for so many people and for such a sustained length of time. How long can one go on doing this without becoming aware of the source in person?

Sandra Keegan Joyce sings *The Parting Glass* a song collected in Limerick. No one knows who wrote the song. All that matters is the music which has survived. That is true also for these people. They will be forgotten but their deeds will endure. A French architect has been selected to build the artists' village for the World Music Centre which now moves beyond the river Shannon at the University of Limerick into Clare. This is not the last hurrah, Brendan O'Regan says, it is the beginning.

The Other Side Of The River

The river has its own limits.
You stand on the other side.

I remain where I am,
in the doorway of my house.

Others enter the river first.
From where you are, you call my name.

The world is still.
Figures in the water grow smaller and smaller.

They swim free of nets cast by fishermen
who pull in their catch.

How particular are these things
and none of them mine.

I only once heard your voice.
Stars appear and rain falls.

The river moves on its course,
leaving me to forget myself or learn my place.[33]

V

MIDDLE ALPHABET

H

Lachlan MacKinnon writing in *The Observer* on Sunday April 7 2002 says about *Finders Keepers* which appeared during this walkabout:

'Heaney has written a manifesto[1] for a poetry committed to strengthening the spirit … but its final effect is to offer us the intellectual autobiography of a poet more canny, self-aware and strange than we may have expected. What also emerges is the portrait of a decent, conscientious, scrupulous man whose artistic swervings have never betrayed his integrity. We cannot have long to wait before someone writes the essay on "Heaney as an Example".'

'Example' is probably not the right word. But something like that is the role Heaney plays in the fashioning of this book and the dream catcher of the future which it implies.

'It is essential that the vision of reality which poetry offers should be transformative, more than just a printout of the given circumstances of its time and place'.

'It becomes a matter of trusting images and emblems rather than conventional readings of the world'.

'Readiness not to commandeer the poetic event but to let insights speak their own riddling truths.'

These three rules from *Finders Keepers* have been guides for what is emerging in these pages.

In the kind of search outlined in this book you follow the red thread of your life, you grasp and hold on to the fragments of a map which your intuition and the Holy Spirit help you to find. You get clues. And every now and then you stumble across a book or a person who can show you a way forward.

Seamus Heaney is one of the guides whose work I stumbled upon

25 years ago. A first attempt to present his poetry[2] as I understood it was attacked by Paul Durcan in the *Cork Examiner* in 1980:

> For those interested in oddity Mark Patrick Hederman continues his sauna bath saga of steamingly stupefied glossology on what he imagines to be the real Ireland (or, worse, the ideal Ireland) ... and discourses on the mystical strain in modern Irish poetry without mentioning the central figure.
>
> In the present issue Seamus Heaney is Hederman's subject or, should I say, victim: for it cannot afford any pleasure to Heaney to see his work so misconstrued ... The title of the article is 'Seamus Heaney: The Reluctant Poet' – never was there a less reluctant poet ... Hederman rounds off this dismal article with a comprehensive misinterpretation of *Fieldwork*.

Such criticism gives one pause, to say the least, and so I decided to send Heaney my thoughts on his new book of poetry *Seeing Things*, before publishing any further misconstruction.[3]

Heaney wrote back on 23 July 1991: 'Your letter and utterly sympathetic gloss on the poems were a great fortification. All the motion and direction that you divine in the opening half, and all the sense of being-there-available which was offered in the second – the way you describe it is the other side of the way I felt for it and towards it. There are some transpositions of course, which you make, forming the drama of the "fiction" into a symptom of the writer/subject – but they are all in order because they do tell a true thing about the way the poems mean for Seamus Heaney ... The overall intimacy and surveillance of your piece and your letter persuade me that you are an anchorage for the air-boats above the oratory ... The way you made clear the mood with which I had assembled tree by poem-tree – the "nets" of "The Biretta" and "The Settle-Bed", the roofed-in versus the unroofed in "Glanmore Revisited" and the other places – "Fosterling" and in *Squarings*, the whole charting of an approach to the open, bare-headed place – all that I see and know to be a true account of what is going on in the book. And your implied direction, to go further, to face into something harder, that of course is scaresome and unwanted, and one cannot quite know how to continue.'

And, perhaps even more touchingly, his wife Marie wrote on the same day: 'Seamus has just shown me your letter and your marvellous reflections on *Seeing Things*. You have certainly made me see things more clearly; things that I guessed at and in a subliminal way knew were there but which have been illuminated by you for me. A compliment indeed from the "one for skylights!"

'I feel you have taken the same journey as Seamus has, onto the heights, into the depths, across the threshold, into the marvellous. I feel very humbled by the insights and responses in your reading of Seeing Things and delighted that someone knows so clearly what he's getting at, the things he's seeing.

'Seamus said reading your letter was "as good as a retreat."

'Thank you for your profound, original insights.'

I give these quotations from private letters not to betray a trust or vaunt some kind of intimacy with the Heaneys, but to defend a possibility that 'poetry' if understood in a certain way can be, and should be, a guide towards the future, an essential voice in the drama of creating a more habitable planet. And that such understanding can and should come from monasteries where people have the time, the atmosphere and the opportunity 'to survey, as from a great height, the whole tortuous errant flow of history; and yet at the same time, like people completely immersed in it, they can see every pebble in its depths.'[4]

I am aware of the dangers of poetry being invited to undertake such a role. It can become 'political', either in the sense that it produces politics or derives from politics. And I do not believe that it should be 'political'. However, that does not mean that the discoveries it makes and the dimensions it reaches should not somehow be incorporated into the structures which are devised to achieve optimum quality of life for the present and future inhabitants of the universe.

Otherwise the pendulum swings into the other danger area, where poetry is syphoned into its own space and cultivated for its own sake, without connection with, or influence on, the way we live. Such limitations relegate it to the level of entertainment.

None of which implies that 'poetry' belongs to the domain of psychology, or that it can be reached by some science or method other than a certain kind of art. It is an ontological space giving access to the transcendent which goes beyond the psychology of the individual. The artist, the poet, can provide access to this space by accomplishing a certain kind of poetic form. It is through the brokenness and vulnerability of such artists that 'history' and culture can cooperate as both continuity and rupture. Art is original. Whenever it happens a new era begins. The poet allows him or her self to be the filter of something beyond that self, something transcendent. This means that the poetry is not the work of their own hands entirely; but it does not mean that they are taken over by some impersonal or sacral force. The original source is open to what is beyond the autonomous powers of the poet's creative activity. Through the particular gifts of the poet what is always new, because never before in history, becomes embedded in the familiar because it emerges in the form of a poem, a palpable work. An artistic metaphysics allows for creation and preservation to be accomplished through the filter of this space. This new 'thing' can be investigated by those who are open and humble enough to respect its originality and study its idiom. The temptation is to capture it in already existing nets and categorise it in familiar overbearing prejudice. Criticism as assault and battery can silence poetry into irrelevance; criticism as creative dialogue can filter the whispering into the bloodstream. Poetry can be harnassed to inform the politics ultimately responsible for fashioning the future. This is how I understand Heaney's imagery of anchoring the altar.[5]

Such anchorage explains the connection between art and history, which is not political but *sui generis*, original. It is not the subjection of history to one's imagination, nor the enslavement of imagination to fate. It is an essentially human movement of history which is neither an inexorable flow of impersonal fate, nor the arbitrary construct of our free will. Between these two 'logical' possibilities, there is the space, which is both uncovered and kept open by the artist, a middle voice between active construction and passive surrender. This third way entails an inner journey through the labyrinth of the poet's own history and situation towards the universal dimension, the open space of transcendence.

However, poetry cannot achieve this on its own. It must be accompanied by a certain kind of critical understanding which will be guarantor of its authenticity and exegete of its accomplishment. In other words, a certain kind of critical thought can facilitate the journey to and from the protectorate of poetry. This space is not a detached and self-contained realm of its own. It is always attached to a particular culture and the poet has to travel through the psychic hinterland of that culture before reaching it. The journey to the top of the world must take you through your own back yard, which might be what Patrick Kavanagh called connecting 'the parish with the universe'.

The 'thought' that accompanies poetry in its specific and demanding task should be cherishing, self-effacing and open to every possibility imaginable. It should be scrupulously vigilant but at the same time humbly aware of its own limited powers of assimilation, its inevitable obtuseness. Such 'thought' is the business of monasteries, the fruit of contemplation.

When I heard the news that Seamus Heaney had won the Nobel prize for literature, I wrote to him (6/10/1995): 'I am sure there are many, as usual, saying that you shouldn't have got it; others saying its all political! And then you saying, maybe they're right!!!'

'So I want to record the reasons why I would have given you my own personal Nobel prize for literature:

'1. 'Life schools our sensitivities and intelligences into souls and our expression into style' (Helen Vendler). You happen to have been born on the same 'last ditch in Europe' (Beckett) as me, and within the same historical time-span. Your poems have been for me, who have lived that time as a monk, 'exemplary documents in both schools' (Vendler again).

'2. In the school of the 'soul' they have been *lectio spiritualis.* Not as pious reading, hortatory injunction, edifying discourse, but as that 'clinking in the darkness' (MacNeice) which confirms that there are other prisoners and that 'Maybe we shall know each other better/ when the tunnels meet beneath the mountain.'

'More than that, your voice speaks of one who has seen some light at the end of the tunnel and your way of Seeing Things helps me forward: 'Me waiting until I was nearly fifty/ To credit marvels.'

'I can better illustrate by quoting Isak Dinesen, who explains what I mean by 'spiritual' reading in her story *Barua a Soldani* (in Swahili it means *The King's Letter.*')

'Her story is a true one. About how she shot a lion while gamehunting in Kenya. It was such a beautiful lion that she gave the cured skin to the King of Denmark where she came from. He sent a letter to her farm in Africa *mokone yake* (written in his own hand) to thank her. She has the letter in her pocket when she comes across a boy who has been badly wounded by a fallen tree. While she waits with him for a car to take him to the hospital, he begs her to give him something for the pain. You must have something for me. At last she remembers and says that she does have something for him – she has a letter from a king. He takes it and holds it against his crushed body. He is convinced that it has helped his pain. The letter becomes famous. It has to be put into a leather pouch to preserve it, and it is taken all over the countryside to people who are in desperate need. It must be kept, however, for the ones who need it most. Those who apply for it because they have a toothache are laughed at. Look at you, you only have a toothache - there is a woman in the next village who is dying. Only the deepest need is deserving of the king's letter. "And we who call ourselves or feel ourselves to be, servants of the word," Dinesen ends her story, "will feel, each of us, as I do, the wish that something we have written, that I have written *mokona yango*, with my own hand, may at some time, in some place, to people in need, be *barua a sultani*" a letter from the king.

'Your writing has been that for me.

'3. In the second school, that of style, I rely on the following quotations to suggest what I mean:

'In his *Peau de Chagrin* Balzac describes a "white tablecloth, like a covering of snow newly fallen, from which rose symmetrically the plates and napkins crowned with light-coloured rolls." "Throughout my youth," Cezanne said, "I wanted to paint that table-cloth like freshly fallen snow ... I know now that one must try to paint only: 'the plates and napkins rose symmetrically,' and 'the light-coloured rolls.' If I paint: 'crowned,' I am finished, you see. And if I really balance and shade my napkins and rolls as they really are, you may be sure that the crowning, the snow and all the rest of it will be there."[6]

'The second is what Yeats said of Synge's style:[7]

Synge sought for the race, not through the eyes or in history, or even in the future, but where those monks found God, in the depths of the mind, and in all art like his, although it does not command - indeed because it does not - may lie the roots of far-branching events. Only that which does not teach, which does not cry out, which does not persuade, which does not condescend, which does not explain, is irresistible.

'And the third is from your meeting with Joyce on your return from Station Island:[8]

> 'Your obligation
> is not discharged by any common rite.
> What you do you must do on your own.
>
> The main thing is to write
> for the joy of it . . .
>
> . . .   And don't be so earnest,
> so ready for the sackcloth and the ashes.
> Let go, let fly, forget.
> You've listened long enough. Now strike your note.'
>
> 'You lose more of yourself than you redeem
> doing the decent thing. Keep at a tangent.
> When they make the circle wide, it's time to swim
>
> Out on your own and fill the element
> with signatures on your own frequency,
> echo soundings, searches, probes, allurements,
>
> elver-gleams in the dark of the whole sea.'

'So, putting the two "schools" together I find your work to be *Opus Dei*, (and as Joyce has hinted in a letter: "The Holy Ghost is in the inkbottle!") it helps me in my own commitment to such work. This can be described only by a poem of Rilke:

> You are at the moment directly approaching the divine;
> more you are flying straight towards it,
> irresistibly surmounting all obstacles.
> But I have been there always, even as a child,
> and I am returning thence on foot.
> I have been sent back, not to proclaim it,
> but to be among what is human,

to see everything and reject nothing,
not one of those thousand transformations
in which the absolute disguises itself,
vilifies itself and makes itself unrecognisable:
I am like a man gathering fungi and healing herbs among the weeds,
who appears to be bent and occupied with small things
whilst the tree trunks around him stand and pray.
But a time will come when I shall prepare the potion.
And yet another when I shall mount upwards with it -
this potion, in which everything is distilled and combined,
the most poisonous and deadly elements as well, because of their
strength.
And I will take it up to God, so that he may slake his thirst,
and feel his own glory running through his veins.'

On 25/10/1995 I got a letter from Heaney: 'This evening I got down
to Glanmore for the first time since the announcement of the Nobel
news and the whole speeded-up phantasmagoria got under way. The
cottage here is both my "bastion of sensation" and my floating world, so
it was right that your letter, so fortifying and so absolving, should have
been waiting here. I greatly appreciated the terms in which you wrote –
"the plane of regard," as Frost (and Brodsky) call it – and I am glad to
report that over the years, and with not a little thanks to you, I have
become the unreluctant poet.'

26 April 1996: I wrote to Heaney: 'Having read *The Spirit Level*,
The Redress of Poetry, and your Nobel acceptance speech, *Crediting
Poetry*, I want to organise a seminar on the spiritual dimension to your
work. This would happen here at the Abbey, but in conjunction with
Limerick University and would take no more than three days. The
structure and shape is not yet clear but the purpose is clear to me: to
allow two important sources of spiritual growth to meet and suffuse each
other with complementary insight.

'The meeting would also inaugurate a centre here for the distillation
of wisdom from every available source: East, West, religious, scientific,
cultural, artistic. I have just returned from the Cézanne exhibition in
London and can see in retrospect the way he changed the focus of vision,
the way of 'seeing things' which we are only now becoming aware of.

Surely, we don't always have to wait 100 years before the still life wakens. A place where science, art, religion (of all denomination) can meet is more likely to give birth to a more imaginative century next time round. Anyway, your contribution to that process would be clarifying, steadying and "close to the bull, Senõr" (as Hemingway would have it) especially where "religion" is concerned – which is at such a rag-end right now: and, for me, your *Crediting Poetry* holds an important key: the key of David, in fact.

'Anyway, the point is this: Will you be there? Can you be there? If so, tell me dates (October onwards) which would be convenient. Obviously there would be readings, but also, I had hoped, dialogue. Enda McDonagh is interesting on the change he finds in the Oxford lectures. Who else should come? We have to drag the great haul out of the depths and whoever can help must do so. We all need each other at this time and everyone needs Ireland as she will be in the aftermath of such suffering. And you have the privilege of being the homilist.

'All this has been on the way for a long time and I believe it is the work of the Spirit.'

4 June 1996: Letter from Seamus Heaney saying among other things that: 'large shyness overcomes me when I think of participating in such a gathering. I am deeply moved that you find such possibility and suggestiveness in my books. I am also aware that the books do proceed from some inner motion of the spirit. But (and you have written about this, in a way) I flee from the promulgation or even the articulation of what all this means. I have some superstition, or instinct, that the work that the books are doing – represented by your own reaction to them - is best left alone. I have watched, for example, a lyric poet of real power become a kind of evangelist. There is absolutely nothing wrong with the evangelical mission, but I think it is a different one from the poetic. This poet's early work operated by a beautiful stealth. His later "missionary" work, which seeks to explicate and apply his intuitions, seem to me to fall into the "how to" vulgarity of American life.

'Now, I am not saying that the kind of sensitive and concerned gathering that you contemplate in Glenstal is to be compared with such hustling of insight. I just want to try to explain to you, in a slightly melodramatic way, the nature of my reluctance to go from the poetic to the pedagogical. Shyness, as I said in the beginning, is probably a better word than reluctance ... Unease ... Earlier, I would have accused myself of shirking a responsibility in this zone, but now I feel it is exercising a prerogative. Maybe I'm making heavy weather of it.

'Well, at least I have answered your letter now. What I desperately need is a bit of time and silence, not a further entry into discourse in public or semi-public. And, alas, I don't see the opportunities for this silence until next year. And then, what my imaginary soul guide is prescribing for me is a full year of refusal of all engagements. Would that not be a wonderful boon? Not a penance, just a kind of duty ... No doubt I'll fail again.'

10 June 1996: The day the peace talks slouch again towards Belfast, I write to Seamus Heaney: 'On this the anniversary of Tolstoy's pilgrimage to the Optina-Pustyn monastery in 1881, disguised as a peasant but accompanied by two bodyguards (carrying a suitcase full of clean clothes) I reply to your welcome and thoughtful letter. Thank you for so painstaking and cautionary a reply to mine. It articulates accurately the dilemma – *Jackson's Dilemma* (Iris Murdoch's latest book). Your letter arrived with one from her. Such synchronicities deserve mention.

'I agree with you about missionary propensities towards the vulgar. My worry for you is that "a bit of time and silence" may be impossible without some delicately spun artifice which surrounds and penetrates with firm unobtrusiveness.

'Also, the inner texture of the Oxford lectures: choice of subject, recurring nightmares, self-perpetuating imagery, which I find rearranged in *The Spirit Level*, make me question whether anyone can hatch them on their own.

'"This man can't bear our life here and will drown"

'The abbot said, "unless we help him."

'Without being importunate, it seems to me that the 'enduring child' in all of this needs mutuality. Not adulation, not jealousy. Some confirmation. Some solidarity with fellow monks. Not any particular group – all those described by, say, Rilke or Dostoievsky. Such contact must be possible without any or all the entanglements, the waste of time and energy, which engagement with a Nobel laureate must bring.

'Such a possibility is what I feel prompted to try to create here in our monastery – something like a 'fifth province' – not as an appropriation, not as an enclosure. And my feeling again is that your presence here would establish the contours, delineate the sketch plans, leave the skinprints behind – filling the element with a signature on the appropriate frequency – to return to Station Island.

'"A crewman shinned and grappled down the rope –"

'The image in my mind is an egg poached in boiling water, which takes on the contours of its own reaction to the crucible.

'However, I do recognise that the crucible must not melt when the ingredients it holds are heated to the point of transmutation. And I am not sure that the monastery is such a crucible. Or that anywhere can be. Gertrude Stein suggested that the twentieth century happened in Paris in the 1920s. Something like that was on my mind and I found confirmation for it in *Government of the Tongue*.

'And perhaps this is "missionary" or even covetous. But it also had to do with you and "us" (in the largest sense) and "The marvellous as he had known it."

'In other words some intuition that the next step must be a combined one – something as awkward as a three-legged race. Not for any communitarian or ethical motivation, but simply because each prisoner has got only one fragment of the map.'

In 1999: 'I find myself stalking you again, like the deer on your Christmas card. I sense the proximity or imminence of a secret which would make all the difference, not just to my own life but to the lives of many people, and it has something to do with the Jewish proverb: "None knows what *hesed* means unless he is prepared to endure shame and disgrace", because the word hesed means two things: "loving kindness" and "shame and disgrace".

'The divination of this area of truth is a matter of synchronicity, both in my own personal experience and in the spiritual crisis of the nation as a whole.

'Somehow the dynamic which you unleashed in poem viii of Lightenings in *Seeing Things*, and have reiterated on several occasions since then, including the Nobel lecture: the dynamic between the altar and the upper air, between the monks and the crewman, between Clonmacnoise and the Celtic Tiger, and between the murky and the marvellous, has sanctioned such an expectation in general terms.'

And again at Christmas at the end of the year 2000:

Dear Marie and Seamus,

I wish you both all the very best I can wish you for this Christmas 2000 and for 2001.

I am sending you my own meagre contribution to the 'turning' of the new century. There is a third volume on the way called *The Haunted Inkwell*. It describes, as I understand it, the connection which might exist between art and spirituality. It will contain the fruits of our dialogue over the last 20 years.

One statement is missing – perhaps more than one! – and it will be from you, Seamus, about the link between the anchor and the altar, the sanctuary and the space-ship, Kevin's hand and the birds that fly.

So, here is a proposal. We are opening here in Glenstal Abbey a very beautiful new library in the spring of 2001. This library has been built with help from a mutual friend whose name cannot be mentioned. It will house 120,000 books eventually. The present collection is over 70,000. It can expand if need be, in several directions.

The official opening will be on a date between 15 and 21 March 2001. My thought is that you might choose this occasion to make your first visit to Glenstal and that Seamus would address us on this issue. Whichever date suits you both between the two above would be the one we choose.

I was at a woodturning exhibition last week which was opened by Thomas Pakenham. He quoted Marie's story about her favourite cherry tree being 'returned' in bowl form. Our woodturner, Ciarán Forbes, who was one of those exhibiting, has chosen out a piece of poplar which he is turning into a bowl for you, 'quicksilvering/ The whole tree in a single sweep'.

Heaney writes: 23/12/2002: 'I look forward to the San Clemente tesserae retesselated and hope to see you in 2003.'

I

Iris Murdoch was born in Dun Laoghaire on 15 July 1919, only daughter of an opera singer and a British army cavalry officer. She was educated and lived in England. From 1938-1942 she studied 'Greats' (Ancient History, Greek, Latin and Philosophy) at Oxford. From 1944-46 she was an administrative officer for the United Nations Rehabilitation and Relief Association, working during the war in Belgium and Austria. Two of her lovers were victims of Hitler: Frank Thompson, whom it was assumed she would marry, was parachuted into Macedonia and was marching with the Partisans towards Sofia, Bulgaria. He was captured, regularly beaten and finally executed by the Nazis. A volume of poems by Catullus and a Byzantine coin found in his pocket when arrested were later presented to Dame Iris by the Bulgarians.

The second was the poet and anthropologist Franz Bauermann Steiner, a scholarly Czech-Jewish refugee from Prague, whose parents were killed in a concentration camp. The suitcase containing his doctorate on the sociology of slavery was stolen from the luggage van on the London-Oxford train in 1942. The year he re-submitted, 1949, he had a coronary and died in 1952.

From 1947 to 1963 she was a tutor of philosophy and a fellow of St Anne's in Oxford. At 35 years of age she began to write novels. Her first *Under the Net*, which was actually the fourth she wrote (two of which she destroyed, the other being the second one she published called *The Flight from the Enchanter*) was published in 1954. In 1956, at 37 years of age, she married her husband John Bayley, later Wharton Professor of English Literature and fellow of St Catherine's College, Oxford.

She wrote 26 novels and 3 major works of philosophy, one book of poetry and three plays. Her last novel, *Jackson's Dilemma* was published in 1995. She developed Alzheimer's disease in 1997. She died 8 February 1999 at 79 years of age. Her husband John wrote two accounts of her last illness and their life together while he nursed her at the end. One of these, *Iris*, became a best-seller.

The above is taken, in abridged form, from obituaries which appeared after her death. I had written in my diary in 1996: 'I have always imagined that at some stage (either in a future novel, or at a future time in myself) a perspective would emerge which would allow me to participate in the Murdoch 'message'. With each novel I feel myself nearer to that goal. Her works have haunted me. Always they seem to contain, although in a different context and proportionality, the images, themes and obsessions which invade my own life. And so, rather than wait until either or both of us were dead I decided to take up the invitation issued through *The Message to the Planet*:

> I don't know where you are in your thoughts – but you should write it down, I don't mean solving it, but just stating, writing it in plain rigmarole, as it were, with all the knots and inconsistencies showing. I know you see it as a sort of cosmic game of patience which would one day come out, and perhaps it will. But meanwhile you ought to write about the state of the game, about the kind of muddle and confusion you're in. (214)

To delineate my state of confusion I wrote to Iris Murdoch in 1996 having just finished reading her novel *The Green Knight*. I sent her a review I wrote for the *Sunday Tribune* of her study of philosophy, *Metaphysics as a Guide to Morals*, which came out in 1992. I took five of her novels: *The Bell* (1958), as an example of the earlier work, and *The Philosopher's Pupil* (1983), *The Book and the Brotherhood* (1987) and *The Message to the Planet* (1989), to describe the way in which her novels always seemed to correspond with whatever happened to be going on in my own life.

She wrote back twice and encouraged me to write again. 'Glenstal Abbey is surely noble and beautiful. Alas, I have never visited it.' I again wrote back describing how her last novels seemed to be harping on similar patterns and the feeling given is that they are either happy prologues to the swelling act or that the act itself has been performed secretly at the deeper level of symbol while the narrative hums away plausibly as a decoy. The overwhelming tremulation tangibly felt by at least this particular reader is that she, Iris Murdoch, in herself or in her writing seems to hold some key, does have an understanding of the mystery of life which it would benefit me to hear. So on 6 April 1996, I wrote to her:

> What a great surprise and excitement to get two communications from you, the second one hoping that you had not forgotten the first. And thank you for giving me the opportunity to write again – not like poor Bellamy in *The Green Knight* who was forbidden so peremptorily!
>
> You see, for at least twenty years you have been something of a spiritual guide, not just to me but to a group of us here who are on a search together (almost in spite of ourselves). Your books have an uncanny knack of saying what is needed at the time. The most forceful of these, I think, was *The Bell*. But we put in our icon chapel at *The Time of the Angels*! From *The Sea, the Sea* onwards I have waited with eagerness the arrival of each novel and in every case it was amazing how it dealt with whatever was happening to us at the time.
>
> Anyway, *Jackson's Dilemma* is the last straw. It describes my life and present project (both as Benet and as Jackson by the way!) so accurately that I am left laughing and gasping.
>
> But, more important than that: James Joyce says that the Holy Spirit is in the inkbottle – and the same Spirit breathes through all your work. It is and has been for me 'spiritual' reading.
>
> And so, what you have not yet encountered is someone searching for God who has also been the beneficiary of your own wisdom and insight and who now wishes to share some of what that means with you.
>
> I was prompted to write because of an article in *The New Yorker* describing your 'religious' beliefs. So Jackson wanted to throw a stone through the window!
>
> It is such a beautiful book – even the dust jacket. And it is all about keys and doors and openings; how to enter and how you can be locked out. About bridges and meetings. The wonderful scene at the end with the boy and the horse. What matter if you are vulnerable, they say.

But you know, dear Iris Murdoch, of course, that Jackson is, in fact, God. Godwithus, Emmanuel, 'Son of this Jack, joke, poor potsherd, patch, matchwood ...' You don't need me to tell you that. But, in some way, you do need me to tell you that.

I want also to thank you for all the richness and the fun over the years. It has been a shared world that has made mine so much more liveable.

I can hardly believe that this will be in your hands before the weekend. So many letters in your books were written by me or to me!

On 5 February 1997 I read in the newspapers that Iris Murdoch had Alzheimers. I got a kind letter from her husband, John Bayley, saying that she would not be able to reply to my letter but would be delighted if I could come and see her.

I only had her work now as my text. I knew that the message was in her novels and especially in her last one. I wrote about this in a book called *The Haunted Inkwell* which appeared in the year 2000:

Jacksons Dilemma[9] is, in fact, Iris Murdoch's dilemma. It hovers over that line or band which separates the two worlds. However, what she 'does' in this novel, which is all about opening doors, building bridges, crossing over divides, leads her to discover that God is, in some frighteningly mysterious way, 'mixed up with dubious history.'

This novel expresses what Heidegger was trying to point towards in his later philosophy both in what it says, especially through the different levels and the interplay of imagery, and in the way it leads Iris Murdoch herself, through its own words, through the mysterious power of language, to articulate a reality which she had expressly repudiated in the 'philosophical' work of three years before.

At the level of narrative, it is about a man (Benet) who lives alone in a particular place or territory, and who is writing a book about Heidegger. 'However, he found it difficult to plan the work and to decide what he really, in his heart, thought of his huge ambiguous subject' (p.13). This, it would seem to me, is the situation for Iris Murdoch also. Like Maggie Verver in the Henry James' novel *The Golden Bowl*, she finds herself doing this 'thought' in the form of a novel, in an art form which incarnates the thought as 'poetry'. 'Heidegger, the greatest philosopher of the century? But what was Benet thinking somehow so deeply about when he turned his mind to that remarkable thinker? It seemed to him that after all his philosophical reflections, there was a sound which rang some deeper tremor of the imagination. Perhaps it was his more profound desire to lay out before him the history of Heidegger's inner life ...' (p.14). 'Benet found himself accusing himself of being fascinated by a certain dangerous aspect of Heidegger which was in fact so deeply buried in his own, Benet's, soul that he could not scrutinise or even dislodge it' (p.13).

The only way to do either or both is to let it deliver itself into the novel. And so, at the second level, the imagery concerns places: two territories divided by a river. The places are forever being locked, barred, bolted, and are connected by bridges. 'The gate, sometimes locked, was now fortunately not locked ... [There was] a scarcely perceptible right of way running steeply down to the River Lip at a place where there was a shaky little wooden bridge. After the river she had left Benet's territory and entered Edward's territory. (They still feuded about the bridge)' (p.39). Those living in both territories are aware of just how tenuous, difficult and dangerous are the territorial ties between them. Part One of the book lands us in the middle of an attempt to solve this relationship in the most 'natural' and 'romantic' way by arranging a match. This is so predictable and 'heavenly'. There is a fourteenth century church on Benet's side of the river where this wedding is to take place the following day. It is as if the Gods have arranged it all, but more especially the ancestral ghosts of Penndean in the person of Uncle Tim (called after Timaeus Patroclus to keep us in the true Graeco-Roman tradition). The night before the wedding 'Benet had firmly laid hold of Edward (the bridegroom owner of the "other" territory), seizing his sleeve ... "Edward, if only Tim were here we would really be in heaven. Well, of course now we are in heaven anyway! I've longed for you to marry that girl."' A guest suggests that it is 'like the end of the Paradiso,' but Benet insists: 'not the end ... it is the beginning.' After which 'they moved back into the house' (p.24). In moments like these, 'and such strange moments sometimes came', Benet 'felt the spirit of Uncle Tim descending upon him, clothing him as it were, and breathing his breath' (p.23). This is the spirit of place, the tribal spirit of possessiveness which drives towards the consolidation of earthly ties, natural kinship between the peoples.

Well it is not to be so. The 'Marian' solution is definitively sabotaged when Maid Marian herself says 'No' at the last minute. And so, the complete cast, in part Two, is thrown out of paradise into 'hell'. Benet retires to his territory 'for some sort of quietness or solitude' and there, once again, is his book on Heidegger and 'Heidegger's central concept of truth or unconcealment'. It all begins according to a lecture which Heidegger gave in 1943 with a certain kind of wonder. 'Wonder first begins with the question, "What does all this mean and how could it happen?" How can we arrive at such a beginning?' ... Benet paused, well what does it all mean, he thought, and why on earth do I go on with it? ... Could one forgive Heidegger or be interested in him ... No, he was just a curious romantic pseudo-historian. He would rather spend his time reading Hölderlin than Heidegger. Really he loved pictures not thoughts' (Pp 68-69).

And so we are led into the real business of the novel: Jackson's Dilemma. Benet's relationship with Jackson and Jackson's connection with history which is Iris Murdoch's 'picture' of what Heidegger really meant by 'truth'.

Benet is forever trying to lock himself into his house. In the last page of part two 'he went round and locked the doors and bolted and chained them'. Then 'he decided to go to bed and to sleep'. The house itself is acoustically ambiguous. 'Those strange sounds were there again: a crackling sound of something on fire, an almost inaudible little wailing sound as by a small creature in pain, then a sharper brief sound not unlike a knock. Of course it was all nonsense, these were familiar noises, he heard them all the time, the natural murmurs of an ageing house, its little secret wounds, wood rotting, tiles slipping ... His ferocious concentration upon Heidegger had for a brief time distracted him'. But, despite his decision, his will to go to bed and lock himself securely within his own territory, 'suddenly he found himself prowling around the house and reflecting upon quite a different matter which now increasingly distressed him. It was Jackson' (p.70).

'Jackson was his servant' (p.48). 'The legend was that Benet had discovered Jackson curled up in a cardboard box late one night' (p.71). In terms of territory, he had first met Jackson in 'that area near to the river' which 'had been, ever since Benet could remember, some sort of gathering place'. But 'Benet himself was not at all sure ... how exactly it had begun. Had he really seen strange eyes looking at him in the dark? ... The idea 'it is fate', was taken up later by Mildred. Had Benet, much earlier, unconsciously, seen those eyes? Can it be that one particular person, sent by the gods, is singled out for another particular person?'

It certainly had to do with trying to find your way into your own home and then hearing a voice, 'a soft voice', 'a cool calm voice' saying 'May I help you? Perhaps I can help you.' 'I can do many things' (p.73). 'Benet had not heard or dreamt of hearing this voice. The voice was hard to place'. He is becoming aware 'that he was not alone'. 'He turned round, annoyed, then alarmed, by the silent unknown figure' (p.71). 'He was troubled by the stranger's silence, and wished he could find somewhere to shake him off'. The novel is a series of attempts to 'shake him off'. 'At last Benet ... turned round abruptly to survey his curious partner. He instantly felt something pass through him, as of an electric shock' (p.81). Getting into his house, finding no light in his house, 'the man was there. Benet said, 'Do you know anything about electricity?'

'Yes'

'Come in'.

That was how it began' (p. 78).

How did what begin ? We are talking again about relationship with what is 'beyond' about the 'deep structures' about the source. We are working through someone who is trying to find his way into his own homeland, his territory, in such a way that he can claim it as his own, accurately delineate it and then secure himself within it, locking it up, barring and bolting the door. But he cannot even find his way in, his way around inside, without the 'help' of 'someone else', a 'voice'. It is a question of finding a key, of electricity, of light even within his own territory.

It is as if nothing works, nothing is possible, nothing exists, without some contact with the territory beyond, with the outside of the house, the space between. Jackson's dilemma is how to pick up the pieces after the apparent disaster occasioned by the explosion of the romantic solution, how to establish another kind of contact, generate another kind of electricity, which would not be the endlessly stereotypical one of the marriage bond. The non-event of this marriage in the church of the Arch-Angel Michael and All the Angels is characterised as almost an anti-sacrament: 'How *wierd* it was, and *terrible*, what an *extraordinary* scene as if some great ceremony were being performed' (p. 37). The italicised words emphasise the numinous dimension of the second sacrament which was taking place by default. And Rosalind, who is Marian's sister, becomes the only witness of the secret return of the bridegroom as a kind of post-resurrection apparition awaiting the arrival of the new dimension: 'She saw something, somebody, just visible from where she stood now . . a man, sitting upon the flat top of a tombstone and looking down' (p 37).

Where she stood now, is the place and the time arranged by Jackson. 'Thank you so much for lending us Jackson, he fixed the thing in no time' (p 56).

So, who is this Jackson who is able to fix 'the thing' in 'no time'?

He is 'our dark angel', Ariel (who, according to Benet, was not an angel), to 'run along the rooftops delivering messages'. He is also Caliban 'who really knew the island, the animals and the plants', the Fisher King in disguise? He is, in fact, whatever or whoever is able to establish contact between the Gods and ourselves. He is 'of the angel order.'

He is God's illegitimate son, as Caliban was Prospero's by the witch Sycorax. He is 'Benet's illegitimate son' (p.65): in both cases, quoting Shakespeare: 'This thing of darkness I acknowledge mine'. Throughout the novel, we all eventually recognise that 'however it may be, in Jackson I recognise my brother' (p.65).

He is 'one of us' and, at the same time, he is beyond us. He belongs to the space between our two territories. '[Benet] walked across in the dark and looked down into the garden below. Jackson lived there, in the little house of his own which Benet called "The Lodge". The light was on in the lodge' (p.65).

In other words, the novel is a description of the relationship between us and God, or 'the gods'. All its imagery of territories, spaces, places, houses etc. is describing a kind of mysticism which architecturally enunciates the 'deep structures' of our lives, the line or the band between us and the 'other' world. The river is the most picturesque analogy for that band. It is called 'Lip' as both the edge and the faculty with which we can achieve that 'kiss' which Eckhart describes as the sublime contact with the 'Other'. Rosalind, as Marian's sister is the other possibility of relationship once the Marian convention has been courageously refused. 'A less courageous person would have felt it was already too late, they would have been ashamed, they would think ... I'm so involved now I'll have to put up with it' (p.59). So that, when Benet goes to visit Rosalind in her 'third floor flat' the imagery of doors, locks, above, below, windows, inside, outside, can be understood in this way: 'He pressed open the front door and began to climb. He heard Rosalind's door opening above – and the pain now came back and the fear, the awfulness of the situation, its bottomless void ... He heard her door opening above and thought, I will recall this.

Rosalind held the door open, then when Benet entered, shut it and leaning against it they hugged each other with closed eyes. Then Benet, holding her by the wrist, led her over to the window where a long seat covered with cushions gave a view down the busy little street dusty with sunshine and a narrow glimpse of the great Catholic Cathedral' (p.59).

The space between, the door between, which has to be pressed upon, opened from inside, is the place of that new kind of relationship between God and humankind. It is a dark place, an 'awful' place: *Terribile est locus iste*, as every mystic has experienced. In the middle of the passage just quoted, Benet tells us 'he knew that beyond these particular matters there was a dark horror which he must not, and indeed could not, thrust away ... Suddenly something out of Shakespeare, the dreadful peril of the bard himself'. This concern, this comparison, this suggestion that

Shakespeare has known this situation, echoes a previous passage where we hear Benet suggesting that Heidegger also was in possession of this terrible secret: 'Heidegger, the greatest philosopher of the century? His ... desire to lay out ... the history of Heidegger's inner life, the nature of his sufferings: the man who began as a divinity student and became a follower of Hitler, and then –? Remorse? Was that the very concept which sounded the bell? What had that pain been like ... A huge tormented life? Was Heidegger really Anti–Christ? "The darkness, oh the darkness," Benet said aloud' (p.14).

This novel is an attempt to articulate such a dimension. And to 'do' the fearful possibility that this is what relationship with God must mean after the times we have been through. Jackson is the personification of such relationship, of such a possibility. 'On the occasion of the key he had refused money, he had, to make this clear, actually reached out his hand, laying it on Benet's hand – his fingers touching the back of Benet's hand. He had touched Benet. Well, what did that mean – a gesture of love? Impossible! He had been closer then than now. Well, Benet's emotion – was there emotion – had soon passed! Yet perhaps the emotion had built up later on: the dream, the return to the river' (p.79).

Having tried to escape from this relationship, having dismissed Jackson, in fact, Benet tries to return to normality, but 'he struggled as if against a power to which he must soon succumb' (p.81). This power has all the outward signs of an hypnotic sexual attraction. This possibility goes through Benet's mind: 'It was also possible, and this occurred to Benet later in the episode, that the fellow was gay and thought that Benet was! He decided that this was unlikely ...' (p.73). And we, also, who have followed Iris Murdoch through her novels know that she is more aware not only of this possibility but of the connection between it and mysticism. A. S. Byatt comments about *The Bell*: 'both Michael and Dora are real and unexpected individuals; Michael as a type, ineffectual homosexual idealist, school–master cum priest, we may have met often enough before, but such a character can rarely have been treated with the completely non–sentimental respect and the patient understanding which Miss Murdoch affords him.'[10]

Both Benet and Jackson could be such characters if Murdoch wished them to be. But they are not. Although, again, this ambiguity is part of Jackson's dilemma and there are times when Benet's 'visions' and 'apparitions' seem to have the homoerotic flavour of some of Thomas Mann's stories, especially 'that curious stroke in Venice' which immediately preceded his first real interview with Jackson (pp.80–85). And when eventually he and Jackson meet up and decide to remain together, it does appear as though either or both of them are 'cruising' along the bridge over the Thames (p.215). However, this is not the kind of relationship which the novel is presenting, even though it might have been the preliminary to it or the occasion of it, which is not stated, but which corresponds with certain Platonic ideas about erotic love which Murdoch explains in her Guide to Morals:[11]

> Plato envisages erotic love as an education, because of its intensity as a source of energy, and because it wrenches our interest out of ourselves. It may be compared with the startling experience in Zen (perhaps a literal blow) which is to bring about enlightenment.

Whatever ambiguities may pervade the context of, or the lead up to, the eventual meeting between Benet and Jackson which seals their fate as committed partners to one another, the actual event, as described in the novel, delineates a specific kind of relationship with the Other, which involves reaching the deep structures of the self and opening that self to the Infinite. Benet first goes to 'the house where he used to live and where Jackson had first spoken to him'. He walks down to that part of it which is beside the river. 'He felt a curious impulse to knock at the door. In fact he knocked, but no one answered.' He goes to the railway station intending to take the train home. 'Why am I here?' he asks himself, 'Oh God forgive me, except that I don't believe in God.' Just beyond was the river Thames. At one moment he was in the railway station about to get on a train, but 'then he found himself standing at the foot of the steps leading up to the railway bridge; automatically he began to mount. Why was he doing this, he felt so tired and so senseless. At the top of the steps he paused. He thought, I am nobody now. He was the beginning of nobody. Now it was dark. The Thames below was full and quiet. It was dark on the bridge ... Benet ... set off slowly toward the other side. Near the centre of the bridge a man was leaning upon the rail, looking down the river ... Nearing, the hideous idea occurred to him of simply passing by ... How this had occurred to him seemed later incredible – certainly it was not contempt or hatred – it was fear' (pp.214–215).

Despite the ambiguities: it could be that either or both of them have gone there to pick up a partner or to commit suicide, the imagery and the thrust of the novel lead elsewhere. Jackson is the bridge. His dilemma is how to entice us to the centre. Once the connection has been made, at the end of part nine, the two men 'walk back towards the station' together' and to do this, we are told, 'Jackson detached himself from the bridge'.

Jackson is the Murdoch version of Heidegger, the reality of the Spirit in our world, the space, the bridge, the pontifex, between us and God, who is not an impersonal fate, but a personal servant. The novel walks us towards the centre of that bridge, which had been philosophically identified in the Guide Book:[12]

> Personal love exists and is tried in impersonal contexts, in a real large world which transcends it and contains other goals, other values, other people. We love in the open air, not in a private room. We know, and this is one of the things we know most clearly of all, which is indeed a knowledge that is 'forced upon us', that the energy of Eros can be obsessive, destructive and selfish, as well as spiritual, unselfish, a source of life. 'Falling in love' may be our most intense experience, when the world's centre is removed to another place. It is difficult to be unselfishly in love, and the lover who lovingly surrenders the beloved may serve as an image of virtue, of the love that 'lets go', as in Eckhart: emptying the soul to let God enter and even, for God's sake, taking leave of God.

Iris Murdoch's last novel, *Jackson's Dilemma*, written as Alzheimers disease was about to make all such writing impossible for her, exudes another energy which takes over and allows the novel to describe the process by which the Spirit intervenes in human lives. The second last paragraph of the book is almost prophetic if one sees it as describing Iris Murdoch's own situation at the time of writing:

> He (Jackson) breathed deeply. Sometimes he had a sudden loss of breath, together with a momentary loss, or shift, of memory. So he was to wait, once more, forgetfulness, his and theirs. He thought, my power has left me, will it ever return, will the indications return? … He had forgotten where he had to go, and what he had to do … How much now will I understand. My powers have left me, will they return – yet my strength remains, and I can destroy myself at any moment. Death, its closeness. Do I after all fear those who seek me? I have forgotten them and no one calls. Was I in prison once? I cannot remember. At the end of what is necessary, I have come to a place where there is no road. (pp.248–249).

In an earlier interview Murdoch had said: 'One can only write from one's own mind, within the limit of one's own understanding of human life. This will be marked by your history, where you've been.' 'What's interesting about the novel is that all kinds of things that you know and feel and think, a great variety of things, are elicited by the art form, so in a way writing a novel is a process of self–discovery – you know much more than you think … The unconscious mind is the great source of the power of art, and all these things will emerge if you wait for them and summon them'. This last novel must have been written very largely from the unconscious, with the discipline and the habit of years of writing helping her to battle against the onslaughts of Alzheimer's.

'You have to explore and extend your limits. This is why reading is so important … another world is pulling you out of yourself, and to get out of yourself is the great thing.'

'I'm very interested in dreams. We are accompanied by a dream world, the unconscious mind teems with strange things. And a work of art is a place where you can formalise and present some of these strange things which are just outside the focus of your ordinary consciousness.'[13]

Iris Murdoch's last novel, written as the curtain of conscious memory was descending, provides us with a most remarkable testimony. Jackson in the novel is the Holy Spirit, son of 'This Jack, joke, poor potsherd, patch, matchwood' that ultimately 'Is immortal diamond'.[14]

20 February 1998: I wrote to Iris Murdoch and John Bayley, saying how moved I had been to meet her, how beautiful she was, how I knew that behind the walls of Alzheimers she was in a monastery with God and that wonderful wisdom was being secreted there. If any manifestations of this wisdom should ever emerge, in however garbled a form, I would like to be privvy to them. I also gave him a dig saying that I had read in the *New Yorker* that he did not believe in God and had persuaded Iris to adopt this view!

03.03.1998: So kind of you to write. Your visit was truly memorable for us both. No, I never advised Iris against God! – wouldn't know how to start – she is the expert, as you say. Alas she can't write or read any more, but she can communicate as your words testify …

In his biography of Iris Murdoch (2001) Peter Conradi notes that: 'In 1996 a Benedictine monk from Glenstal Abbey in County Limerick wrote to Chatto to say, 'I would like to speak with her. More than that, I feel I should speak with her': the monks at Glenstal felt inspired by their understanding of some of her 1980s novels to reorganise their abbey' (p.587). John Bayley records the eventual conversation which I had with Iris in his memoir *Iris* (1998):

> [W]hen the tall monk and Iris sat down together, things changed at once. They became extraordinarily animated – she starting sentences, or ending them – he appearing to know at once what she wanted to ask, and filling the words they were failing to make with a professional abundance of loving kindness. And yet his face looked really transfigured: so, a few moments later, did hers. They were soon on about his childhood, why he joined the order, most of all about his plans to make discussion of her works a regular thing at Glenstal Abbey. He assured us that two of her novels, *The Book and the Brotherhood* and *The Good Apprentice*, could be said to have inspired the recent setting–up of the monastery, and the way they wanted it to go (p.127).

12 December, 1998:

> Dear Iris and John,
> You must think me very strange to keep on plying you with proofs of an underground, providential plot to make something emerge

which is connected to Iris, and will make her work a source of important guidance for people in the future. However, as long as the impulse remains as powerful as it does presently, I shall continue to do so! Happy Christmas to you both.

Apart from the physical appearance of first editions of her works at confirming times in whatever place I happen to be, New Mexico (*Henry and Cato*); Boston (*The Sea, the Sea*); Clonakilty (*An Unofficial Rose*); Oxford etc. I walk into a shop and these books reach out to me, or they are sent in the post, as *The Sacred and Profane Love Machine*, last month, which was the right text for the right time. In this group which we form, *The Black Prince* was our spiritual reading this summer.

After my last visit to you, with Dermot Rooney, we bought the *Elegy for Iris* in Oxford and read it right through. I was interested in what you said of my visit, a private conversation which then became part of the coded message, which it is, particularly the two books you quote, *The Book and the Brotherhood* and *The Good Apprentice*. These are being acted out here, as it were.

It is a narrative with a different purpose. That purpose being to show that Iris is still 'being' in an extraordinary way and that is continuous with and burgeons from the wonderful way she has been all her life. And you are the key witness to that very important reality and one which this present world needs to be educated about. I also am a witness. But mine is at the level of intuition which bears none of the burden of intimacy, which is both your privilege and your passion, in every sense of the word. I pray for you both and for the patience and the vision necessary to endure.

I arrive home and waiting for me is a photocopy of an interview Iris had given in 1986 to an Edward Whitley in a book about Oxford called *The Graduates*. On page 73 it says:

'Miss Murdoch's characters often experience moments of surprise when they recognize something passing between them which takes them half out of their own lives and half into each other's. In *The Sandcastle*, Mor is aware of this sort of feeling … [By the way *The Sandcastle* dedicated to you, John, is the only remaining novel which I do not have in a first edition and I know that this one is being kept last because it is going to 'appear' as confirmation of some decisive moment in this ongoing saga, so akin to the interior mechanisms of a Murdoch novel, because so akin to her own interior spiritual life.]

'Do you think such epiphanies are actually possible? the interviewer asks, 'Especially amongst older middle–aged people?'

'Yes, of course, people retain this capacity. I think that these "epiphanies" are happening all the time. If people have any strong relationships at all, and most people do (the family is very important), then these discoveries and these dramas happen all the way through life.'

You describe my visit with Iris as such an 'Epiphany' which I also experienced. Then you go further and you describe yourself as writing the novel *The Red Hat*, (which in the Roman Catholic tradition is how you describe someone being made a cardinal – which, for instance Newman was and which Iris should be) as an attempt to either imitate Iris or to extend her spirit, almost as if you were writing the novel for her. I had written to you last August that such a collaboration might now be happening and compared it to Yeats' writing *A Vision* through the mediumship of his wife.

Anyway, on the morning of my departure for Boston, last month, your book, which I had ordered, arrived by post, in time for me to read on the plane. I love the cover. When I bought it in Boston 'for a friend' the American edition wasn't half as striking. And it is so witty and a great read. But, there was more in it than that for me: I kept on realizing that the first half is told by the woman (and this seemed to me to be Iris talking of her relationship with God, as in *Wuthering Heights* and Emily Bronte's poetry – sex is that communication symbolically – in the lift (ecstasy, ascension, upwards, towards 'my' room) and with the dark stranger who walks through doors. 'At first it did nothing for me, having sex with him,' she confides – and the androgynous nature of the boy/girl in the picture and in the novel and the way they had sex. 'I let him do what he wanted to do the first time ...' It is sexual imagery for relationship of an extraordinary kind, as in *A Passage to India*, *The Good Apprentice*, *Jane Eyre*, *Wuthering Heights*, *The Idiot*, etc. The second half of the novel is then told by a man and his version of the relationship, even his terrified run to escape, is all creation of his own imagination: perceived assessment of the dark stranger. An article in the New Yorker, I think, which I can't lay my hands on, has Iris saying that she believed in God until you persuaded her that such existence was impossible. You certainly didn't persuade the novelist Iris Murdoch, and the wonderful lines you quote between yourself and herself re *Jackson's Dilemma* – 'perhaps he is a woman – I don't know if he has yet been born' – are all about the life of the Spirit which is emerging and which the works of Iris Murdoch are there to elucidate and testify to.

Some of what I say should ring a bell with you, with her ... or something should turn up which would corroborate ... Synchronicity, coincidence = God's way of remaining anonymous. I was deeply moved by your elegy (and indeed by your writing in general, so humourous, so accurate, so down–to–earth and unpretentious yet subtle and open to the mysterious) it gave me quite a different picture of you. I had suspected that you were preventing her from some kind of spiritual activity even now and, I suppose, projecting on to her situation the scenario she describes in *The Good Apprentice*. Anyway, I take all that back. Both Dermot and I were uplifted by our recent visit. We were silent for most of the day afterwards. We felt we had been in the presence of sanctity. You and she, like two little garden saints in a very dilapidated cuckoo clock. By the way, you are living next door to an Admiral of the Fleet who cannot understand such inefficiency ... how they can't get that bell mended!

I do hope I shall have occasion to visit sometime in 1999. It is now, as I write this, the anniversary of my first visit to Oxford in the Blue Van. (That might be the title of another novel – sequel to *The Red Hat* – which needs at least a third part to complete the first two).

I wish you all the very best I can wish. If you feel up to it, we would love you to come and visit our monastery. You only have to get a plane to Shannon (I think from Gatwick, two hours from you) and I would meet you at the other end and drive you to the monastery (about an hour's drive at most.) Meanwhile I hope Christmas is peaceful and 1999 a year of grace for you both.

15/2/1999:

Dear John,

I am glad for Iris that she has slipped away and for you that you do not have to hold her any longer as too long a sacrifice makes a stone of the heart. And yet, I feel so sorry for you as this wrenching away of the second half of your being must be an amputation almost too cauterizing to bear. And then to have to listen to the world chattering at her funeral. The newspapers, the programmes on radio etc. Thomas Mann says that 'nothing sounds sillier to us than praise of someone whose true worth we think ourselves better able to gauge than anyone else … "Ass!" muttered Petepre into his folded arms … "What is he jabbering about?" … Jabbering was pretty bitter too. But the dwarf was not to be put off.'

And so this dwarf also must jabber to you, who alone know who and what Iris Murdoch is, was and always will be. I heard her, in her own voice, saying on an interview from the 1970s that she was an only child and that she created the characters in her novels as so many brothers and sisters. And when the novel was over it was sad because it was as if they had packed up and gone to Australia or somewhere. But, in fact, they had gone out to find other brothers and sisters. For thirty years of my life, Iris has been like a big sister to me. And more than that, a wonderfully deft, amusing, accurate guide in my spiritual life, my life as a human being.

Her first lover, Frank Thompson, died in the year I was born. He wrote to her from the war front: 'If we should meet again, then why we'll smile, if not – why then those that will follow us will be able to smile far more happily and honestly in the world that we are helping to make.' That is true for me and for many others. Thanks to Iris Murdoch I am incrementally more alive as I read each one of her novels throughout those years. I was in Belfast and in Dublin on the day she died. That same day my friend, Dermot Rooney, who visited you both with me last October, posted me from Oxford a first edition of her 1971 novel An Accidental Man. Such 'accidental' coincidences have made my life into the Murdoch mould: chance occurrences that weave the delicate web of a spiritual destiny.

I believe in God because of icons of the divinity (as in *The Time of the Angels*) which have touched me in ways that make denial impossible. The life of Iris Murdoch is one such icon and the inspired scripture she has left in her wake is positive proof that the Holy Spirit was with her and breathed through her. The last novel *Jackson's Dilemma* is a letter of love written marvellously through her, in her already faltering hand.

My last communication from John Bayley, dated Oxford, 14 October 1999:

I believe you are <u>right</u>! Dear Jackson – so good, so simple and so mysterious a figure. Alzheimers is mysterious too, and not all bad, but yes – you are right! Bless you.

J

On 10 June 1904 James Joyce met 20-year-old Nora Barnacle who worked in Finn's Hotel. From their first walk together on 16 June she changed his view of the world and of the secret forces underlying it. This became 'Bloomsday' the day of *Ulysses*, the most important day in Joyce's life. They left Dublin together on Saturday, 8 October 1904.

In 2004, a hundred years after the first Bloomsday, a letter from James Joyce to Nora Barnacle was discovered. It was written on 1 December 1909. Joyce's biographer Richard Ellman, thought that 'Joyce's letter of 1 December 1909 has not survived.' It had survived only coming to light a century later. It was hidden in a copy of *Ulysses*. The letter was auctioned in Sotheby's in July 2004. The collection included a telegram from Nora with the one word *si* (yes) – the last word of Molly Bloom's soliloquy and of *Ulysses* – with a purse like a religious reliquary which Joyce had made to contain it. The fervour of Joyce's relationship with Nora, expressed so graphically in their correspondence, underscores the importance, both for an understanding of Joyce himself, and for the hidden exegesis of his written works, of such letters.

Two everpresent antipodal dimensions to their love represent the paradox which his life and his work struggled to resolve.

But, side by side and inside this spiritual love I have for you there is also a wild beast–like craving for every inch of your body, for every secret and shameful part of it, for every odour and act of it. (2/12/09).

Quite early in the career of Stephen Dedalus, as described in *A Portrait of the Artist*, we are given several indications about his sense of vocation. The director of Belvedere College questioned him on this score and the whole movement of the book carries the soul of Stephen Dedalus along 'two paths, the path of the priest he might have been and the path of the artist he is to become.'[15] Boys of his intelligence and sensitivity were often coaxed into the order.

The one element in his personality which prevented this possible outcome was his unusually precocious sexuality. For a boy of his age in a Dublin day–school he seems to have had considerable sexual experience. His sexuality formed the warring partner in the struggle towards his ultimate destiny. He realised that the call to priesthood meant the eradication of this vital aspect of himself. He saw the Catholic Church as a call to a certain kind of perfection which demanded emasculation and evisceration.

A Portrait of the Artist as a Young Man describes the bitter and lonely struggle between these two realities in an almost unbearably sensitive youth. The famous sermon on hell was the final blow to the possible vocation to the priesthood. 'Before the rector had delivered himself of his last word, the developing priest was slain in Stephen Dedalus; the developing artist, like a waiting animal, stared watchfully and did not move.'[16] Joyce decided to remain true to his own nature and to reject the way of life proposed to him and endorsed by all who surrounded him. He decided to defend the orthodoxy of his own humanity against the orthodoxy of Roman Catholicism as this was presented to him. This involved him in the three famous rejections, of family, faith and nation. His mind began to 'feel its way towards some comprehension of the actual nature and dimensions of the work imposed upon him by his own nature and qualities'.[17]

> Do you know what a pearl is and what an opal is? My soul when you came sauntering to me first through those sweet summer evenings was beautiful but with the pale passionless beauty of a pearl. Your love has passed through me and now I feel my mind something like an opal, that is, full of strange uncertain hues and colours, of warm lights and quick shadows and of broken music.

This is Joyce writing to Nora on 21 August 1909, three months before the newly found letter was written.[18]

The word opal comes from the sanskrit *úpara* meaning 'lower,' which is the comparative of *úpa* meaning 'under.' At base it is a silica mineral, the principal constituent of most rocks. Disseminated impurities impart colours to this durable base. Impurities, imperfections, inhomogeneities, gas–filled cavities, are what cause this kind of beauty. Joyce defends in his life and his work the orthodoxy of such beauty, its right to a place in the hall of virtue.

Whereas opals are the effect of outside invasion, pearls are the product of war against invaders. Molluscs (the Latin word *mollis* means 'soft') invertebrate and soft–bodied, usually surrounded by a shell, are the creatures which produce this second kind of beauty. Molluscs with double shells, such as clams, oysters and mussels, lay down pearl (*pernulla*, Latin for 'unattested' 'nothing gets through') as the inner layer of their shells. The mother–of–pearl, as it is called, consists largely of thin layers of calcium carbonate, the chemical of which chalk is composed.

When some foreign matter, often parasitic larva, gets into the body, the mollusc forms a small sac around the foreign body, isolating it, and then builds layer upon layer of calcium carbonate around the sac, imprisoning the invader for ever and creating a pearl.

Natural pearls are rare. Only one oyster in a thousand contains one. Yet this lonely, defensive, self–contained perfection is the only model proposed to the artist as a young man as worthy of the name of beauty, virtue, sanctity. Joyce refused to abandon everything about himself which was declared to be anathema to this ideal of perfection. Instead of Prometheus, Lucifer and Faust, those bachelors, disobedient sons, and brilliant failures, he conjured up Ulysses, Dante, Shakespeare as his prototypes, men of substance and family whether they were voyagers, exiles, or homekeepers.[19] He saw himself as having barely escaped the fate of Faust: the unmarried, arrogant, doomed, pointless rebel. It was the fact of meeting Nora which saved him from the pearl–like perfection of Aloysius Gonzaga, patron saint of youth as proposed by the Jesuits. He liked to think of himself as Ulysses and, as Ellmann says, 'it is not surprising that Joyce's description of Ulysses as pacifist, father, wanderer, musician, and artist, ties the hero's life closely to his own.'

In a 1906 letter to his brother Stanislaus he says: '... if I put a bucket into my own soul's well, sexual department, I draw up Griffith's and Ibsen's and Skeffington's and Bernard Vaughan's and St. Aloysius' and

Shelley's and Renan's water along with my own. And I am going to do that in my novel (*inter alia*) and plank the bucket down before the shades and substances above mentioned to see how they like it: and if they don't like it I can't help them. I am nauseated by their lying drivel about pure men and pure women and spiritual love for ever: blatant lying in the face of the truth.'[20] Ulysses has been controversial since its publication in 1922. The director of public prosecutions in Britain ensured its infamy by banning it as vulgar and obscene. The novel, acclaimed by the critics, finished by few readers, is a love letter to a city from an exile who could not live there. It offers another orthodoxy, a vindication of the nature which makes up its basic tenets: vulgarity and obscenity as hypocritical misnomers for humanity and sincerity.

Joyce's paradoxical temperament drove his several antagonistic aspects to the furthest limits of his personality, forcing him to be a completely different person on different occasions. The obvious example is to be found in his letters. Here, as he says himself, 'Some of it is ugly, obscene and bestial, some of it is pure and holy and spiritual' but he adds, 'all of it is myself'. The cultural and other pressures exercised upon him from early youth forced him into such a psychic bifurcation – the different parts of him which made up the 'all' of himself were scattered and diversified. Nora was the only person he ever met in his life whom he trusted fully. This meant that he was able to confide in her to the point of displaying all the most obscene and bestial impulses which had been driven to the frontiers and turned into perversions of their real meaning by the overbearing ethos of the time.

> As you know, dearest, I never use obscene phrases in speaking. You have never heard me, have you, utter an unfit word before others. When men tell in my presence here filthy or lecherous stories I hardly smile. Yet you seem to turn me into a beast. [3/12/09, p. 182]

The overall impression is of disconnection between the opposite poles of his make–up and a capacity to behave, under different circumstances, in a way that seems as opposite as Jekyll and Hyde. The most spiritual and lofty aspirations coincide with the most carnal and obscene thoughts and actions. The Jesuit Joyce and the seducer Stephen abide under the same roof. The one is petulant and almost prudish about other people using foul language or obscenities in his presence, the other is secretly writing letters to his 'whorish wife' Nora which are among the most scatological in the history of letter writing. Then, at a certain point in his life, this discordance melts away. The obscene passion dies out of him to such an extent that Lionel Trilling in his study of Joyce's letters suggests that although 'the substance of the marital correspondence at forty is not different from that of the twenties' there is a change in the quality of Joyce's passion and that this 'devolution from his early egotism of the world to the later egotism of nullity is a biographical event that asks for explanation'.[21] The biographical event which Trilling demands as explanation for the transformation of the scatology of Joyce's early letters is the eschatology of *Finnegans Wake*.

Joyce became the direct mouthpiece for such dislocated reality. Whether by disease or natural genius he was able to situate himself in a psychic dimension, which for others is only available in such unconscious states as sleep, and retain his consciousness sufficiently to allow expression of this dimension to filter through into a text. Jung calls this 'visceral thinking' (in which case he points to the presiding bodily organs in episodes of Ulysses as significant) or 'conversation in and with one's own intestines' which describes a process 'of almost universal "restratification" of modern man, who is in the process of shaking off a world that has become obsolete'.[22]

Gossip and scandal inside and outside the normally dull and unruffled stream of literary research have created an almost tabloid notoriety about the so-called 'dirty' letters of Joyce to Nora. These 'pornographic' letters were published in full by Richard Ellmann in *Selected Letters of James Joyce* which appeared in 1975. It is understandable that the couple's grandson, Stephen, should be affronted by the breach of privacy which publication of these letters entailed. These, in his view, were intimate, personal, private letters never intended for the public eye which have been sold and pirated in an intolerable shameless invasion of privacy. He has published his disapproval in a letter to the editor of the *International Herald Tribune* of 10 July 1984, where he names both Stanislaus Joyce's wife Nelly and Richard Ellmann as two of those who contributed to the publication of the letters.

Another Stephen takes a different view:

> –Bosh! Stephen said rudely. A man of genius makes no mistakes. His
> errors are volitional and are the portals of discovery. [Ulysses, 179]

Whatever about his grandson's reservations, the fact is that the
letters are now in the public domain and have become an essential part
of the mystery which it is our business to understand. These letters are
available in unexpurgated form in *The Selected Letters* referred to above.

In the introduction to that volume Ellmann says:[23] 'Frank as these
letters are, their psychology can easily be misunderstood. They were
intended to accomplish sexual gratification in him and inspire the same
in her, and at moments they fasten intently on peculiarities of sexual
behaviour, some of which might be technically called perverse. They
display traces of fetishism, anality, paranoia and masochism' but '[t]hen
too, the letters rebuke such obvious labels by an ulterior purpose; besides
the immediate physical goal, Joyce wishes to anatomize and reconstitute
and crystallize the emotion of love.'

Denis Donoghue introducing *The Golden Bowl* of Henry James[24]
gives insights and terminology helpful towards articulating the portals of
discovery being prised open in Joyce's scatological correspondence:
'there are no words for supernatural or otherwise sublime experiences;
there are only ordinary words, to which unusual pressure may be applied
in the hope of driving them beyond themselves.' The letters written to
Nora are made up of words 'to which unusual pressure' is applied. The
words are written with sexual energy. They ride like a ping–pong ball on
top of a fountain until they achieve the end for which they are designed:
orgasm for the author. Henry James, according to Donoghue, could
heighten the intensity of the words he used 'mainly by accumulating
qualifications and corrections of their complacency (xiii).' His writing of
such ordinary words transfigured these to unrecognisable imposture.
His brother William wished he would call a spade a spade. Was this novel
about adultery? 'Henry insisted on his freedom to move between the
accepted name of things and other possible forms of them which he
undertook, on authority entirely his own, to imagine (xiv).' After reading
The Golden Bowl we can never use the word 'adultery' with the same
smugness and self–evidence which the word possessed before its
dissection under the novelist's scalpel. 'James evidently felt confident

that he could make his last fictions not as a moralist but as a prophet; or a moralist in the sense – as we now see his programme – in which Neitzsche and Lawrence were prophets; imagining new forms of life rather than enforcing old ones (xvii).' *The Golden Bowl* transfigures the word 'adultery' into a new form of life as opposed to a relentless chloroforming category. Leavis finds this morally repellant and thinks that 'James had died to moral life in projecting it (xvii).' The same could be said for those 'portals of discovery' which Joyce's life and work were prising open. Civilisation at that time held up its hands in horror at the very suggestion of removing these hubcaps, at unscrewing the coverlids into such sewers.

The recently discovered letter, which is the first of the 1909 correspondence, was sold in Sotheby's 08/07/2004, for £240,000, a record price for literary memorabilia.[25] If indeed, as rumour suggests, it was found inside a copy of *Ulysses*, and was sold in a lot along with the telegram from Nora containing the last word (on), as well as of, Ulysses, with the leather pouch in which Joyce kept it on his person at all times, these coincidences point us in a certain direction if, one hundred years later, the prophetic words with which Ellmann opens his biography of Joyce are to be realised: 'We are still learning to be James Joyce's contemporaries, to understand our interpreter.'

The orthodoxy of the pearl versus the heresy of the opal. The ethics of the underground cathedral require inclusion of all aspects of our humanity. An exaggerated emphasis on the 'spiritual' and corresponding vilification of the carnal or physical; concentration upon self–contained identity (pearl) as contrasted with inescapable being–with–others as our inevitable situation in the world, has coloured our relationship with ourselves and with others from our very earliest contacts. Such an option for the pearl as opposed to the opal dictates that our role models and preferred heroes will be solitary, celibate, rugged and ascetic (usually) males. Those of us who cannot or will not embrace and realise these ideals will feel second–rate and frustrated. Such a programme towards perfection produces in us a repressive reflex with regard to the physical. We cultivate an ingrained fear and guilt about all bodily, especially sexual, self–expression.

Such ideals of virtue, however unrealistic and arbitrary they may be, can and do fashion certain exceptional individuals, do inspire exotic and awe–inspiring feats of asceticism, but these only promote in the ordinary lives of most people a despairing tension. Disregard for the emotional and sexual aspect of ourselves and the other–oriented structure of our bodies and personalities has two consequences: we develop the defence mechanisms and outer armour which allow us to survive in the desert without nourishment for our philanthropic appetites and we remain illiterate and undereducated in our relational faculties. Those who fail to become beautiful and impressive pearls or hermits have to stumble through the market–place of life guilty, insecure, awkward and angry.

While not condemning the valid and valuable vocation of the few to the contemplative life and the life of the hermit, the beauty of the pearl, those promoting the equally valid formation of the opal suggest that a life of contact and intimacy with others has its own rigours, discipline and demands, which we must be taught and we must learn to speak as a quite different and very specific language. The emotional and sexual sides of ourselves must be understood as an essential part of our human growth and development.

The most serious aspect of these divisions is the suggestion that Christian, especially Catholic orthodoxy is irrevocably aligned with the first of these attitudes. Christian teaching and principles, and therefore the belief structures of many people defend and support the primacy and purity of the pearl. Opals are at best fornicators, at worst heretics. If we are faced with a choice between supposedly 'Christian' values and more contemporary 'heretical' discoveries we create once again oppositions which were never meant to be pitted against each other, certainly not by the founder of Christianity, whose salvation was sent to reach the ends of the earth. These oppositions are entirely of our own making. No one has the right or the mandate to deprive Christianity of any aspect of our humanity. Everything we discover about ourselves should be integrated into our Christian anthropology.

Joyce's original intention, according to Ellmann, was to make the Penelope episode of *Ulysses* into a series of letters from Molly. The ease with which he wrote the episode in the summer and autumn of 1921 was owing to the delivery in March of Nora's obscene letters of 1909 which he had kept in a private and sealed briefcase. He had written to Ettore Schmitz in Italian (5 January 1921):

The Circe episode was finished some time ago. The Eumeus

episode, which is almost finished, will also be ready around the end of the month. According to the plan, *Ulysses* will appear there [New York] around 15 June next. Now for the important matter: I shall soon have used up the notes I brought with me here so as to write these two episodes. There is in Trieste in the quarter of my brother–in–law in the building bearing the political and registry number 2 of Via Sanità and located precisely on the third floor of the said building in the bedroom presently occupied by my brother, in the rear of the building in question, facing the brothels of public insecurity, an oilcloth briefcase fastened with a rubber band having the colour of a nun's belly and with the approximate dimensions of 95 cm. by 70 cm. In this briefcase I have lodged the written symbols of the languid sparks which flashed at times across my soul.

The gross weight without tare is estimated at 4.78 kilograms. Having urgent need of these notes for the last incident in my literary work entitled *Ulysses* or 'His Whore of a Mother', I address this petition to you, most honourable colleague, begging you to let me know if any member of your family intends to come to Paris in the near future, in which case I should be most grateful if the above–mentioned person would have the kindness to bring me the briefcase specified on the back of this sheet.

So, dear Signor Schmitz, if there is someone in your family who is travelling this way, he would do me a great favour by bringing me this bundle, which is not at all heavy since, you understand, it is full of papers which I have written carefully with a pen and at times with a bleistiff when I had no pen. But be careful not to break the rubber band because then the papers will fall into disorder. The best thing would be to take a suitcase which can be locked with a key so nobody can open it.

It seems clear from this letter, and Brenda Maddox[26] has built a convincing case to this effect, that the 'notes' for which he has an 'urgent need' in order to compose 'the last incident in my literary work entitled *Ulysses*' are indeed the scatological correspondence between himself and Nora which are 'the written symbols of the languid sparks which flashed at times across my soul.' 'Do you notice, he had written to Stannie [9 October 1906] how women when they write disregard stops and capital letters.'[27] And to Frank Budgen (10 December 1920) 'I am going to leave the last word with Molly Bloom – the final episode *Penelope* being written through her thoughts and body Poldy being then asleep.'[28] And again to Frank Budgen (16 August 1921):

> *Penelope* is the clou of the book. The first sentence contains 2500 words. There are eight sentences in the episode. It begins and ends with the female word yes. It turns like the huge earth ball slowly surely and evenly round and round spinning, its four cardinal points being the female breasts, arse, womb and cunt expressed by the words *because, bottom* (in all senses bottom button, bottom of the class, bottom of the sea, bottom of his heart), *woman, yes.* Though probably more obscene than any preceding episode it seems to me to be perfectly sane full amoral fertilisable untrustworthy engaging shrewd limited prudent indifferent *Weib. Ich bin der [sic] Fleisch der stets bejaht.*

Ellmann translates as 'I am the flesh that always affirms.' And says that 'Joyce is playing on Mephistopheles' identification of himself in Goethe's Faust Act I: 'I am the spirit that always denies.'[29]

The letters hold a secret key just as ALP's letter in *Finnegans Wake* tells the hidden truth about HCE and cryptogrammatically about the world in which we live. The world, created by the Word, is a conglomoration of 96 elements. *The Wake* created by Joyce is a conglomorate of words, combinations of 26 letters. Both these kaleidoscopes of world and Wake can be jostled towards readable configuration if we find the appropriate viewing–point, adjust the focus, and discover the key. The epitome of *Finnegans Wake* is a teastained letter about a woman who is a river, a man who is a city. Nora Barnacle knew that this was the important work: 'What's all this talk about Ulysses?' she said to Maria Jolas some time after her husband's death, '*Finnegans Wake* is the important book.'[30]

Joyce felt obliged to explain the ways of humankind to God. Having rejected the orthodoxy of the Catholic Church he embraced with passion and rigour the orthodoxy of humanity. He realized that there was more to humanity than Jesuit philosophy had ever dreamed of and he was determined to explore that reality. In this sense he was   a contemporary in spirit of the Surrealists, of Proust, of Freud, of Jung, of Rilke and those who sensed new dimensions opening up. Not that he was in anyway appreciative of his contemporaries. He despised Freud and Jung, for example, referring to them as Tweedledum and Tweedledee. He felt that they were pillaging a reality which artists alone were capable of expressing, and exploiting this for particular practical needs. They were reducing it to the limited categories of their own minds, whereas he was opening himself and allowing this reality to spread through him so that every organ, channel, category, or compartment, was flooded.

The reason why Joyce had to use the style he eventually forged for himself in *Finnegans Wake* is because 'one great part of every human existence is passed in a state which cannot be rendered sensible by the use of wideawake language, cut–and–dry grammar and go–ahead plot' as he wrote to Ezra Pound. Lionel Trilling holds that 'James Joyce, with his interest in the numerous states of receding consciousness, with his use of words which point to more than one thing, with his pervading sense of the interrelation and interpenetration of all things, and, not least important, his treatment of familial themes, has perhaps most thoroughly and consciously exploited Freud's ideas.'[31]

The ethics, or way of conducting one's life, of the underground cathedral which Joyce elucidated, sought to join heaven and earth, the body with all its urges and imperfections and the soul, sexuality and mysticism. In all of these he was not far distant from the ancient monks, whom we have come to know as the Desert Fathers:[32]

> We can appreciate why sexuality had come to bear so unaccustomed a weight among the finest exponents of the desert tradition …
> [T]he body, in which sexuality lurked with such baffling tenacity, had come to be viewed in the searching light of a new, high hope: "What is this mystery in me? What is the purpose of this mixture of body and Soul?" "Everyone should struggle to raise his clay, so to speak, to a place on the throne of God."[33]

> The desert became the powerhouse of a new culture. Origen's spirituality remained that of an urban study group … It was the precise meaning of Scripture, pondered by highly literate men and women, that caused the heart of the Christian 'to burn' … in The Life of Anthony and in successive layers of monastic spiritual

guidance, we can detect the emergence of an alternative. The monk's heart was the new book. What required infinitely skilled exegesis and long spiritual experience were 'movements of the heart,' and strategies and snares that the Devil laid within it.

Examination of the heart was not something to be undertaken on one's own. A suitable partner had to be found. 'Such movements were best conveyed orally to a spiritual father'.

The shift from a culture of the book to a *Cultura Dei* based largely on the non–literate verbal exchange of a monastic 'art of thought' was rightly hailed as the greatest and the most peculiar achievement of the Old Men of Egypt: it amounted to nothing less than the discovery of a new alphabet of the heart.

Joyce's life and work centred around the invention of such an alphabet of the heart. Not being a string of pearls it could only be a rosary of opals. It could not be constructed in his own mind. He had to find a partner whom he could trust wholeheartedly. This person would have to be one to whom he could pour out his heart unreservedly and to the dregs without fear of misunderstanding or rejection. Sexuality in this alphabet of the heart became a privileged ideogram.

You know how to give me a cockstand. Tell me the smallest things about yourself so long as they are obscene and secret and filthy. Write nothing else. Let every sentence be full of dirty immodest words and sounds. They are all lovely to hear and to see on paper even but the dirtiest are the most beautiful.

Write the dirty words big and underline them and kiss them and hold them for a moment to your sweet hot cunt, darling, and also pull up your dress a moment and hold them in under your dear little farting bum. Do more if you wish and send the letter then to me, my darling brown–arsed fuckbird. (9/12/09 p.186).

In the spirituality of the Desert Fathers 'Sexual desire revealed the knot of unsurrendered privacy that lay at the very heart of fallen man. Thus, in the new language of the desert, sexuality became an ideogram of the unopened heart.' Purity of heart was achieved by revealing to another the fullest extent of one's secret thoughts and desires. 'Sexual lapses were a fact of desert life. Monks were known to have become the fathers of sons. Older men harassed the novices ... Bestiality with the monastery's donkeys could not be ruled out' (p.230). The content of these thoughts and desires was as irrelevant as it was extravagant. The important thing was the trust and the humility which allowed you to express this fully to another person who then became your spiritual father, a father in the desert of the heart, the one who had the power to change that desert into a place of growth. 'The abatement of sexual fantasy in the heart of the monk – an abatement that was held to be accompanied, quite concretely, with a cessation of the monk's night emissions – signaled, in the body, the ascetic's final victory over the closed heart' (p 230). 'The sexuality of the emission created a disjunction between his public, daylight self and the last oasis of incommunicable, privatised experience' (p.231).

Finnegans Wake is 'nighttime emission' transfigured into absorbent language. The change which Lionel Trilling detects in Joyce from his earlier to his later correspondence with Nora is the result of his confessions to her and his transformation of the stuff of his deepest yearning into the creative word of his artistic work. Nora in this way was his spiritual guide. 'The aim of spiritual guidance,' in the spirituality of the desert was 'the total expropriation of the inner world of the disciple. The inner world must be turned inside out'. At this level sexual thoughts served as barium–traces, by which the Desert Fathers mapped out the deepest and most private recesses of the will. The correspondence between Joyce and Nora Barnacle is such a clearance of the Augean stables, a sharing of the deepest recesses of their wholehearted humanity. To reach the foundation beneath this grim reality, as Richard Ellmann suggests: 'They must share in shame, shamelessness, and unashamedness.'[34] What happened between them at the level of private correspondence a hundred years ago must take place at the level of public national consciousness today if we are to become Joyce's contemporaries, if we are to really understand our interpreter.

The last chapter of *Ulysses*, the Circe episode, which was originally envisaged as letters from Molly Bloom is certainly indebted to the scatological correspondence between Joyce and his wife. Her letters to him which seem not to have survived would appear to provide the substance of the text itself, transformed by the artist into literary form.

A further transformation seems to have taken place in and through the composition of *Finnegans Wake*. The cerebrospinal system which normally provides the channel for writing in our civilisation, is here anaesthetised, mostly through the daily imbibing of large quantities of Joyce's favourite wine: Fendant de Sion. This Swiss white wine he referred to as either electricity or *Orina d'un'arciduchessa* (urine of an archduchess). Having diverted the normal channels to the brain he was then able to engage the nervous and sympathetic system directly by accomplishing an intensity of authorship akin to the excitement of masturbatory word secretion issuing from the unconscious self. The double pression thus exercised caused the language to squirt onto the page in new and unprecedented shapes and forms.

The artist of language in this capacity is the guardian and shepherd of being as it expresses itself through the traces of all recorded human utterance, the anatomy of language. 'When the call comes, he shall produce nichthemerically from his unheavenly body a no uncertain quantity of obscene matter ... with this double dye brought to blood heat ... through the bowels of his misery ... this first till last alshemist wrote over every square inch of the only foolscap available, his own body, till by its corrosive sublimation one continuous present tense integument slowly unfolded all marryvoising moodmoulded cyclewheeling history.'[35] The artist 'reflecting from his own individual person life unlivable' creates a text 'transaccidentated through the slow fires of consciousness' which is 'perilous, potent' and 'common to allflesh'.[36] Language here is 'the squidself which he had squirtscreened from the crystalline world' of the unconscious. It becomes a history of our unconscious life.

Such a use of language allows Joyce to 'psing a psalm of psexpeans, apocryphul of rhyme' (FW 242) which exploits every aspect of the syllables which compose the words, 'for to concentrate solely on the literal sense or even the psychological content of any document to the sore neglect of the enveloping facts themselves circumstantiating it is just as hurtful to sound sense ...' (FW 109). This is not a scientific use of language which would translate reality into clear–cut and unambiguous terms. It is a surpassing of the principle of non–contradiction by a supralogical use of words, each one containing at least 'two thinks at a time'. (FW 583) The pun, in Tindall's phrase, is mightier than the word because it uses the referential medium of sound to spark off correspondences simultaneously tangential to those suggested by the shapes. The artist of such a language does not fly in a cerebral fashion over the forest of language, he situates himself in the thick of the jungle and hacks away at the roots of vocables until he reaches that 'root language' which holds 'the keys of me heart' (FW 626). He has learnt to produce 'nichtthemerically' (a word that combines the ideas of 'night–time,' 'nonthematic' and 'numerically') 'from his unheavenly body.' And this unheavenly body is source of the only orthodoxy he is willing to endorse. Salvation which bypasses or supersedes blood–and–guts physiology is sham. Unless some correspondence is devised between ourselves as we imagine ourselves to be, and ourselves as we have been revealed so painfully to ourselves to be, in recent relentlessly ubiquitous and all–pervading scandals of abusiveness, there can be little hope for humanity of the future.

K

My correspondence with Brendan Kennelly dates from 1984. I had written a review of *Cromwell* for the *Irish Literary Supplement*. He wrote to me (8/3/1984):

What can I say? You seem to have struck very close to the heart of the poem, and to have done so with the sort of energy that can come only from accepting that sympathy, hard to define, that most critics are afraid of because they want to be 'intelligent.' I feel, after reading your article a few times, that I understand the poem better. And yet to be truthful I have never worried about this – being more interested in the 'victim – victor blood' of the last piece than in any 'understanding.' So much of understanding as we blandly accept the term is only distortion – a way of releasing ourselves from the deeper pain of experience. I think Cromwell is about that pain of experience, the experience of daring to use the mind to nail the dream because in itself this nailing may be a sin, a genuine obscurity.

You're right about challenging poetry – I mean the very act, the arrogance of writing, the implicit criminality of the 'creative process,' that sense of violation at the heart of expression.

What right have we to 'fiddle' with God's dream of us? If there is a right, it is generated by our own human (here, English and Irish) capacity for obscurity, all the ongoing time–defying commitment to the spread of that pain which it is pain to contemplate. I said the poem is imagistic, but its more accurate to say that it is contemplation of, and through images, of things otherwise unthinkable.

There are two streams of Irish poetry. One might be called poetry of the singing head; the other, of the singing heart. The first has been strengthened by a mainstream European tradition and our composing in English. The second stems from an older, wilder oral tradition. Brendan Kennelly belongs to this garrulous and untrammelled company of bards.

Fionn Mac Cumhaill, the Irish mythological hero, was once in the service of a giant. So successful was he at his job that the giant gave him his ring to wear. The ring was so tight that he could not take it off his finger once he had put it on. Later they had a row and Fionn blinded the giant. The giant begins to chase our hero to kill him. *'A fhainne, ca bhuil tu?'* (Where are you, my ring?), he calls out. And the ring answers: *'Táim anseo ar mhéar Fhinn Mhic Chumhaill.'* (I am here on the finger of Fionn Mac Cumhaill.') The giant gets nearer to Fionn. Fionn cuts off the finger with the ring, and throws it into the deepest lake in Ireland. The giant calls out again. The ring answers from the depths of the lake. The giant follows and is drowned.[37] Such is the relationship between Ireland and Brendan Kennelly. Kennelly's capacity to strip himself and fight in naked combat with the giants that plague us, make him Ireland's most endearing and reckless poet. His overriding quality is generosity, from which both his strengths and his weaknesses derive:[38]

> The flaws in my writing, which are considerable, have to do with spontaneity ... I would cite my native flaw as someone who transfers from an oral tradition to a written tradition.

'Poetry returns again and again to the same themes, like a ghost compelled to return and haunt endlessly a house that symbolizes everything it has known and loved' he says in the Preface to his *Selected Poems* in 1969.[39] Although he believes that 'what matters is vision and the uniqueness of vision,' he is opposed to authoritarian creeds, doctrinaire philosophies, dogmatism of any kind. 'Poetry must always be a flight from this deadening authoritative egotism'.[40] The poet, as visionary, is 'riddled with different voices, many of them in vicious conflict'. The poet provides in his/her person an arena, an acoustic chamber, where every voice can be heard. The democracy of imagination uses this humble, neutral parliament to 'speaksing' its 'individual stories'. The matter for debate coincides with the recurring obsessions of the poet who presides over the hearing. He summarises these in the 1990 collection in terms of power: 'power in love, religion, education, politics, work.' The aim of the debate is to achieve 'vision' which is no less than 'an attempt to make sense out of the world'. The poetry issuing from this process caresses the poet's 'bewilderment into intensely lucid personal knowledge'.

Kennelly gives us a guided tour of the process as it happened in the creation of, perhaps, his most famous and most anthologized poem 'My Dark Fathers'. A talk given by Frank O'Connor on the effects of the Famine on the Irish character; a woman of fifty who dances on the Kerry shore; perhaps the most frightening consequence of the famine in Ireland, the death of music and dance. A man named Paddy who put his wife's feet inside his shirt against his bosom to warm them before they both died of starvation; the pit or communal grave used to bury famine victims. 'These images of the pit, the woman, the rows of dead, the terrible silence, were on my mind.' Then, shortly afterwards, he was at a wedding where a boy was asked to sing. He did so with his face turned to the wall, his back to the audience. In his averted figure, the poet saw Ireland as a place where art has been repudiated by historical and sociological disaster, yes, but also through censorship, apathy, complacency and ignorance. Out of these images and this realisation the poem was born. If it has achieved the 'clarity' which the poet hopes for it, then this is what it 'means.' If the poet has been true to his craft, then 'no human being can say exactly what a poem means. Only the poem can say that'.[41]

So, what entitles or qualifies him to speak for 'otherness'? Is he not also irretrievably consigned to his own identity? One of the sources of self–knowledge that leads beyond self to what is other than self is one's past as 'savage educator' of one's present. In an interview[42] he admits that 'your own trouble – whether alcoholism, depression or whatever – is the biggest kind of education'.[42]

But it is not enough to suffer or to descend in one's own life to the depths of human misery and despair with however fine a sensibility and capacity for self–expression. The secret of otherness is in the gift of self. Kennelly is a poet because he has understood in the depths of his being that poetry is language speaking through him. He is not the master of language; he is, in a certain sense, its victim. Poetry is the inversion of the usual relationship between us and language. The strange task of the poet is to listen and to empty him or her self so that language itself can speak. The greater the poetry the purer the capacity to hear, the more scrupulously untrammelled the acoustic chamber.

At every stage of his poetic career, Kennelly has both acknowledged and celebrated this 'giveness' of poetry. His 1990 collection begins with the 'Gift' and ends with 'Am'. As poet he *is* that gift. And 'I give therefore I am' is the nature of the poet: 'I spill / Myselves'. Poetry is essentially 'The Gift' and the poet is essentially a beggar who never appropriates the source of what can only be understood by the receiving of it. The essence of poetry is hearing accurately and then letting go.

His obsession with otherness finds its most demanding and appropriate protagonists in Oliver Cromwell and Judas Iscariot, archetypal enemy and icon of apostasy in the Roman Catholic Irish psyche:[43]

> I don't think any Irishman is complete as an Irishman until he becomes an Englishman, imaginatively speaking. I was reared to hate and fear Cromwell, the legends, the folklore of my own parish, the unquestioning hatred of him, which was then transferred to England. That appalled me when I began to try to think … Cromwell is an ordinary experiment in my own psyche: that I am giving voice to a man who made trees wither. The worst thing you can say in the part of the country I grew up in is 'the curse of Cromwell on you' and I wanted to turn that curse into a blessing.

One thing this poem shows for certain: Kennelly has got guts. And a large portion of these are served up here. The book is not for the squeamish.[44]

The two major characters, Cromwell and Buffún, are like the villain and the clown in a pantomime: Frankenstein/Faustus versus Falstaff/Sancho Panza. The imagery is violent and sexual, jerky and iconoclastic. The language is stark, crude and, at times, shockingly funny. We could almost shrug off the responsibility to face up to it by declaring it off–limits as some kind of video nasty. But, after the initial shock, we find it doing something dangerous but decisive. As Kennelly suggests in his introductory 'measures':[44] 'The butcher walked out the door of my emptiness, straight into me.'

The poem itself seizes Kennelly, assumes his character and through him reveals this 'glittering darkness.' 'I do not want this dream but it dreams me.' (C 101) Nothing in our tradition or culture can provide a method or the equipment necessary to describe such a visitation. Kennelly's craft and practice have served him well in netting this shoal of nocturnal images. He has heaved them out of the depths into enduring shapes, which allow the rest of us to see.

Our nothingness, according to the poem, is defined by hatred. This hatred is paralysing and corrosive. Although we may think that we have an identity which allows us take our place among the nations, we have been reduced to that saliva of resentment which keeps regenerating itself in our throats, in our culture. Our high–sounding words about 'Irishness' are hypocrisy which helps us to swallow the self–perpetuating spittle which panic keeps pumping.

> 'Jesus Christ! burst Cromwell, 'I saw this spit
> Right in the main street of Caherciveen.
> I nearly threw up at the sight of it.
> As you may realize, I have seen
> A few things to make any man throw up
> But this black yellow slimey spreading heap
> of muck was, in any tongue, the last straw. (C 82)

This substance of ourselves 'echoing curses soaked in verbal bile' gives us a psychic size, shape, smell. We have developed a stooping, pain–expectant gait: (C 102):

> Propelled, as ever, by this electric sense of wrong
> That I cannot define but cherish, nevertheless.
>
> I have an enemy somewhere, that's for sure.

And this energy of hatred and self–pity releases a spoor in our orbit which attracts any Cromwell within striking distance. Not just Cromwell as an historic figure, but as ever existing counterpart to such a psyche. In other words, the relationship between Cromwell and Ireland is kinkily symbiotic: 'Our destinies are mingled, late and soon'(C 101).

> I hate and fear you like the thought of hell.
> I can never hate you enough. That is my shame.
> Every day I pray that I may hate you more.(C 103)

This alienating deformity makes the cromwellian settlement a permanent and incurable feature of the Irish psyche.

With Cromwell behind him and eight years of 'clearing a space,' Kennelly moves to the other archetypal enemy: Judas. *The Book of Judas*[45] is a 378-page epic, which combines a labour of Hercules with a forgotten book of the New Testament. The 'labour' is cleaning the stables in the Irish psyche and rehabilitating a scapegoat who has been the convenient peg for all our treacherous hang–ups.

Christianity in Ireland, and Kennelly believes 'that the culture of these islands is, broadly speaking, Christian', has developed into such a simplified version of the original that 'this culture is now in an advanced state of self–parody. Or, if you wish, in an advanced state of self–betrayal, playing Judas to itself' (J 9). Christy Hannity (Christianity as 'he' has become in Ireland), is Judas, 'the most accomplished castrator of God's creatures in our pious island' (J 333).

The oversimplification is partly the refusal to admit the necessity of exploring our underground sewer. Christian hypocrisy in this regard is a betrayal of essential humanity. Are we not, as Judas possibly was, 'a shrewd refuser of what might have made him loveable and vulnerable?' The obstruction of an essential part of our make–up, its oversimplified and sterilized caricature and banishment, inevitably creates a lawless untrammelled underworld where parts of us live on in dangerously schizophrenic isolation. The poem gives tongue to the Judasphere:

> Got a job in the sewers. With
> Helmet gloves rubber clothes flashlamp
> I went down below Dublin
> From Kingsbridge into O'Connell Street
> Flashin' me lamp in the eyes o' rats
> Diabolical as tomcats. Rats don't like light
> In their eyes. (J 43–44)

We have to marvel at the almost unlimited capacity of this poet to act as ventriloquist, in the original Latin sense of 'speaking from the belly', to evacuate these inner spaces:[46]

> And clear a space for himself
> Like Dublin city on a Sunday morning
> About six o'clock
> Dublin and myself are rid of our traffic then
> And I am walking.

After Brendan Kennelly had read my essay on his Book of Judas, he wrote me a letter including the following:

> The most revealing criticism for me is the kind that, while I'm reading it, begins to read me. After I'd read your essay a few times I began to realise you knew more about the poem than I did, and much more about the strange dreams, at once shadowy and obsessive, it came out of and seemed always to be passing through and, despite moments of lucidity, drowning back into. The second thing (it necessarily follows from your deeper knowledge) is the sense of the presence of the power I constantly sought and sometimes seemed to achieve in startling ways, even shocking ways, – the sense of connection. Once one dispels the illusions rampant in chronology, one is at the mercy of various intensities – 'Before Abraham was, I am' – the real presence is the eternal presence – reality is eternal is now – and these intensities are sane and connective – well, sanity is connection – and you connect the basic intensities on which the poem is built with charming (in the true sense of that word) clarity. Good criticism partakes of magic as much as good poetry; and the hypnotic sense of order in your perceptions has its own charms. You read the poem with wondrous attention and made it real for me again. How can one give years to something and then find it becomes a dream which one witnesses in daylight as if one were a complete stranger to it? Thank you for bidding me into the presence of the poem as something real again.

Ace de Horner is the poet in the collection *Poetry My Arse*, which among other things, is an epic poem about Dublin as a post–colonial city, and about poetry as blind tapping in the dark, 'often wearing a mask of boisterousness, in what is probably the most garrulous city in Christendom.'[47] 'His life is a fierce healing of a disease he never understood' (p.58) and his poetry is 'the perfect no–ending to a story forever incomplete' (p.134). He travels around Dublin with a ferocious pitbull terrier called Kanooce, who, as energetic, violent, carnivorous brute, represents the 'severed emotional' predator in most of us.

Poetry is again an autonomous river of language. The poet is syphon of 'sound bubbling up out of infinite emptiness' (p.209) and the poems are 'swirling bobbiting Dionysiac bubbles' (p.345). Language is the creator of this poetry. Unlike the poets of the *bien fait* tradition of stolid craftmanship this is linguistic madness ('shameless madness singing beyond itself' (p.201)) or lingual possession, where the river of language takes over control of the poet. 'Some who play with words may never know/ how words may play with them' (p.142). Poetry has to reappropriate and rehabilitate words which have become unacceptable in a genteel society of bourgeois hypocrites. There must be such a word as 'spiritfuck' and no word should be off-limits to the 'beastmanpoet' who has to 'swim through spittle to freedom' (p.331). The task of this kind of poetry to turn 'the geography of darkness' into 'a map of freedom' (p.334).

To achieve this poetry of nothingness the first thing to be got out of the way is the head. It has to be 'split open …' 'till his head/ was a pure clean wound bleeding shyly' (p.335). Having achieved this existence as nobody, the poet has to transcend the self go 'through it and out the other side'. 'By the way,' he asked, 'who are you?'/ 'Me?' I replied. 'Nobody. I'm just passing through.' (p.276)

When he 'passes through' to the 'other side' he is taken over by the river of language. He becomes its spokesperson. And 'poetry has a life of its own' … 'the life that had the right to breathe in its own/ way, not his'. He has to prepare himself to be 'the river he would become …' (p.214).

12/10/1996: 'I could see the creative act of attention you pay to what poems are trying to explore. And your idea of dialogue is the quintessence of sanity and grace in this manjungle … You do in criticism what I try to do in verse – make these connections which, unmade, seem ludicrously unthinkable and, made, a new kind of light. It is a tingling experience to read criticism that sees through and true and even has in it (or so I believe, and am delighted by) moments of laughter. But it is your thinking power of bold connection that makes your writing exhilarating, a network of perceptions, a dialogue with poetry at the edge of the cliff or the mad blackness of the backyard where the rats gather to invade the cradle. The dialogue gets the poetry talking to your philosophy which listens patiently and hears clearly – then speaks out to shape what it has heard from the poetry but also from itself because of that electricity of connection. Even dialogue then begins to sound like *one* voice, new and vigorous freshly lonely, embarking on its own journey. This voice-journey becomes 'criticism,' making its way through attention-paying minds. Your whole approach is an act of attention to mindlife, that rage and calm, that dark fury and seated restfulness … I think your book will be a bit of a revolution. It has its roots in service and its aim is mastery.'

19/2/1998: ' To say so much in so few pages is quite astonishing, but even more so is the sense I get that you have said, more clearly and more powerfully, what I was trying to say in the poems. Is it that the philosopher can distil, can extract the essence of poetry in a tight, concise, dynamic way ? Some of your lines contain chapters. Its like walking into and through a forest, and walking back out into the light with the secret of trees in your fist.'

One of the first invitations I received when I began walkabout in the Holy Spirit in earnest was to address the Brendan Kennelly Summer School in Ballylongford in July 2002 on *A Man Made of Rain*.

Kenosis is a word which can be used to describe the essential characteristic of both Brendan Kennelly and his poetry. It is a Greek word and a theological term to describe the 'self–empying' which allowed God to become a human being, to be made flesh, to become one with us: body and soul. Again, in the preface to his *Selected Poems*[48] of 1969 he described his work as 'an attempt to express some kind of personal philosophy,' to 'try to define the nature of personal vision'. Although he believes that 'what matters is vision and the uniqueness of vision' this did not mean religious vision as such. Twenty years later in his 1990 collection of selected poems, he says that the poet, as visionary, is 'riddled with different voices, many of them in vicious conflict'. The aim of the debate is to achieve 'vision' which is no less than 'an attempt to make sense out of the world'.[49]

I have read most of what this poet has written. I have published articles about himself and his work,[50] about his poem Cromwell,[51] and about his Book of Judas,[52] I have been in correspondence with him for about twenty years, so it is not as any naïve interloper that I tell you and, indeed him, that having lived with, what I consider to be his most important book of poetry, over the last five years, I recognise in it, what I have written about extensively in a book called *The Haunted Inkwell*,[53] God's gift to him in return. This is certainly poetry of 'vision'.

At the launch of *The Man Made of Rain* I could not believe that the poet was asking me who 'he' was – who on earth could he be – The Man Made of Rain?

The Man Made of Rain records a vision which the poet had the day after his operation for a quadruple bypass. The book records an out of the body experience after major heart surgery. He saw at the end of his bed the day after he woke from the anaesthetic, a man made of rain:[54]

> Isn't it always raining
> in North Kerry, that's where the snipe
> wear wellingtons and swallows from Africa
> swim through the summer. (MMR 54)

The poem is a map, 'a wonderplan' (MMR 58), a physiognomy, an autopsy of a presence: 'He taught me the meaning of presence, what it means to be truly and fully in somebody's presence, a process of complete dreamsurrender to another's emotional and intellectual reality at its most articulate and vital' (MMR 7). This 'real' presence haunted the poet. 'The man made of rain would not leave me ... until I let his presence flow in the best and only poem I could write for him' (MMR 9). So, whatever we think of this poem, it's the best we're going to get and the only one of its kind. It is a trace left behind, a presence.

> 'Don't worry if you lose sight of me,' says
> > the man of rain,
> 'Something of me lingers
> where I am not.' (MMR 31)

Kennelly by default has become a witness of the resurrection of the body. 'When he happened my world outgrew itself' (MMR 33).

Resurrection of the body is nothing more or less than:
A human being
longing
to flow forever,
to pour forever, yet be contained (MMR 33).

The poem is about love and love as 'a singing wound' which is the way
the body endures into eternity.

'What is my body?'
'What is my blood?'

The occasion of this presence is the very physical operation on the heart
which the poet underwent in 1997. An evocative painting of Louis le
Brocquy on the cover called 'Isolated Being' acts as a visual aid.

The series opens like a wound with questions that reiterate the
words of consecration reenacting the real presence of the quadruple
bypass on Calvary. The wounds of Christ are the bypass to eternity. The
Latin word for wound is the same as our word for vulnerability. This
poem is a eucharistic prayer, a prayer of thanksgiving.

The task of writing such a poem is like screwing the poet's head into
a light socket, replacing the bulb, which should transform the electric
current into manageable wattage, which can then spread domesticated
light throughout the living room. The tiny head is asked to contain such
voltage and replace for the time being a nuclear transformer. 'It's a light
striding sound' (MMR 31). It can only be done while the heart is being
by–passed.

It was a time when I'd no words
but I let him happen
to me as he
had pleaded

And he poured through me
with a look
with a smile
with a line

not mine, although I witness it, not mine.

Kennelly has always been the most generous of men. Generosity is the analogical attribute he identifies with God. He had to wait until he was sixty to actually have his own heart cut open, employ 'a knife with a mind of its own to stab cut and save my life' so that he could 'thank the heart of sickness for the man of rain' (MMR 94).

> I said, 'There's no way
>> I could ever say
>> You.'
>
>> 'Say I'm the lost spirit–currency
>>> you found
>>> and are learning to spend.
>
>> 'Say I could be your friend.' (MMR 24)

The man of rain is resurrected bodiliness, what comes after the opening up of the heart, it is the possibility for each one of us having shuffled off this mortal coil. All of us as human beings are 'dying into wonder beyond wonder' (MMR 58). The man made of rain is pleading to us: 'Let me happen to you. Let me happen to you'. It is what happens when we allow ourselves to rise from the dead. Meanwhile 'solid bodies walk unresolved,/ trapped in their solidity.' (MMR 66) The only thing between us and resurrection is ourselves:

> I wanted to rise and follow quickly
> but something heavier than the world prevented me,
> whispering, Stay, you cannot do without me. (MMR 60)
>
> My flesh is hot and thick.
>
> Past, present, future. The three–card trick. (MMR 61)

Flesh is 'a kind of everything waiting to be nothing' (MMR 60) And if it accepts to be nothing it can be transformed. Flesh can become 'a garden/ where love walks and meditates on all/ that is not itself but may yet be part/ of itself' (MMR 31).

And yet flesh is an essential part of what we are and of what resurrection is and of what poems must be:

> [M]eanwhile the man of rain sits
> on the edge of the bed, he suggests
> a flick of the brain from flesh to rain,
> from solid to flowing, I try to comply
>
> I know that smile, he's taking the side
> of flesh right now, backing the way it is
> supporting the way we flourish and rot from day
>
> to day, that's the secret, out in the open,
> but nothing's out in the open, not completely, his smile
> supports that too, it's a necessary style,
>
> he always has mercy on style which must
> exist if flesh is to continue
> its long adventure through bone and sinew,
>
> itself, as it is, now.
>
> It's a matter of time.
>
> Give me the courage
> To rise and flow with the tide. (MMR 64)
>
> Rain is like praise, it flows everywhere, like music.
>
> My rain is music, can you hear it?
>
> Let your music out, let my music in. (MMR 71)

'Love is particular and fluent' (MMR 91). It is first person singular, present tense. The man made of rain is Brendan Kennelly at his very best.

In 2003 I was invited to preach before the University of Dublin,

Trinity College, on Trinity Monday, 12 May. The words given to me on this occasion were these:

'On this day in 1911 the first non–stop flight from London to Paris took almost four hours.

On this same day in 1961, 50 years later, the Russian cosmonaut Yuri Gagarin became the first human being to orbit the earth. His journey lasted 108 minutes.

'Progress?

Yapping, he can't stop yapping, sitting,
walking on his own.
He is a mobile phone ...[55]

Commemoration and thanksgiving are eucharistic exercises, works of the Holy Spirit. Only those inspired can actually tell us what happened. Anamnesis, epiclesis, the liturgical experts confound us with words.

The Spirit of truth will make it known to you.

Only the Spirit of truth can reveal what actually happened. The rest is stereotype.

The past is inaccessible to us as is the future. Everything we do is a mystery beyond our comprehension. The mystery of the past like the mystery of the future are dimensions which we do not understand:

The most trivial experience ... is imprisoned in a vase filled with a certain perfume and a certain colour and raised to a certain temperature. These vases are suspended along the height of our years, and, not being accessible to our intelligent memory, are in a sense immune, the purity of their climatic content is guaranteed by forgetfulness, each one is kept at its distance, at its date'.[56]

Samuel Beckett who wrote those words would have been 97 years old tomorrow, if he had lived, and if we are to believe his birth certificate.

Facts and figures. Facts and figures, we are told, matter only to those who have never really lived. What, then, is life beyond my perception of it?

On this day in 1866, the trustees of the College of California gathered on a hillside overlooking the Pacific Ocean. Below them were 200,000 acres of clear land that would one day become the University of California. One trustee recalled a poem by Bishop Berkeley. Moved by the moment, the others agreed to name their town-to-be after the bishop. Who now remembers, who gives thanks?

> Some truths there are so near and obvious to the mind that a man need only open his eyes to see them. Such I take this important one to be, to wit, that all the choir of heaven and the furniture of earth, in a word all those bodies which compose the mighty frame of the world, have not any subsistence without a mind, that their *being* is to be perceived.[57]

Esse est percipi ... Is it? We've had 250 years to work it out.
 'Progress?

> Progress is another name for now
> Yet when I try to imagine grace
> I glimpse a young man, tiring,
> who said he always made
> an awkward bow.[58]

Commemoration. Memory. We give thanks for the newly opened Usher Library. It is part of the work of a university to provide a memory bank, especially for a nation suffering in the main from amnesia and, in part, from selective recall.

Thanksgiving is another matter. It requires a High Priest and the appropriate anaphora. Fortunately for us all you have both in this hallowed place. And so:

> I take the mystery of giving in my hands
> And pass it on to you.

> I give thanks
> To the giver of images
> The reticent god who goes about his work
> Determined to hold on to nothing.

> I give thanks

I listen to the sound of doors
Opening and closing in the street.
They are like the heartbeats of this creator who gives everything
away.
I do not understand
Such constant evacuation of the heart,
Such striving towards emptiness.

It is this little
That I give to you
And now I want to walk out and witness
The shadow of some ungraspable sweetness
Passing over the measureless squalor of man
Like a child's hand over my own face
Or the exodus of swallows across the land

And I know it does not matter
That I do not understand.'[59]

3 June 2004: Brendan Kennelly posts me from Trinity College a copy of
his *New and Selected Poems 1960-2004*.[60] 'I hope you enjoy dipping into
the years of this book which blew my head to assemble. I hadn't realised
the power of poetry to make one re-live. Living is one thing. But
Re–living is a fascinating, challenging, troubling, uplifting thing.'

L

This last section of the middle alphabet is correspondence during the walkabout with Louis le Brocquy.

23/03/03:

Dear Mark Patrick,

Sometime around the month of January I happened to turn on the car radio, and there you were before me! I questioned again – as I believe both Joyce and Jung were inclined to – the nature of coincidence. What affected me most, I think, was the sudden presence of your spirit.

A stupid head-first fall I had six weeks ago has not helped, but I hope to be back at work next month.

The episode, however reminds me of previous thoughts, thoughts shared by Anne, that we might ask you whether you might perhaps consider saying a few words at some ceremony following my death when it does arrive?

On the whole we both favour the background of St Patrick's Cathedral, primarily because of my mother's interest in Swift (her books, *Cadeus* and *Swift's Most Valuable Friend* are to be published again in one volume by Lilliput shortly.) Maybe, too, the choice is vaguely ecumenical, embracing that larger Christian message which I accept with all my heart.

Let me know very frankly what you might feel about this.

Meanwhile much love from us both.

Louis

25 March, 2003, Feast of the Annunciation:

Dearest Louis,

Synchronicity! My life has been a following of this reality from September of last year. I am on walkabout in the Spirit, searching for a new consciousness which I sense is trying to emerge. I am going wherever the Spirit prompts and keeping a log–book of what happens. It has been very wonderful and I am both humbled and awestruck by the concatination of coincidences, God's way of working anonymously.

And so, ten days ago on Martha's Vineyard I was watching with Fanny Howe a video on Samuel Beckett. You appear on the screen speaking about your friend. This morning, as your letter arrives, Fanny's does also asking me to write something about her forthcoming book, *The Wedding Dress.*

The Millennium Spire in O'Connell Street, completed this year, was likened by its architect to the spire of an underground cathedral. It does seem to preside over an alternative cathedral hewn from the underworld. I see Joyce on a side street squinting up at it and then Francis Bacon from his studio, now in the Hugh Lane Gallery so appropriately. Sam Beckett and yourself make up the pillars of this new foundation. Of course, Yeats and Swift are there and so many wonderful women we are beginning to hear about. So, I agree with St Patrick's Cathedral as the older site of a 'vaguely ecumenical' possibility 'embracing that larger Christian message' which we both accept and promote with our lives and work. Our generation has been privileged to breathe the air of this planet with so many warriors of the spirit: your depiction of these, their noble heads, does much permanent justice to their struggle. You yourself are the great warrior painter in their midst.

April 2003:

Little did I think when I wrote to you that you could respond with such generous reassurance and sympathy as to encourage me to believe that my life and work might be seen on the whole as positive. This in itself means much to me, haunted as I am by regrets and thoughtless inadequacy in the past.

All the more do I rejoice in your own on-going 'walk-about in the Spirit.' And wish you well in what our mutual friend, Seamus, referred to as this 'knowledge-freshening wind.'

I like the architect's description of his spire and your Dante-esque vision of those great spirits 'squinting up at it' (but leave me out of this distinguished equation.)

Dear Patrick, there is no question of our discussing any content within your wonderfully concerned acceptance of my request. Let us leave all that in grateful silence on my part.

10 September 2003:

Dear Louis,

After your invitation to me to speak at your funeral in St Patrick's Cathedral – I knew, when the initial shock dissipated, that this was a prompting from the Spirit to understand what your life's work is essentially about. Several previous hints during the year had indicated that necessity. And so I spent some time this summer looking at all the paintings (so beautifully reproduced in various books and catalogues which you have sent me over the years) and reading the dossier of those who have written about these works. And so I enclose the log–book of this exploration which I have found so worthwhile and so connected to my own life's journey, especially during this particular year which has been given over to walkabout in the Holy Spirit. 'You don't have to do anything' I was told, 'whatever is significant will be pointed out to you'.

Coincidences: I also went to St Gerard's school in Bray, although some years after you. Anne quotes you as saying there: 'I am on my own' (p.14) which is the meaning of 'monos' the word for a monk. She says you were 'religiously inclined, secretly believing (you) would become a monk' (p.16). And you did become a monk. The secret of this is described by Thomas Kinsella: 'There are certain staying qualities that help an artist to major achievement. The gift of concentration is one (in the sense of economy as well as of intensity), and so is steady energy. Le Brocquy has these qualities to a degree unique among Irish painters or designers since the death of Jack B. Yeats. He also has that individual force stemming from tireless curiosity, which gives coherence to a career – the kind of force that insists on artistic growth, or change, and ensures that any stimulus, however seemingly random, finds a central response.' This capacity to allow any stimulus to find a central response is one I share with you as a monk. This year, I was told by a visionary woman, as I followed the path of the Spirit, I would not have to search myself, but the essential things would be pointed out to me; I would only have to recognise and record these. Certain coincidences would map the path. In this instance, there was our meeting at the funeral of Dorothy Walker; then there was a video about Beckett which I saw with Fanny Howe on Martha's Vineyard, in which you appear along with her mother, Mary Manning. The three part exhibition of Anne's 12 doves, her talk on the artist's way, and the video of her transfiguration in blue of the church in the south of France. Your 'Isolated Being' on the cover of Brendan Kennelly's *Man Made of Rain*: these were some of the preludes to this journey through your work which I here annotate.

THE WHITE LABYRINTHS OF LOUIS LE BROCQUY

'We Irish, born into that ancient sect
But thrown upon this filthy modern tide
And by its formless spawning fury wrecked
Climb to our proper dark, that we may trace
The lineaments of a plummet–measured face'.
W. B. Yeats.

'I wish to be the maker of a new sign of my inner movement,
for in me is the path of the whole world'. Malevich.

You must have been one of the loneliest persons in Ireland from the beginning of the new state. Born at its birth in 1916 you were and are a seer among the visually impaired. This solitude, which is not so much solitary confinement or any active effort on the part of your co–habitants on the planet, results from an innate gift of X–ray vision, which allows you alone to see the skeleton where everyone else is looking at the smiling face.

Some are born into dysfunctional families which gives them forever the excuse for being dysfunctional themselves. You were born into a family, *tout court*, with nothing to shield you from that fact. 'I am the son of a man and a woman' as Lachelier noted at the age of 26, 'that disappoints me, I thought I was a little more than that.'

Travelling people, prisoners condemned to death, these are marginalised exceptions for most of us; for you they were the norm: human existence writ large.

Meeting Anne some 40 years later allowed that solitude to become cradle of genius.

John Russell picks this up: They lived in 'a sophisticated hermitage' 'a place of retreat and concentration in which the news of art has no one local tinge'.

Here your 'leprosy' was given miraculous fruitfulness; the albino was allowed full scope for achromatism: 'When whiteness was the rule and all else the exception ... Louis le Brocquy was laying seige to whiteness ... traps sprung in stillness'.

'And then just white, the thought of white' (Beckett's *Watt*). 'A white thought in a white shade' made you the intrepid explorer of those arctic regions, Captain Ahab forever obsessed by the white whale:

Is it that by its indefiniteness it shadows forth the heartless voids and immensities of the universe, and thus stabs us from behind with the thought of annihilation, when beholding the white depths of the milky way? Or is it, that as an essence whiteness is not so much a colour as the visible absence of colour, and at the same time the concrete of all colours; is it for these reasons that there is such a dumb blankness, full of meaning, in a wide landscape of snows – a colourless, all–colour of atheism from which we shrink? ... pondering all this, the palsied universe lies before us a leper; and like wilful travellers in Lapland, who refuse to wear coloured and colouring glasses upon their eyes, so the wretched infidel gazes himself blind at the monumental white shroud that wraps all the prospect around him. And of all these things, the Albino Whale was the symbol. Wonder ye then at the fiery hunt? (Herman Melville, *Moby Dick*, Chapter 42)

Yours was not an academic training, an art learnt in the head; it was an apprenticeship. 'Art is something you go to see'. 'What was exciting about Rembrandt' you say 'was the paint itself'. Paint like spittle smeared on the eyes of the blind.

'Jesus took the blind man by the hand and led him out of the village. Then, spitting on the man's eyes, he laid his hands on him and asked, "Can you see anything now?" The man looked around. "Yes," he said, "I see people, but I can't see them very clearly. They look like trees walking."' ['Spanish light turned his world inside out. Shadows became more real than substance, hot colours entered the shade, and cool colours the heat; matter dissolved in the blinding white light' (Dorothy Walker); 'he became fascinated by the impression that the shadow of an object in strong sunlight appears to be of greater solidity than the object itself' (Anne Crookshank).] 'Then Jesus placed his hands over the man's eyes again. As the man stared intently, his sight was completely restored, and he could see everything clearly.' (Mark 8:22–26).

There are two moments in this cure of blindness. First you see people 'like trees walking' and then you see clearly. Again it was Anne who led you like the angel to 'fresh inspiration', 'a new human significance'; 'the spirit within the reconstituted ancestral head' (p.145).

The mystery of the person. The face.

Everyone quotes Francis Bacon. I think this quote appears at least three times in Dorothy Walker's book: 'Louis le Brocquy belongs to a category of artists who have always existed – obsessed by figuration outside and on the other side of illustration – who are aware of the vast and potent possibilities of inventing ways by which fact and appearance can be reconjugated'. This enigmatic assessment needs unpacking.

For you, in your own words: 'Art is neither an instrument nor a convenience' 'Art does not survive being used or manipulated.' 'It is another way of seeing, the whole sense and value of which lies in its autonomy, its distance from actuality, its *otherness*'.

'There is a brain in the hand ... yet that hand does not seek to express its own personality'. 'Jerked into coherence by a series of scrutinized accidents'.

Again you say: 'There is something in the struggle with the artist's material in which the personality is ... reborn in the form of a new convention, a painterly restatement of the reality which preoccupies him.'

This is the 'personality' of the lonely 'monk' who, far from rejecting the Christianity which was his childhood companion, reinvents it:

The vision of Christ which thou dost see
is my vision's greatest enemy ...
both read our bibles day and night
but thou readst black where I read white. (William Blake)

Dorothy Walker had, according to herself, asked you why you never painted a face of Christ (DW p.68). You replied that you 'needed at least a possible feature, or detail of actual physical appearance.' But, in my view, you were being much more faithful to the real mystery of Christ which is twofold: one, that 'Christ is nothing, never forget it Christianity' (Kierkegaard), he emptied himself, obliterated himself, painted himself white on white; the other is the mystery of the Holy Spirit which is the face of Christ as that face is realised in the art–work which is each one of us. At the deepest level of ourselves, as work of the Holy Spirit, we are *alter Christus*, without ever being anything less than our selves for all of that: me, as myself at my most profound.

For Christ plays in ten thousand places,
Lovely in limbs, and lovely in eyes not his
To the Father through the features of men's faces.

This is the mystery of the communion of saints, the mystical body of Christ, the 'face' of Christ, his image, as the total assembage of those 'glorified' by the Holy Spirit. It is beautifully represented in your tapestries and your illustrations for Kinsella's poem translations.

'The Táin is an Irish word meaning "hosting" or gathering of a large crowd': The tapestry 'is a very large work (407 x 610 cms) with its surface completely covered in multi–coloured heads, all facing the spectator. These heads retain that relentless individuality of single beings having no relationship to their neighbour; lacking Roman order, there are no military ranks, no imposed external form, the mass of heads is held together by an inner, inherent order, like a flock of plover. "In this tapestry I have tried to produce a sort of group or mass emergence of human presence, features uncertain ... each individual head is conscious only of the viewer vertically facing it. This I think is the secret of their mass regard. Each head is self–contained, finally a lump of presence. No exchange or incident takes place between their multiplied features.' 'I was not nervous of the fragmented or multiplied image. On the contrary, it was this image which encouraged me by suggesting a way in which the head–unit might be transformed into a vast honeycomb or mosaic, giving some kind of cohesion or vibration to the architectural surface' (DW 52–53). 'The minute, irregular "features" of the faces, even on this tiny scale, assert the individuality of the members of the crowd'. 'A permanently open, breathing connection with the snowy sheath from which they strive to release themselves' (Jacques Dupin).

This is as good a description of what happens to 'Christianity' after the strange miracle of Pentecost as I have found outside of Russian theology, and I think especially of Bulgakov's last work on 'The Paraclete'. But it also is the subject of Anne's recent icons of the spirit which she again compares to Hopkins' poem 'The Windhover'.

So, we are all being led, most especially through your work (*Opus Dei*) to the core of the mystery of the person, which is essentially the mystery of the face–to–face. ('While his paintings are always seen to be concerned with the head image, he never paints the head but only the face'. Dorothy Walker again). And you keep on saying that your work is not entirely yours, 'it seems to me that the image tends to emerge on its own gradual insistence.'

Jean François Jaeger, in my view, is also: 'getting nearer to the truth of the painting, perceiving both its freedom and its rigorous control as well as that insight through which a few improvised touches can conjure up such diverse qualities as energy, movement, variability, density and that radiance which is the essence of the inspired human being ... And how can one escape thinking of painting once again in the light of its original vocation as a great art – as a means of knowing – when, as here, it can commit itself completely to the service of a revelation ... Before the most potent of these images, those which opened up completely the widest field of metamorphosis ... I was led to understand better that there are hidden within the formation (or deformation) of those magically evoked archetypes, various secret truths which both justify and condition the form of a 'portrait' idealised by a particular consciousness. Images of the Christ or Buddha, or of Mayan, Tibetan, African or Oceanic deities all proclaim the very same transcendental impulse, modified only by the cultural style which produced them. Each is sufficiently universal to transmit its message to us, to belong to us.

A veritable adventure in itself is implied in the choice of the subject, in the nature of the personality which the artist evokes – and in the wide–open risk of letting himself be invaded by that subject even to the point of abandoning all thought of an individual style.

... I shall await your new images, hoping they will be ever more open, evocative and radiant with that element which, in the life of the exceptional beings you paint, reaches far beyond their human condition.'

Of course, at times, you wonder about the appropriateness, the possibility of blasphemy:

'It seems to me ... that one is trying to do something which is perhaps impossible, worse than that, unsuitable. One is trying not merely to imply but to realize by palpable means, in paint, an impalpable thing; that is to say the inner reality of the human presence beyond its merely external appearance ... The preoccupations of painting are very difficult to talk about because they seem to me to be innately private, one is speaking about a personal search ... involving even the problem of one's identity. I often think of painting as being a kind of personal archaeology, I feel one is digging for things and suddenly something turns up which seems to be remarkable; something apparently outside oneself, which one has found in fact within oneself' (DW 69).

This is, again, the mystery of the Holy Spirit as that divine principle which loses itself in love at the profoundest point of my own person: Christ incarnate in our humanity; the Spirit inspiring each of our personhood; it is also the mystery of genuine creativity, of inspiration.

'I think they mark out a singular path ... towards the person and the poetic idiosyncracy' (Claude Esteban)

And you choose those great saints of our monastic order who have searched relentlessly for the orthodoxy of our humanity. Talking of the heads of Joyce, you say: 'I was also thinking constantly of the extraordinary adventure that had taken place in that head. Because he really did push the boat out, didn't he, sailing into realms that very few people dare to enter'.

Your works, dearest Louis, are prophetic in that 'all are paintings of interior meaning rather than of detailed, particularised content' and 'one of our pleasures and one of our difficulties in relation to artists is that

they are in their very nature ahead and beyond us in thought and feeling'
(Anne Crookshank).

And the result of this dedicated search for the mystery of the human
person is the radiance now present in your own most noble face which
has a serenity and grace recognisable as the work of the greatest artist of
all. I recognised this most clearly in the very special moment when we
embraced at Dorothy Walker's funeral mass.

31 October 2003:

Your deeply impressive letter and essay lie before me still, too
meaningful to be lightly, or even promptly answered. First let me say that
I do not recognise myself in the picture you have painted of me. I am
humbled to be thus seen. Nevertheless your account means much to me,
if only because it describes something of what I have aimed to be in my
work and in my life. And I need not say how very much it means to me
that you will be willing to speak when the time comes.

Already I feel moved and privileged that you should associate me
even referentially to your profound spiritual adventure. I myself have not
been given the certainty of faith revealed to you and, since the age of
twelve or thirteen have become agnostic, in the strict sense of the word.
I simply do not know.

What moves me most of all, perhaps, is your association with the
paraclete, the counsellor and infusor of knowledge. As a child I
wondered about being human, believing that I might just as well have
been born – if at all – as a goat or a hedgehog with a purely instinctive
view of reality. So I suppose I was always fascinated by the miracle of
human consciousness, into which – as I see it – we have evolved.

As to *how* this evolved is another matter. It is for the open–minded
agnostic to ask silently the metaphysical question: might not the
Paraclete – latent throughout the Cosmos from the beginning of time –
have ineffably realised consciousness within us human beings?

Looking back I can see that my work has always been concerned, in
one way or another, with this inner consciousness which is, I imagine,
our most profound reality. It is of course not possible to paint a concrete
image of what is impalpable, but it would seem that my life as a painter
has been largely spent in reaching towards an image implying its
existence.'

3 December 2003, (on a card of Louis le Brocquy 'Procession with lilies'
printed in aid of the United Nations Children's fund):

> Dear Mark Patrick,
> This is to bring you my thoughts as Christmas approaches in your
> journey alongside the Holy Spirit. Pray, if you will that I be given
> greater insight.'

8 December 2003:

> Dear Louis,
> This is like a mystery story. Thank you for two cherished
> communications since my last to you. And in that time I have
> received no less than three reproductions of your 'Procession' which
> I shall see at the Taylor Gallery before Christmas. Also, another clue
> is contained in Brendan Kennelly's *A Man Made of Rain* which has
> your 'Isolated Being' on the cover.
>
> It seems to me that the point being made by the Spirit with
> humour and aplomb is that you have already unveiled this real
> presence for us all in your work and that no one has any right or
> need to introduce you further!
>
> 'Procession' was the technical term for the way in which the
> Holy Spirit *is* – as distinct from the Son who was/is 'generated.'
> The Greeks had two words for such forms of emergence whereas the
> Latins could only rise to one. This caused the rift between the
> Eastern Orthodox Church and the Catholic Western Church in or
> around the eleventh century.
>
> What I am being prompted by the Spirit to surmise is that no
> one has been more assiduous than yourself in pursuing the Spirit's
> presence in the world and your works are ungainsayable testimony
> to this truth: 'One is trying to realise by palpable means, in paint,
> an impalpable thing, the inner reality of the human presence beyond
> its merely external appearance' as you yourself say in a recent
> interview.[61]
>
> Give me time – I'm getting there!'

13 May 2004: I have dinner at Bono's Clarence Hotel with Anne and Louis le Brocquy. I try to persuade Louis that he is in fact an iconographer of the Holy Spirit. The day before while staying chez Louise and Risteárd on my own, I discover among various videos one which Benedict Tutty had given me about Louis le Brocquy, made by Michael Garvey for RTÉ in 1986 (with music by Seán Ó Riada). It holds some clues.

'1957: concentration on a single image emerging, dragged from the light, from the depth of the white canvas, in which pictorial composition in the conventional sense of the word had to be destroyed or ignored.'

This led to a long series of white paintings or presences.

At no point did he leave the figurative tradition.

But these prefigure the later work.

'Painting is not virtuoso performance, dominating a theme, a subject: painting is groping towards an image, discovering, uncovering, revealing, archaeology of the spirit. The painter is a watcher, a supervisor of accident. Like an archeologist, you disturb surface reality, provoking the possibility of a further accidental discovery. Reverence, compassion, wonder.'

'I don't think a painter consciously chooses his way. He does not have much say in the matter, not much decision. He simply does his best to catch some kind of inner tide, to avoid being stranded.

'Often I am stranded. But then I catch a sort of ebbtide. I return to a simple state of being to birds and flowers and inanimate things, emerging in their own nature, filling out their little volume of reality with the various natural possibilities of their forms. Perhaps this is simply a temporary relief from the heads, their intense reflective consciousness, their tragic aspect.'

West of Ireland. A cleft in the rock, a cave, a doorway to the mysterious aspect of the ocean, the deep.

'In this vaulted place are two worlds, an outer material world of fact, and an inner world of the mind, seem to overlap as they do in painting. "O nature and O soul of man, how far beyond utterances are your linked analogies. Not the smallest atom stirs or lives in matter but has its cunning duplicate in mind." [Ahab in Mellville's *Moby Dick*]

The open mouth as cave, as entrance within the evident face to some inner less tangible human reality.'

In Celtic myths the head substitutes for the whole person. The mysterious box which contains the spirit, magical, central, essential. Erwin Schroedinger proposes that 'consciousness is a singular of which the plural is unknown'.

'To see is to transform; art is a transformation. To allow the paint, while insisting upon its own palpable reality, to reconstitute the object of one's experience, to metamorphose into an image. Not in a representational fashion, not to describe. The object has become paint; the paint is transformed into the experienced object. Reality is stripped down to a deeper layer and the ordinary is seen to be marvellous.

Painting has its own recognised *objets trouvés*.

The painter perseveres and induces something further until an entire image may emerge.

'It searches for what is possible, conceivable, not what is actual or phenomenal. The painting itself dictates. It is autonomous. It emerges under the painter's hands.'

I gave Louis both these letters as reproduced here and a quotation from Naum Gabo, which had been one of Benedict Tutty's favourite texts:

Nahum Gabo[62] was born in Briansk, Russia in 1890. He issued his famous Realistic Manifesto in Moscow in 1920 and held his first exhibition. He became an American citizen in 1952:

The state of mind in which humanity finds itself today is indeed disturbing. I am distressed but I do not despair, because I believe that life is indestructible, and the force that makes it indestructible is human constructive consciousness. I believe that human consciousness is a growing force given to us with life, and that its growth is as yet far, far indeed, from reaching its potential limits. It is a force which cannot be broken up into pieces and parts. It does not depend on any one individual's wanton will and whim. It grows and perfects itself with a power all its own.

It is within us, and our life is sustained by it. Human life without its presence is not only meaningless, it is not human. Its presence is revealed to us not by our experiences alone but by the images and conceptions which our consciousness enables us to create as a guide for our action.

Very often, it must be admitted, we make misconceived images, but nothing in our history shows us that our consciousness has ever failed us; it never loosened its control of life when our mistakes became a danger to it.

The greatest mistake we are apt to make is to turn these images into absolutes, and I see that the reason of our ailment today lies in the fact that the images we have made have proved mistaken; let us say, ineffective.

We are faced now with the task not so much of discarding the old images – they are already falling apart by themselves – as of creating new ones to sustain the growth of our culture.

I see the course of human culture as a continuous and unending thread, consisting of innumerable filiaments tightly interwoven with each other and having a single direction. Following the course of its history we discern in a distinct sequence of phases; we observe here and there changes in its volume. Here it gets thinner; there it thickens, and then it begins to turn, winds back on itself and binds itself into a knot; for a while it looks as if it is slowing down; it takes some time to make the knot, but then we see that the thread has never stopped moving; it flows out of the knot, preserving its main characteristics and following the same direction; we see that, at the phase when it was seemingly slowing and forming the knot, its growth was still uninterupted.

This is how I see the development of human culture. These phases are vital for the sustenance of the growth of culture. There is no adequate word to signify these phases. The words 'style' or 'tradition' could serve that purpose had they not been so much misused in common parlance that they have almost lost their proper meaning.

'Style,' for instance, is so vulgarized as to be a synonym for fashion, a term of taste that can be imposed by an advertising agency one day and changed by another the very next day; whereas styles when we study them in their proper historical array are accumulative results of a formative process of culture when it reaches the highest point in its development and growth.

A style can neither be imposed nor predicted, it grows organically out of the human consciousness in any given epoch, signifying the form and the substance of that epoch.

A tradition also should not be understood as something static, a permanent set of rules handed down from generation to generation in strict unchangeable patterns which allow no transformation from within; whereas when a tradition reaches that state of permanence, it signifies only one thing, that its growth is exhausted and that it is ready to die.

It is my strong belief that we are now experiencing just that kind of turn in our culture. History is making another knot in its course, and a new tradition, a new style, is being formed where many filaments of the old are going to be thrown off; many will remain in culture's later continuation.

Holding this belief, I do not share the common feeling of distress that we have lost our moral and aesthetic sense. We cannot lose these senses, because they are attributes of our consciousness, the mainspring of our drive for life. It is the images, the conceptions, made of them in previous civilizations that are being broken up.

Our forefathers kept beauty and goodness on separate pedestals in a divine garden outside themselves which only some were allowed to enter, if and when their deeds were considered good and beautiful according to the standards of those who created those two goddesses.

They did not know that nothing we make is made forever. No image which we create of our experience can claim an eternal existence.

The images of goodness and beauty which our forefathers created are not valid for us any more. I believe that beauty and goodness cannot be separated. I do not share the view of those philosophers who assert that 'ethics cannot be expressed'; ethics can and has been expressed, but not by philosophic systems nor by the winding arguments of their logic. Ethics has been expressed by prophets and poets through many millennia of our history. The Ten Commandments are not philosophical treatises; neither is the Sermon on the Mount.

Their commanding poems appealed to the core of human consciousness by the force of their concise and compelling imagery, penetrating deep and wide into the hearts of men, making them resonate with the poet's invocation.

Therefore, what we cannot express by the art of thinking, by the art of Science or philosophy or logic, we can and should express by the poetic, visual, or some other arts. It is for that reason that I consider morals and aesthetics as one and the same; for they cover only one impulse, one drive inherent in our consciousness – to bring our life and all our actions into satisfactory relationship with the events of the world as our consciousness wants it to be, in harmony with our life and according to the laws of consciousness itself.

15 May 2004:

Dear Mark Patrick,

It was a joy for Anne and for me to have you with us last Thursday and to talk with you in the context of your own revelatory adventure which means so much to us both.

You kindly suggested I might read and comment on your texts. I have read them, need I say with the greatest interest. Gabo's extraordinary insight and faith in human consciousness is perhaps even more relevant today than it was half a century ago.

As I've said or implied, I cannot see myself in the kindly image you drew, but it does manage to recall to me something of my aspirations over the years, half realised as they are. For this and much else I am grateful.

One small thing: on the tenth page of the text I might be seen to say that my work comes from the *Digitus Dei*. Alas I have no such conviction. All that I myself know is the awareness that the images I paint tend to emerge 'on their own' rather than being consciously conceived by myself. What prompts that emergence I do not know.

Forgive me accordingly if I have therefore altered my own account of this. As also my reference to the Holy Spirit, which you yourself specifically refer to in this context on the following page. Again let me say, dear Mark Patrick, how much I enjoyed and appreciated our meeting *à trois* on Thursday and to wish you well in your profound spiritual adventure.

19 May 2004:

Dear Louis,

That was a most radiant evening for me, sitting with you and Anne at Bono's table in the Clarence Hotel, in the very setting of your Procession studies!

My own conviction is that our present dialogue was initiated not by either of us but by the Holy Spirit so that we might be coaxed into elaborating a phenomenology of his or her presence, based on the experience of your work both as emergence and as accomplished standing stones which remain as signifiers.

So, even if it is true that you have no conviction that your work comes from the *Digitus Dei* but do admit that it emerges 'on its own gradual insistence,' I would suggest that what you are stumbling upon, especially in those works which seek out the deepest mystery of the most remarkable human persons, is, in fact, the mystery of the Holy Spirit which blends itself with the deepest recesses of personality as such. That is the ultimate mystery of the Holy Spirit, as I understand this: the indwelling self-effacing love which *is* each one of us, both as ourselves and as ourselves resurrected. It is almost like the fire which allows terra cotta to dry itself out of mud into an enduring form. Here's what Cyril of Alexandria [370-444] has to say in his commentary on St John's Gospel:

(and this text was read out in our church on the morning I received your letter, so again I say that it was pushed at us by the Holy Spirit to help us forward in the search for Him or Her self!):

> With regard to our unity in the Spirit, I shall follow the same line of reasoning and say again to begin with that we have all received one and the same Spirit, the Holy Spirit, and so in a certain sense are mingled with one another and with God. For although, taken individually, we are many, and in each of us there dwells the Spirit of the Father who is also the Spirit of Christ, nevertheless this Spirit is one and indivisible. According to his peculiar mode of being, through himself he binds together into a unity all the spirits that are broken off from the common unity, and in himself he makes all people appear again as one.

For just as the power of the sacred flesh unites in one body all who receive it, so too, I maintain, the one Holy Spirit is not divided among all those in whom he has come to dwell, but brings all to a spiritual unity.

If we put aside the natural way of life, and surrender once and for all to the laws of the Spirit, it is incontrovertible that, by denying, in a sense, our own life and assuming the heavenly form of the Holy Spirit so that he becomes woven into our being, we are transformed, so to speak, into another nature. We are no longer just human beings but sons and daughters of God; we receive the name of heavenly because we are made partakers of the divine nature.'

Add this to what Naum Gabo and Teilhard de Chardin are saying and you have a presence of the Holy Spirit within human consciousness, which not only prompts the evolutionary appetite of the species towards the point omega of fulfilment, but you also have a clear and arresting manifestation of the face of that Spirit within the deepest pools of consciousness abiding in the depths of the eyes of those who really search for this in our world.

And so you say about your portrait of Picasso: 'Fame and photography have made Picasso's remarkable head familiar to us all. Each one of us has formed an image of his face. Yet the face itself remains ambiguous, both masking and revealing a consciousness too explosive to be wholly contained within its exterior appearance. And so I have not attempted to paint the appearance, the material fact of Picasso. On the contrary, I have deliberately effaced the well known likeness so that from the depths of that palimpsest (piece of writing–material on which original writing has been removed to make way for new writing. Palin = again; psestos = rubbed smooth[63]) might emerge some ulterior image of this extraordinary man.'

That is, to my mind, a description of the mysterious presence of the Holy Spirit in each one of us : our faces remain ambiguous, both masking and revealing a consciousness too explosive to be wholly contained within our exterior appearance. We are all of us personalities on palimpsest: the ulterior manifestation of our personhood is that white hot firing that makes us divine without disturbing or losing one drop of what it means to be human also. And you have been able to reveal this ultimate presence in the face of The poet: 'not as a figure of fame but of heroic consciousness.' This is particularly revealing in the case of your images of Shakespeare: 'Apart from the much restored bust at Stratford, the only authenticated portrait is a poor engraving and as Dorothy Walker says: As there is no authentic visual material available, it is all the more startling to encounter Shakespeare's very live eye glistening through a mass of paint'. All of which comes at the end of a long period of exploration and development.

But lest it might seem that this Holy Spirit is reserved for the great personalities and poets of the world, it has been clearly pointed out to me that 'Procession with lilies' is perhaps your most important, poignant and transparent manifestation of this mystery. Procession is the technical term used in some theologies to describe the way in which the Holy Spirit proceeds from the Father and the Easter Lily remains the traditional flower of Easter, symbolic of a resurrection, as lilies rise from earthy graves as scaly bulbs, and bloom into majestic trumpets, embodying beauty, grace, tranquillity. Barthololmeus Anglicus had this in mind when he wrote in the 13th century: 'The Lily is an herbe with a white flower; and though the leaves of the floure be white, yet within shineth the likeness of gold.' So goes the saying, 'To gild a lily is to attempt, foolishly, to improve on perfection.' To many artists and poets it seemed that, if any flower could have one, the lily had a soul. Which, in other terminology, means that the lily was white transparency allowing the golden needle at its base to be glimpsed.

The exhibition which I was again led to see in the Taylor Gallery in Dublin on the 11th December 2003, was also shown in 1985 as an attempt to complete what you describe as 'this microcosmic circle,' by which you implied that you were somehow giving back to Dublin, Bloomsday of 1939, in some form or other. Yes, indeed, Bloomsday is the one we all await; the day when the spirit in each one of us bursts into bloom (something too explosive to be contained within the photograph of School children returning from church, feast of St Anthony, after the blessing of the lilies in the evening Herald 16/6/1939, sent to you by Robbin Dobbin).

This white procession along the liffey from Merchant's Quay, along
Bachelor's Walk and O'Connell Bridge, 'Riverrun past Eve and
Adam's' you associate with Joyce's attempt to make manifest 'the
Spirit of Dublin.' You describe it as a 'curiously arrested moment of
fluid succession of presences, fleeting image I had never witnessed
myself.' You hadn't witnessed it yourself but you had the gift of
revealing it to the rest of us. Going back into the dark room of your
studio you could develop it for us into a manifestation of its mystery.
'And here I am today still painting these schoolgirls, these
temporarily white beings, momentarily related in their progression
within space and time, rounding a Dublin corner into the Evening
Herald, as it happened, of Bloomsday 1939.'

And this year is the centenary year of Bloomsday, during which
I hope we can take the 'microcosmic circle' up one further notch on
the spiral of epiphany, until the procession emerges in the light of
the Holy Spirit. If that is not the very definition of gilding the lily!

18 June 2004:

Dear Louis,

There is some trap being sprung by the trickster Spirit and it circles
around 'procession' and your obsession with this image and this
work. It is as if the Spirit is trying to use me to show you something
(a manifestation an epiphany) that is startlingly obvious and
radiantly present in your own work. Something about lighthouses
attracting 'many birds.' Thanks for your card from Beara on Whit
Sunday. I was in Mexico that day. Procession with lilies took place
on the feast of St Anthony 13th June 1959. W. B. Yeats's birthday
in 1865.

I went to the National Library on June 3rd and looked up the
Evening Herald for June 16th 1959. The picture which Robin
Dobbin sent you was not there. I looked back over previous
editions. It was in the Evening Herald for 14th June 1959. I asked
them to make two photocopies and to send these to my sister's
address in Dublin. They said it would take about a week. I went to
Mexico and Wales. I came back to Dublin for the week of
Bloomsday and sure enough the photocopies reached me on

Bloomsday 2004 at 12.45 a.m.

Why did Robin Dobbin send you that picture? There must have been some relation of his, or yours, in the photo? They must be still alive – who are they now? Somewhere in this process there is a secret known only to you which is the white stone of the Apocalypse with your real name written on it.

555

POSTSCRIPT

SUBLIME GENEROSITY

Then new events said to me,
'Don't move. A sublime generosity is
coming toward you.'

And love said, 'Stay with me.'
I said, 'I will.'

You are the fountain of the sun's light.
I am a willow shadow on the ground.
You make my raggedness silky.

The soul at dawn is like darkened water
that slowly begins to say Thank you, Thank you

Then at sunset, again, Venus gradually
changes into the moon and then the whole night sky.

This comes of smiling back
at your smile.

The chess master says nothing,
other than moving the silent chess piece.

That I am part of the ploys
of this game makes me
amazingly happy.

[Rumi]

I will stand on my watch towerand take up my post on my battlements watching to see what he will say to me … then Yahweh answered and said, 'write the vision down inscribe it on tablets to be easily read, since this vision is for its own time only: eager for its own fulfilment, it does not deceive; if it comes slowly, wait, for come it will, without fail.' Habakkuk, 2:2-3.

I am aware that during this year, 2005, something is secretly happening which is mostly the ingenious work of the Holy Spirit. I find myself sitting tight, hibernating somewhere beneath the waterlevel of consciousness, praying and mechanically moving from one basket-weaving distraction to the next, within the wheelhouse of the monastery, almost as if sweating oil into the machinery which will loosen joints into conformity with the plans of the Spirit. I had thought that this Walkabout was over. The script had been ready before the end of 2004 and I was planning to have the book out before the end of that year. Brian Lynch suggested that spring of the following year would be more appropriate and we set our sights on April 2005. So many things happened to prevent this deadline being met. And now as I sit here in front of my computer at 10.20 a.m. on Friday 19 May 2005 I know that next Monday 23 May is the final date for handing over this text to the printer for the last time. This date is arbitrary in one way; it is determined by the publishers who want the book to appear in June; but it does not cause me any scruple at this time. I am as sure as I can be that the task I was given has now been done and that the most comprehensive and complete account of it is contained in these pages. I realise that this does not make it either easy to understand or manageable as a dossier, but at least it is there. All the time I was on this search I kept on hoping to have sufficient evidence that what I was doing was actually happening and not just my own invention. As I began to knit the wool which eventually became the book which you are now reading, I kept on examining it to see whether it hung together in a coherent way, and by its size, shape and texture to make some initial actuarial calculation of the length it was going to be, and the time it was going to take. All these things were determined by the trapeze artist who originally placed my two hands on this swing.

This is not my script. I have been secretary to another presence. It has been enjoyable and exhilarating but never within my creative control. I have sewn it up into a number of ungainly portmanteaux, with the impatience and frustration of one with too much stuff lying around which has to be crammed into a limited number of shapeless holdalls. I am sure it could have been shorter and clearer, but I was afraid of losing the diamonds in the refusacks of straw. As I sit here having read over the page-proofs (dated 05/05/05, the day I returned from the USA and Canada) I am aware that an unusual form of consciousness is trying to present itself through this Walkabout and in these pages, and that this particular perspective is one which allows the traces of the Holy Spirit to be seen through the windowpane. This makes both the complicated circumlocution and the effort to read it worthwhile. It is as if one required a periscope and as if the extent and the detail of what needs to be perceived required both microscopic and telescopic lenses at the same time. Multifocussed and peripheral contact lenses are required. Normal vision and customary consciousness miss the point. That is why I have suggested mythic intelligence and symbolic awareness as descriptions of the kind of mindset to which we need to adjust ourselves. If this sounds complicated, it isn't. The adjustment is a matter of turning off the normal everyday formatting to which we have been programmed since our early childhood by our education.

The difficulty is that as I write the picture gets bigger and recedes. The temptation is to start again on a smaller canvas. The smallest. Everything here could be boiled down to one page if I had the appropriate synthesizer. Not only am I aware that the journey has spilled over into 2005 but I am also aware that certain happenings in this year are essential to the tapestry and that others have roots in undetected seeds sown during the last four years. For instance, in October 2003, June Fennelly invited me to Waterford to address her community of Ursuline sisters there. During lunch I was sitting beside Bishop Russell of Waterford. He had been in the diocese of Cashel and Emly before he became bishop of Waterford and Lismore and had known the Glenstal community. He told me about Vincent Lebbe, the so-called Apostle to China (1877 – 1940) whose brother Bede Lebbe had been a monk in Glenstal Abbey for some years as appointed superior. Vincent Lebbe was working in China for much of his life. He returned home every now and then and came through Paris. As he did, he always enquired about

Chinese students who were studying there and would meet them to see if they were settled in. On one occasion he met a group of such students and asked them if there was anything they needed. One of them said he would much appreciate a wrist watch. So, Vincent Lebbe took off his own wrist watch and gave it to him.

Very much later when he was in charge of a hospital in China and there was a war going on between the forces of Chiang Kai-shek and the revolutionaries led by Chu-en-lai, he was advised with his staff to leave the hospital and retreat. They did so and some days later a plea came by radio to have them return to run the hospital as there were very many wounded and no one able to help them. Chiang Kai-shek warned Vincent Lebbe and his staff that they should under no circumstances return. It was a trap and they would all be killed. Lebbe explained that he and his medical staff had taken various professional oaths when they became doctors that they would always try to save lives. So they all went back. Not only was it a trap but they found to their horror that they were to be executed one person a day as a lesson to the government forces and any others who would try to stop the rebels. As Vincent Lebbe was in charge he was the last one to be killed. The night before his execution as he was preparing himself in his room the door opened. A man came in and asked him if he had once given his wrist watch to an impoverished Chinese student in Paris. He said that he had done so. The man gave him back his wrist watch and told him he was free to go. The student he had helped in Paris was Chu-en-lai. Perhaps, said June Fennelly, the reason for your coming here today was to meet Bishop Russell. For whatever reason, when I got back to the monastery, Terence, who is archivist in our community, had found in our archives two parchments of Chinese writing in Vincent Lebbe's own hand. He must have given them to his brother, Bede, while he was here in our monastery. Terence had put these on display in our common room, probably because of his own great interest in China where he has been at least twice in the last number of years. The Chinese calligraphy reads: *In Manu Dei* and *Pro Dei Amore*. Such coincidences and synergies have provided much of the causal connections on this Walkabout, a causality of chance which is the way the Spirit moves without being detected.

The second such incident involves colour. I had met Jaime Zobel de Ayala and his wife Bea while in Barons Court with Peggie and Gordon

Richardson on 25 May 2003. It was a most beautiful weekend and we had a picnic on the lake around Belle Isle with James and Sacha which remains one of the great moments of meeting of my Walkabout. Jaime is himself a very remarkable photographer but he very vehemently recommended a film to me called the *Three Colours Trilogy*. I thought no more of it until, this year, the same film was recommended to our cine-club by Br Martin Browne. I happened to be in the Irish Film Centre and saw these three CDs and bought them. We showed them on the first three days of Holy Week. Tuesday morning all became clear to me. Krzysztof Kieslowski, the Polish director of the films, died on 13 March 1996, 9 days before Benedict Tutty (22 March 1996). Each of the films represents one person of the Trinity. The three women Juliette Binoche, Julie Delpy, and Irene Jacob represent us as earthlings. Although, of course, blue, white and red are also the French flag, and the colours can betoken liberty, equality and fraternity, it is also clear symbolically that blue is 'the Father,' white, the son, Jesus Christ, and red is the Holy Spirit. As if to confirm this, a phone message was left on my answering machine on Holy Saturday afternoon from Sr Paula of Glencairn, who is an iconographer and with whom I have never had any real contact, so I presume she intended the message for someone else: She felt sure I would be interested to know that 'on the seventh day God created rest because he himself rested on that last day. He stopped creating but created rest. Our Lord was therefore resting on the cross in his last words. Therefore the blue background was relaxing; it was a peaceful restful colour. It says that in the liturgy, the blue donated rest, tranquilized.'

Saturday 2 April: Pope John Paul II died at around 9.00 p.m. I went to Maynooth to talk with Enda McDonagh at their theological society. During the funeral I am rung by the Marianne Finucane radio programme just before midday to ask me what I think about the huge crowds attending the last rites for the Polish pope. I say that it is an archetypal cultural phenomenon: the death of the twentieth century. Strange and moving that so violent a century should end so peaceably. We are all mourning the death of the father. And we are grieving for ourselves. I had heard several students being interviewed in tears saying 'My father is dead.' This pope was a leader and a father figure. John Paul II had been named 'Man of the Century' by several biographies and by

Time magazine. And, indeed, so he was. But as one women poet put it, that makes him, perhaps, half a person. It is time now for all of us to move forward into the twenty-first century.

I was moved by the simple coffin made of wood and by the fact that the pope had asked to be buried in the earth and not in some marble catafalque high above the ground. Most striking of all was the red book of the bible lying on top of the coffin with its pages being blown over in the breeze. The Holy Spirit is in charge in the interim period as well as during the reign of whichever pontiff.

Some weeks before Easter the Icon Chapel was completely buried, cut off by preparations for new buildings taking shape in the monastery. On Holy Saturday it was caged in with rusty squares of iron reaching above the entrance door. James Scanlon had a problem with his heart around the same time. He was looked after by Peter Kearney, whose mother was a devotee of the healing icon. Some days later Ciarán was at the Crawford Gallery with Virginia Teehan. There was James completely recovered. His next assignment would be the icon of the Holy Spirit which is to be shining in through the new entrance to the icon chapel.

Both Gregory and I feel that Pentecost (15/05/05) this year will be important. I add to that 05/05/05 which is the day I return from USA landing in Shannon at 6.10 a.m. Gregory gives the talks during the Easter Triduum. Abbot Celestine, who is in Jerusalem, sends me greetings from Cardinal Christoph Schonbörn, who is there for Easter.

My last journey takes me from Ohio to San Francisco. Staying with Fanny Howe we learn that the new pope is Benedict XVI. She has been to Sky Farm and has to admit that the place looks well and seems to be very much more capable of achieving its silent harvest than it was under Dunstan's supervision. It is my ninth time in San Francisco. I think of Tom Hayes and Tom Jordan. There is a picture of Christoph Schonbörn in the *Newsweek* coverage of the new pope. I am staying with Diarmuid and AC and give a seminar on the Tarot in the Mercy Centre on Sunday 24 April. This is the same day as the inauguration of Pope Benedict XVI. The triple tiara with which the pope used to be crowned has now been abandoned definitively. Paul VI laid it aside after his own coronation and John Paul I did not use it at all. His was the first papacy by installation rather than by coronation. The present pope is the first to remove the triple tiara even from his coat of arms.

I am asked the question: 'What does the pope say about the Tarot cards?' I do not know, but at present am more concerned about what the Tarot cards say about the pope.

The fifth card, which is the pope, represents as the number suggests a quintessence of the spiritual quest. Just as we have five senses and five fingers with which to probe the world around us so this pentagram will be significant in probing the world of the spirit. The pope is called pontifex which in Latin means bridgebuilder between two worlds. This card represents a blessing or benediction. Benediction, from which the name Benedict comes, is nothing less than the power of God. Whoever is entitled to give such a blessing is putting into action divine power. Such exercise of the divine will transcends all individuality of thought and of will-power either in the one who is blessing, or in those being blessed. This card presents us with an essentially sacerdotal act.

The design of the card describes a circular movement of prayer and benediction passing from the left hand side to the right. Two disciples or acolytes kneel before the pope. The one on the left has his hands raised in prayer; the one on the right has his hands lowered and open to receive the blessing from the pope's right hand. Moving up from the head of the suppliant is a triple cross which carries the prayer heavenward. A similar movement downwards from the descending tiara through the red folding robes of the pope leads the blessing of his right hand to the head of the second acolyte. The three heads and the two pillars of the throne behind the pope make up the sign of the pentagram. On their own the two pillars and the tiara form a tryptich which mirrors the parallel lines of the triple cross, which in turn designates the three layers of the tiara. This mitre shaped crown decorated with three-leaved shamrock templates beside what looks like keyhole openings has the appearance of a beehive. It is indeed a beehive of the invisible. The complex weave of the trinity issues through the blessing into several streams of prayer: 'Thy kingdom come' as addressed to the Father; 'Thy will be done' as expressed through the Son; and 'Give us this day our daily bread' as uttered by, with, and through, the Holy Spirit.

The pentagram of the five wounds is the effective sign. Under this sign, the benediction flows. Each of the wounds of Christ are effective against the five dark currents of human motivation: the desire to be great, the desire to take (the prerogative of the right hand), the desire to keep (prerogative of the left hand), the desire to advance at the expense of others (prerogative of the right foot), the desire to hold on to, at the expense of others (prerogative of the left foot). The five wounds of Christ were a five sense breakthrough into our world of the greedy senses and covetous limbs. His wounds are five vacuities which result in the five currents of the human will being filled from above by absolutely pure will, the will of God. This is the principle of the grace of the pentagram of the five wounds.

The fifth wound as is suggested by the fifth card of the major arcana of the tarot is where the fingers of the pope are pointing: it is the wound of organic humility, the wound of the heart, which replaces the natural current of the will-to-greatness. This wound penetrates from the right-hand side.

The only wound through which such power can flow is the freely opened heart and will of an authentic lover of God. Such a person is the one represented in this card. No amount of worldly pomp or pagentry can create such an office. The only lightning conductor which can harness the power of God is the loving will of a genuine pontifex. It does not matter how we break down these walls between the two sides, it may require quite different kinds of wounding in the case of each individual. However, what is ungainsayable is this: The bridge is created through the open wounds on both sides. The triple cross of the pope's crosier is the victory sign of the divine breakthrough. It is the power of salvation. So potent is this staff that no human being should touch it without a gloved hand. The freedom we have been given is so powerful and so dangerous that it can lead us through every one of our five senses to a hell of our own construction. That is what freedom means: the free choice of surrender to heaven or construction of hell from our own sweating selves. The secret wisdom hidden from the beginning of time is the mystery of God's love for us. And so powerful is this secret wisdom that the five gates of hell shall never prevail against the formula of the five wounds.[1]

The major arcana of the tarot also present us with a female pope, a corresponding archetype, Sophia, the kind of wisdom we must have in order to approach the mysteries hidden since the world began. Somehow such wisdom must be incorporated into the hierarchy of the church if the twenty-first century is to begin.

In this card number two, the woman is seated. Sophia is the seat of wisdom. She carries a book in her lap which is opened with both her hands. This book is the distilled embodiment of her life and being as a channel of wisdom, as an incarnation of obedience to the word. On her head she also wears a triple tiara which represents the threefold wisdom that filters from above into her open heart and soul and mind, until it becomes flesh in her and then is reborn as word once again in her holy book. The three levels are inspiration then reflection and memory followed by active expression in her own words. It is a process similar to giving birth. Her work is, at every level, inspired. The card shows very graphically the descent of revelation from the small uppermost circle on her tiara down to the open book on her knees. She is seated in a way that graphically depicts relationship between the vertical and the horizontal: the circling, descending vertical rings of the tiara which covers her head and the arrival of this into a horizontal and outward plane in the square pages of the book. Such is the way in which tradition is born. It is necessary to be seated. This describes active-passive state of being which allows for attentive listening in silence. The complete figure is the human being as attentive ear. 'I am all ears' we say when attentive to what another person says. The book lying open at the base of this waterfall allows the wisdom to be handed over, handed on. But a book never contains the fullness of the wisdom which is embodied in this extraordinary person. Not all the books in the world could contain the sum total of this mystery.[2]

Benedict XVI in his sermon today, instead of putting forward a programme, simply commented on two liturgical symbols representing the inauguration of the petrine ministry:

The first symbol is the pallium, woven in pure wool, which will be placed on my shoulders. This ancient sign, which the Bishops of Rome have worn since the fourth century, may be considered an image of the yoke of Christ, which the Bishop of this City, the Servant of the Servants of God, takes upon his shoulders. God's yoke is God's will, which we accept. And this will does not weigh down on us, oppressing us and taking away our freedom. To know what God wants, to know where the path of life is found – this was Israel's joy, this was her great privilege. It is also our joy: God's will does not alienate us, it purifies us – even if this can be painful – and so it leads us to ourselves. In this way, we serve not only him, but the salvation of the whole world, of all history. The symbolism of the pallium is even more concrete: the lamb's wool is meant to represent the lost, sick or weak sheep which the shepherd places on his shoulders and carries to the waters of life. For the Fathers of the Church, the parable of the lost sheep, which the shepherd seeks in the desert, was an image of the mystery of Christ and the Church. The human race – every one of us – is the sheep lost in the desert which no longer knows the way. The Son of God will not let this happen; he cannot abandon humanity in so wretched a condition. He leaps to his feet and abandons the glory of heaven, in order to go in search of the sheep and pursue it, all the way to the Cross. He takes it upon his shoulders and carries our humanity; he carries us all – he is the good shepherd who lays down his life for the sheep. What the pallium indicates first and foremost is that we are all carried by Christ.

The symbol of the lamb also has a deeper meaning. In the Ancient Near East, it was customary for kings to style themselves shepherds of their people. This was an image of their power, a cynical image: to them their subjects were like sheep, which the shepherd could dispose of as he wished. When the shepherd of all humanity, the living God, himself became a lamb, he stood on the side of the lambs, with those who are downtrodden and killed. This is how he reveals himself to be the true shepherd: 'I am the Good Shepherd ... I lay down my life for the sheep,' Jesus says of himself (Jn 10:14f). It is not power, but love that redeems us!

The second symbol was the ring of the fisherman.

Diarmuid, AC and I arrive in Canada where we stay with Miriam and Stephan in Nelson, the final Cóiced, interrupted and inspired by Adonia their daughter who is 18 months old. They have started 'Next Step Foundation,' whose purpose is 'Advancing Consiousness for an Integral Tomorrow.' Our meetings bring up a question about the meaning of song which we find answered unbeknownst by Ciarán in an email:

The Return of Song. 'The swans are singing again,' said to one another the gods. And looking downwards, for my dreams had taken me to some fair and far Valhalla, I saw below me an iridescent bubble not greatly larger than a star shine beautifully but faintly, and up and up from it looking larger and larger came a flock of white, innumerable swans, singing and singing and singing, till it seemed as though even the gods were wild ships swimming in music. 'What is it?' I said to one that was humble among the gods. 'Only a world has ended,' he said to me, 'and the swans are coming back to the gods returning the gift of song.' 'A whole world dead!' I said. 'Dead,' said he that was humble among the gods. 'The worlds are not for ever; only song is immortal.' 'Look I look!' he said. 'There will be a new one soon.' And I looked and saw the larks, going down from the gods.

We visit Morning Star where I sense a tryst made in India and embedded in this countryside between the northern deck of the main house and the Valhalla mountains, which is the name of this range. I gave two radio interviews and a talk on the 'Tarot and the Unconscious' in Nelson on Wednesday 27 April. These are picked up by Philipp Gawthrop who joins us with Jonathan Rheans and Jonathan Taylor to discuss what that next step might be. Somehow the meeting senses that Nelson holds a geography and a history recalcitrant to the Spirit and San Francisco may be too open and too raw. Portland which is halfway between the two, and is AC Caldwell-Rooney's home in Oregon, suggests itself as a possible compromise. Nóirín sends us a dream: we will all be directed by a white cat, pangur bán!

05/05/05 I returned to Glenstal ending my Walkabout. I had visited twelve countries during this time: the Bahamas, Canada, England, France, Holland, Ireland, Mexico, Russia, Scotland, Switzerland, USA, and Wales. At vespers that evening Nóirín and Oscar Mascarenas were singing in the main body of the church. Representatives (he from Mexico) of another kind of revolution in the Holy Spirit, Cinco de Mayo, 2005.

Brian Lynch had sent proofs of this book to Canada but they did not arrive. Several delays prevented the book from being published in April, and I knew that this day which ended my trip to Canada and the USA was meant to be the final date, which explains this postscript.

The night from the 4th to the 5th of May, I [Simon Mason] had a dream: I was with Sybille in the basement of a sky scraper, there was a strong earthquake, I was sure the building would topple, we would be crushed. A doctor said it would not be a good moment to do a ceasarian, his hand would shake too much. The top of the building swayed back and forth. Then the earthquake stopped, the building was still standing, we walked out of the basement, people had to repair the water system that had been damaged. The sun was shining.

Sunday 8 May was the Ascension. I had agreed to go to Dingle to address Féile na Bealtaine on 'Harry Potter and the Da Vinci Code' in An Diseart Chapel. The invitation had come from Mícheál Ó Coileáin. Dingle through the Conor Pass in May is beautiful. I walked down the street and am hailed by Matilda McManamon. She drove me to the opening of Tomás Ó Cíobháin's exhibition in the Greenlane Gallery. 'The Irish word *dúchas* is hard to translate but when I see your work it's the word that comes to mind. The dictionaries say it can mean "inheritance, native place or land, connection, affinity or attachment due to descent: inherited instinct or natural tendency" – and all of those meanings have a bearing on the way you see your subjects. There's a boldness in the paintings that tells us the artist is somebody who knows and loves his place – not just his place in the physical world but also in the world and tradition of Irish art.' So Seamus Heaney had written to the artist in February 2005.

Later Monsignor Pádraig Ó Fiannachta and I have a dialogue after my talk. 'I have always felt uneasy about the notion of being adopted children of God,' he said, 'There is an Irish word *dúchas* which tells me that it is much more than that.' I agree with him. The use of that same word confirms the reality here involved. We are 'family' in this regard, fully paid-up members of the Blessed Trinity. And we don't have to wait until the last day for Resurrection either. I quote Pasternak: 'You rose from the dead on the day you were born only you never realised it.' Resurrection is now: it is the different kind of time, the different kind of space available to us as walkabout in the Holy Spirit. It is as if I have been led to Dingle to hear this wise Priest-Shaman saying it in Irish.

Christine Sophia Murphy brings Matilda and I to her home. She and Finbarr her husband had been at the Sophia Conference in Glenstal in 1999. We had known at that time that we would meet again. There is a completely white cat in the house. They have even written a little book about this Pangur bán. Their daughter, Deirdre, is a professional clown, working in hospitals and with a troupe called Paradoxos. She makes up the Cóiced on this evening in the Dingle starry.

The icon chapel is accessible again on Pentecost Sunday when Nóirín, Simon and I visit it. I preach at the main Mass today. Gerbera with its green stem, yellow sunburst and red petals, is saying the same thing as the ceiling of our church: green for the creator of the universe, two shades of blue for the wooden crosses throughout the universe, like a world war cemetery, for the second Person of the Trinity laying down structures of infinity; and bright red for those rivers of blood, with tongues of fire moving through the centre. Everything on earth this day is speaking in tongues of the Holy Spirit.

Tuesday 17 May: Jackie Nickerson arrives in the guesthouse. Her task as a photographer is to show the Catholic Church in Ireland through the faces of ordinary people who believe. Even though the institutional church has been rocked by scandals and betrayals, there is still the Church of the Holy Spirit alive and vibrant. She will show this face of the Spirit in the book of photographs she is presently creating. The Son shows the face of the Father; the Spirit shows the face of the Son; but the face of the Spirit is only revealed in the collage of all those faces who make up the communion of saints, the gathering of the faithful. Her book will show enough of such faces to establish an outline.

Endnotes

II THE BOOK OF ICONS

1. *The Icon and its Significance*, From the visions of Joa Bolendas, JOM verlag, 8876 Filzbach, 1979, Switzerland, translated by John Hill. Photographs: Samuel Künzli. This book was later retranslated and incorporated into *So that you may be one, from the Visions of Joa Bolendas*, translated by John Hill, Lindisfarne Books, 1997, New York.
2. Robert Graves, *The Crane Bag and other Essays*, Cassell, London, 1969.
3. Alan McGlashan, *Savage and Beautiful Country*, Hillstone, New York, 1966.
4. *The Crane Bag*, Vol 1, no 1, Spring 1977, p 3–5.
5. Thomas Mann, *Joseph and his Brothers*, Vol IV, p. 431.
6. Mark Patrick Hederman, 'The Future of Glenstal Ecumenical Congress,' *Doctrine and Life*, October, 1983, Pp 486–490.
7. I have since developed these paragraphs into a book: *I Must be Talking to Myself, Dialogue in the Roman Catholic Church since Vatican II*, Veritas, Dublin, 2004.
8. Seamus Heaney, *The Government of the Tongue, the 1986 T. S. Eliot Memorial Lectures and Other Critical Writings*, Faber & Faber, London, 1988.
9. Interview in *Link–Up*, a journal for the Dublin Diocese, March 1994.
10. Enda McDonagh, 'Bruised Reeds and the Mystery of the Church,' *The Furrow*, October, 1995.
11. Evmarie Schmitt, *Cézanne in Provence*, Pegasus Library, Prestel, New York, 1995.
12. Andrew Cyprian *Love, Musical Improvisation, Heidegger, and the Liturgy, A Journey to the Heart of Hope*, Studies in Art and Religious Interpretation, Volume 32, The Edwin Mellen Press, Lewiston, Queenston, Lampeter, 2003.
13. John Moriarty, *Dreamtime*, The Lilliput Press, Dublin, 1994, p 208.
14. Rainer Maria Rilke, *Letters on Cézanne*, edited by Clara Rilke, Vintage Books, London, 1991.
15. Mario Botta, *La tenda–La tente–Das Zelt*, Edizioni Casagrande, Verlag für Architektur, Bellinzona, 1991.
16. Eventually published by New Island, Dublin, in 2004 as *An Arid Season*.
17. Joseph Jaworski, *Synchronicity: The Inner Path of Leadership*, Berrett–Koehler Publishers, San Francisco, 1996. Edited by Betty Sue

Flowers with an Introduction by Peter Senge.

18. Isaac C. Rottenberg, *The Turbulent Triangle, Christians, Jews, Israel*, Red Mountain Associates, Pennsylvania, 1989, p 91. I have not been able to verify whether this prayer is one of John XXIII. It is not included in his *Journal of a Soul*.

19. Dunstan was born in 1923 in Illinois. His father who was baptized a Catholic but raised by Protestants, died of pneumonia after he came back from the First World War when Dunstan was nine. Dunstan became a baptized Catholic when he was a Senior at Notre Dame and he joined the Diplomatic Service and served for 2 years in Egypt. He studied later in Frieburg and eventually joined a Benedictine monastery down the Illinois River called St Bede's Academy. He did his novitiate year in St John's Minnesota. He was dean of St Bede's where he was ordained in 1953 and stayed for 15 years. Still pursued by his desire for solitude, his abbot gave him permission to join the Camaldolese – Italian eremitical branch of the Benedictines – who had arrived in California. He did another novitiate with them. He then got permission to live in solitude under the direction of Jacques Winandy, a retired French abbot living on the island of Martinique, a former French colony in the Caribbean. He lived under Winandy's direction in solitude for 4 years. He would see him once a week and later every six weeks. He saw no one else. They were joined by others, so he left Martinique, went to New Mexico and ended up on Vancouver Island in Canada. 'On the feast of John the Baptist, 1967, the bishop visited me. He told me to return to the world and I knew that Winandi must have prompted him. So I left Vancouver 30 years ago with $50 in my pocket. I studied pottery with Marguerite Wildenhain, originally from the Bauhaus, for two summers. Also to try to get a way to support myself.'

'Don't dare present a pot to the public until you've made five thousand pots and thrown them away' was Wildenhain's catch–cry.

He worked as a janitor while he threw those trainee pots. The bishop of Santa Rosa who oversees the territory from Marin County up to Oregon, allowed him to go around and substitute in parishes where they needed a priest. He was sent to Sonoma for two weeks. He stayed for two years. He met Pop Norrbom who wasn't a Catholic but whose secretary was. Dunstan brought her communion on first Fridays and met Norrbom. They used to sit in silence together.

Norrbom's father was one of the early Swedish settlers. He owned hundreds of acres. Pop's mother was Irish. He knew Dunstan was a priest and a monk who wanted to live as a hermit. He left Dunstan 120 acres in his will in 1975. So that is how Sky Farm came to be. And now Dunstan, who visited Glenstal last summer, believes it was meant to go to Glenstal. 'I'd like Sky Farm to offer the possibility of a venture into the unknown. And if I were to be more specific, I think I'd be betraying what the situation is here, and what the offering is here. I think of my painter friend Prasanna sitting before the canvas, sometimes for weeks. He speaks of being on the edge. He has to wait there at the edge of the unknown, for the unknown to manifest itself.'

Dunstan lived on Sky Farm without electricity and on his own for the first 15 years of its existence for less than $100 a month. He mowed the grass himself with a scythe twice each year, mostly for fire protection. 'You have to let the poppies and the blue lupins flower but you can't leave it too late or it gets too tough'. He now has 4 buildings and two hermit's huts on the property and a backup account of $10,000 which he doesn't touch. The original inheritance was 120 acres. He sold half this property to Sam Keen for $100,000, less than the minimum price he was advised to ask. He did this because Kean was a protegé of Paul Tillich and an authority on Gabriel Marcel. He has since regretted it. Sam Kean is a guru of popular psychotherapy, one of the 'Pied Pipers of our culture.'

In the beginning when Dunstan inherited the property the local bishop wanted him to hand it over to the diocese. He refused, saying that monks were independent of the diocese. The bishop then deprived Dunstan of his authority to exercise the duties of the priesthood in the diocese. Since then the bishop has 'retired' because of various scandals, financial and other.

20. Later published in *Anchoring the Altar*, Veritas, Dublin 2002, Pp 112–146.
21. According to the founder of the Limerick Fancy Pigeon Club, Paul Hogan.
22. John Hill, Anthony Keane, Ronnie O'Gorman, Simon Sleeman and myself.
23. John Hill translator's foreword to *So That You May Be One, From the Visions of Joa Bolendas*, Lindisfarne Books, New York, 1997, Pp. 37–38.
24. Later incorporated into the complete volume of Joa's visions, *So That You May Be One, from the Visions of Joa Bolendas*, Lindisfarne Books, New York, 1997, Pp146–176.
25. Taken from the Gregorian Chant antiphon for the Feast of the Transfiguration, 6 August, the day after this conference ended: '*Et ecce vox de nube dicens: hic est Filius meus dilectus, in quo mihi complacui: ipsum audite, alleluia.*' which is to be found on page 1000 of the Antiphonale Monasticum, Tournai, 1934.
26. So that you may be one, *op.cit.* p 35.
27. These were later published in Joan McBreen, *Winter in the Eye*, Salmon, Co Clare, 2003.
28. Castletroy Park Hotel, Ma Feeney's Expandable Meatloaf Recipe. Ingredients: 2lbs ground beef, 10 oz. seasoned breadcrumbs, 2 tsp of tabasco sauce, 10 oz catsup, 1 chopped onion, 3 eggs, 1 tbsp salt, 1 tbsp pepper. 1. Mix all ingredients in a large bowl. 2. Bake in oven at 320F for forty minutes. If any other friends show up, add three slices of bread per friend until colour of meatloaf turns white. Then, add more catsup to retain brown colouring.

III WALKABOUT

1. *Wandering Joy, Meister Eckhart's Mystical Philosophy,* Translations and Commentary by Reiner Schürmann, with an Introduction by David Appelbaum, Lindisfarne Books, USA, 2001.
2. *THE SHOp: A Magazine of Poetry*, issue number 7, Autumn/Winter, 2001 pp.32–39.
3. Mary Ryan, *Hope*, Headline, London, 2001.
4. Orlando Figes, *Natasha's Dance*, Allen Lane, London, 2002.
5. Carlos Castaneda, *The Fire From Within*.
6. All information about the construction of this bridge is taken from the

official report of 'The Angle Ring Company (who) undertook the bend forming of tubular steelwork used in the construction of the James Joyce bridge in Dublin, Ireland'.

7. Anna Achmatova, *Selected Poems*, translated by D. M. Thomas, Penguin, 1988, p.87. Sent to me by Joan and Kate Newmann. It arrived 8 March 2004.

8. Taken from Breda O'Brien's report of the proceedings posted to participants in September 2004.

9. Paul Valliere, *Modern Russian Theology, Bukharev, Soloviev, Bulgakov, Orthodox Theology in a new key*, T&T Clark, Edinburgh, 2000.

10. Mark Patrick Hederman, *I Must be Talking to Myself: Dialogue in the Roman Catholic Church since Vatican II*, Veritas, Dublin, 2004.

11. *Love Impatient, Love Unkind*, The Crossroad Publishing Company, New York, 2004.

IV MOSAIC OF TIME AND SPACE

1. From 26 February to 7 May 2002 there was an exhibition in the National Gallery London called *The Image of Christ*. A book of the same name was published to accompany it. Jane Daggett Dillenberger gave a copy of this book to Diarmuid and AC Rooney in San Francisco.

2. G. K. Chesterton, *The Resurrection of Rome*, pp 340–42.

3. William Butler Yeats, *Four Years 1887–1891*, The Cuala Press, Dublin, 1921, pp.4–5. later published in *Autobiographies, op. cit.* pp 115–116.

4. Walter J. Ong, *Orality and Literacy, The Technologizing of the Word*, Routledge, London & New York, 1982, This Edition, 2000 Hereafter in this text referred to as (Ong + page number).

5. John Carey, 'Poetic License,' *The Sunday Times*, 9 March 1997, sec. 8, p.1.

6. A. N. Whitehead, *Science and the Modern World*, p57.

7. Charles Dickens, *Hard Times*, Book the First, Chapter I, page 1, begun by Dickens in 1853.

8. *Modern Russian Theology, Bukharev, Soloviev, Bulgakov, Orthodox Theology in a new key*, Paul Valliere, T&T Clark, Edinburgh, 2000. 'In dogmatic terms Mary's link to the divine may be expressed as a special connection with the Holy Spirit. The archangel's words at the annunciation are explicit about this: 'The Holy Spirit will come upon you, and the power of the Most High will overshadow you' (Lk 1:35). Through the Spirit's visitation Mary became Mother of God (Bogomater'). Her moral purity and receptivity made her 'transparent for the Holy Spirit.' The permeation of Mary's being by the Spirit was so complete that she should be regarded not just as a supremely 'spiritual' person but as 'the Spirit-bearing Person'. Mary received the Holy Spirit with her whole being and bore its unique gift – the Son – into the world. She was the 'Spirit-bearer', the Spirit's 'living abode' in the world.

Bulgakov draws an even bolder analogy when he likens Mary's relationship with the Third Person to Jesus' relationship with the Second. In Mary the Holy Spirit found its perfect human image, just as the Son found his perfect image in Jesus. As Spirit-bearer Mary co-ordinates humanity with the Trinity by linking it to the Third Person as Jesus the God–human links it to the second. A restored humanity in the image of the Holy Trinity will therefore manifest both bogochelovechestvo and bogomaterinstvo, the humanity of God and the motherhood of God (The translation involves predicating motherhood of God as well as of Mary p.326), as in the icon of the Mother of God with her child. 'The God–human and the Spirit–bearer, the Son and the Mother, revealing the Father through the Second and Third hypostases, respectively, manifest also the fullness of the divine image in humanity, or conversely, of the human image in God.'

The Son is 'begotten' by the Father and executes the divine will for the world through incarnation. The Spirit 'proceeds' from the Father and executes the divine will for the world through vivification ('the Giver of Life') and sanctification. Bulgakov sees these distinctions reflected in the creaturely images of the divine hypostases. Hence Mary is not God incarnate because incarnation is not the Spirit's work. As the humanity of the Holy Spirit she is the perfectly sanctified, revivified, deified human being, to such a degree that her mortal flesh is glorified and assumed into heaven at the dormition. But Mary does not anticipate Jesus' work any more than Jesus recapitulates hers. Their missions are distinct, though co–ordinated and equally integral to the humanity of God. So Mary is the perfect image of the Holy Spirit: Now the Spirit gives life, the Spirit sanctifies, that is to say, inspires, nurtures and strengthens the children of God. In both respects the Spirit's work may be described as a kind of mothering. Even in the inner life of the Trinity the Spirit has a maternal function. Bulgakov states this unambiguously:

> The Holy Spirit, proceeding from the Father to the Son, finds the Son already begotten but actualizes Him for the Father through Itself. In this sense the Spirit is as it were a hypostatic motherhood proceeding from the Father to the Son, 'the giving of life' being the special property of the Holy Spirit.

For Bulgakov, then, bogomaterinstvo is a life–giving and life–nurturing force far vaster than the motherhood of Mary, although the latter is the perfect creaturely image of it. The work of the Spirit is nothing less than 'a kind of universal, cosmic motherhood of God'. Annunciation looks ahead to Pentecost and beyond when 'creation will appear as Christ in the process of being born, human existence as the God–bearing womb, the whole world as the Mother of God.' (p.327)

9. Matthew 27: 50.
10. Luke 23: 46.
11. Matthew 2: 2;12.
12. Cf: Serge Boulgakov, *Le Paraclet*, Éditions l'Age d'Homme, Paris 1996, Pp 229–230.
13. Rev 5: 1–6.
14. John 'invisibly shepherds his flock (by) prophetically inspiring it.' Johannine primacy is thus a primacy of prophecy as well as of love, which again distinguishes it from Peter's primacy of office and authority.' (p.302) 'In the church of Peter dogmatics is a retrospective discipline; it expresses what has been duly taught by the line of successors going back to the rock of the church. In the Johannine church dogmatics is a prospective discipline; it expresses what is yet to come or just beginning to dawn. This, too, is an apostolic calling, though necessarily more provisional, more experimental, more conversational than the Petrine vocation. The prophetic principle

reminds the dogmatic theologian that "no pre–established forms are prescribed for church tradition – the Spirit living in the Church blows where it wills".' Paul Valliere, *Modern Russian Theology, Bukharev, Soloviev, Bulgakov, Orthodox Theology in a new key*, T&T Clark, Edinburgh, 2000. (p.303)

15. This was the reading at Morning Office, 21 May, 2004, Augustine on St John's Gospel, Homily 124,5,7.

16. John 21: 24–25.

17. St John of the Cross, Commentary on Stanza 39 of The Spiritual canticle, nos 3 & 4, in *The Collected Works of St John of the Cross*, translated by Kieran Kavanagh (1999), pp. 622–623.

18. All information about the construction of this bridge is taken from the official report of 'The Angle Ring Company (who) undertook the bend forming of tubular steelwork used in the construction of the James Joyce bridge in Dublin, Ireland'.

19. Richard Ellmann, *James Joyce, op.cit.* p 524.

20. *Ibid.*

21. Richard Ellmann, *James Joyce*, the first revision of the 1959 classic, OUP, 1982, p 546.

22. David Sylvester, *Interviews with Francis Bacon*, London, 1975, p. 58.

23. *Ibid*, p.53.

24. *Ibid*, p. 105.

25. Seamus Heaney, *Opened Ground, Poems 1966–1996*, Faber & Faber, London, 1998, p 364.

26. *Reading The Future, Irish Writers in Conversation with Mike Murphy*, (Dublin, Lilliput Press, 2000) p 90.

27. Seamus Heaney, *Opened Ground, op. cit.* p.19

28. Louis MacNeice, 'Coda', *Collected Poems*, Faber & Faber. London, 1966, p.546.

29. W. B. Yeats, *Essays and Introductions*, London, MacMillan, 1961, p 272.

30. *Ibid,* p 271.

31. T. S. Eliot, from 'Little Gidding,' in The Four Quartets, *The Complete Poems and Plays*, Faber & Faber, London and Boston, 1969, p.192.

32. Alexander Solzenitsyn, *The First Circle* (Fontana, 1971) p.358.

33. Joan McBreen, *Winter in the Eye*, Salmon/poetry, Galway, 2003, p.31.

V MIDDLE ALPHABET

1. Seamus Heaney: *Finders Keepers Selected Prose 1971–2001*, Faber & Faber, London, 2002

2. 'Seamus Heaney, The Reluctant Poet', *The Crane Bag*, Vol 3 no 2, 1979, pp.61–70.

3. Mark Patrick Hederman, *The Haunted Inkwell*, Columba, Dublin, 2001, pp.172–185.

4. Alexander Solzenitsyn, *The First Circle*, Fontana, 1971, p.358.

5. Mark Patrick Hederman, *Anchoring the Altar*, Veritas, Dublin, 2002.

6. Maurice Merleau–Ponty, *The Phenomenology of Perception*, Routledge & Kegan Paul, London, 1962, 197–98.

7. W. B. Yeats, *Essays and Introductions*, London, Macmillan, 1961, p 341.

8. Seamus Heaney, *Opened Ground, Poems 1966–1996*, Faber, London, 1998, pp.267– 268.

9. Iris Murdoch, *Jackson's Dilemma*, Chatto & Windus, London, 1995.

10. A. S. Byatt, *Degrees of Freedom, The Early Novels of Iris Murdoch*, Vintage, 1994, p.224.

11. *Op. Cit.* P 345

12. Irish Murdoch, *Metaphysics as a Guide to Morals*, Chatto & Windus, London, 1992

13. Interview with Iris Murdoch by Edward Whitley published in his book *The Graduates*, Hamish Hamilton, London, 1986, pp 63–74.

14. Last line of Gerard Manley Hopkins's poem 'That Nature is a Heraclean Fire and of the comfort of the Resurrection'.

15. Louis Golding, *James Joyce*, London, 1933, p. 55.

16. *Ibid.* p 56.

17. *Ibid.* p 35.

18. *Selected Joyce Letters*, edited by Richard Ellmann, The Viking Press, New York, 1975, p 161.

19. Richard Ellmann, *James Joyce*, New and Revised Edition, Oxford University Press, 1982, P 393.

20. *Selected Joyce Letters,* ed. R Ellmann, New York, 1975, p 129.

21. Lionel Trilling, 'James Joyce in his Letters', *Commentary*, February 1968, pp.57–58.

22. C. G. Jung, 'Synchronicity: An A–Causal Connecting Principle', in *The Collected Works*, vol. 8, (Bollingen Series XX, New York, 1960), Pp. 513,119.

23. Richard Ellmann, *Selected Letters of James Joyce*, Introduction, Faber & Faber, London, 1975 p xxv.

24. Henry James, *The Golden Bowl*, Oxford World Classics, 1999

25. As I write these lines 09/07/2004, headlines in the *Irish Independent* tell me that a mystery buyer paid £240,000 for this letter yesterday at an auction in Sotheby's in London.

26. Brenda Maddox, *Nora, A Biography of Nora Joyce*, Minerva, London, 1989.

27. Richard Ellmann, *Selected Letters of James Joyce*, Faber & Faber, London, 1975 p.116.

28. *Ibid.* p.274.

29. *Ibid* p.285.

30. Richard Ellmann, *James Joyce, New and Revised Edition*, Oxford University Press, 1982, p.743.

31. Lionel Trilling, *The Liberal Imagination*, London, 1951, p.40.

32. Peter Brown, *The Body and Society*, New York, 1988, p.229.

33. John Climacus, *The Ladder of Divine Ascent*, 15: 904A; p 186; 26:1064A; p 248)

34. *Selected Joyce Letters*, edited by Richard Ellmann, The Viking Press, New York, 1975, p.xxv.

35. FW 185–6

36. FW 613

37. I got this version of the story from my friend and fellow monk, Seán Ó Duinn.

38. Interview with Richard Pine, *Irish Literary Supplement*, Spring, 1990, p.22.

39. Brendan Kennelly, *Selected Poems*, Dublin, 1969, p. xii.

40. *A Time for Voices, Selected Poems 1960 – 1990*, Bloodaxe Books, 1990, p.12.

41. *Selected Poems*, 1969, p. xii.

42. Interview with Katie Donovan, *The Irish Times*, 19/12/1991

43. Interview with Richard Pine, *Irish Literary Supplement*, Spring, 1990, p.22.

44. Brendan Kennelly, *Cromwell*, Breaver Row Press, Dublin 1983. All references here are to this edition and are noted as C with the number of the page.

45. Brendan Kennelly, *The Book of Judas*, Bloodaxe, 1991, hereafter referred to as J with the page number. I have written a more detailed and comprehensive study of this book in *The Listowel Literary Phenomenon*, Ed. Gabriel Fitzmaurice, 1994, Pp. 116–130.

46. *A Time for Voices, Selected Poems 1960 – 1990*, Bloodaxe Books, 1990, p.124.

47. Brendan Kennelly, *Poetry My Arse*, Bloodaxe, 1995, Preface p.14. Hereafter referred to as P with the page number.

48. Brendan Kennelly, *Selected Poems*, Dublin, 1969, p. xii.

49. Brendan Kennelly, *A Time for Voices, Selected Poems 1960–1990*, Bloodaxe Books, 1990, p 13.

50. Mark Patrick Hederman: 'Such Striving towards Emptiness' The Poetry of Brendan Kennelly, *Neuropa*, 94/96, Anno XXVI, 1998, Pp 29–35

51. Mark Patrick Hederman: 'The Monster in the Irish Psyche', *Irish Literary Supplement*, Fall, 1984, p 15.

52. 'Singing to me of who and why I am' Brendan Kennelly's Judascape, *The Listowel Phenomenon*, Ed. Gabriel Fitzmaurice, Cló Iar–Chonnachta Teo, 1994, pp.116–129.

53. Mark Patrick Hederman, *The Haunted Inkwell*, The Columba Press, Dublin, 2001.

54. Brendan Kennelly, *The Man Made of Rain*, Bloodaxe Books, 1998 (from here on referred to as MMR with the page number).

55. Brendan Kennelly, *Glimpses*, Bloodaxe, 2001, p 92.

56. Samuel Beckett, *Proust*, 1931, reprinted by Grove Press, New York, 1957, p.55.

57. George Berkeley, *The Principles of Human Knowledge*

58. Brendan Kennelly, *Glimpses*, Bloodaxe Books, 2001, p 92.

59. Brendan Kennelly, 'A Giving' *A Time for Voices*, P 106.

60. Brendan Kennelly, *Familiar Strangers, New & Selected Poems 1960–2004*, Bloodaxe Books, 2004.

61. *Cara*, July/August 2000 p. 38.

62. Naum Gabo, *Of Divers Arts*, The A.W. Mellon Lectures in the Fine Arts, 1959, Bollingen Series XXXV 8, Pantheon, Washington, 1962.

63. My explanation, not Louis le Brocquy's.

555 POSTSCRIPT

1. This is taken from my book *Tarot: Talisman or Taboo?*, Currach Press, 2003. In my Walkabout during that year of the Holy Spirit, it was a surprise to me to find that these cards were a potential place of revelation for that same Spirit.

2. The book which has provided me with inspiration for much of what is written here about the Tarot was composed by an anonymous author who had his work published after his death in 1973. He was born in Russia in

1900, became a disciple of Rudolph Steiner before converting to Catholicism. His major work called *Meditations on the Tarot, A Journey into Christian Hermeticism*, was originally written in French and was completed in 1967. The German translation which appeared in 1983 contained a preface by one of the great Roman Catholic theologians of the twentieth century, Hans Urs Von Balthasar, *Die Grossen Arcana des Tarot, Meditationen, mit einer einführung von Hans Urs Von Balthasar*, (Herder, Basel, 3rd edition 1993, 2 vols). The introduction is from pp. ix to xvi.